An OPUS book

INTERNATIONAL RELATIONS
IN A CHANGING WORLD

International Relations in a Changing World

Fourth Edition

JOSEPH FRANKEL

Oxford   New York

OXFORD UNIVERSITY PRESS

Oxford University Press, Walton Street, Oxford OX2 6DP

Oxford New York Toronto
Delhi Bombay Calcutta Madras Karachi
Kuala Lumpur Singapore Hong Kong Tokyo
Nairobi Dar es Salaam Cape Town
Melbourne Auckland Madrid

and associated companies in
Berlin Ibadan

Oxford is a trade mark of Oxford University Press

International Relations first published 1964
Second edition 1969
Third edition, entitled International relations in a Changing World, 1979
Fourth edition first published 1988 as an Oxford University Press paperback

British Library Cataloguing in Publication Data
Data available

Library of Congress Cataloging in Publication Data
Frankel, Joseph.
International relations in a changing world.
Bibliography p. Includes index.
1. International relations. I. Title.
JX1395.F682 1989 327 87-28165
ISBN 0-19-289217-7 (pbk)

7 9 10 8 6

Printed in Great Britain by
Biddles Ltd
Guildford and King's Lynn

Preface

Although completely rethought and rewritten, this book remains almost identical in format with the first edition published in 1964. This requires a word of explanation.

The student wishing to be introduced to international relations today faces a situation vastly different from that in 1964: both states and international problems have multiplied; instead of the few books then available he now has a large choice from a confusingly varied specialist literature and is confronted with an avalanche of news and views in the mass media, often in an extensive and sophisticated form. Though over-abundance has replaced the scarcity of information and analysis, the basic need of the student remains the same: he requires some general framework for understanding. The trouble with the various sources of information and instruction is that they do not add up: their relationship is obscure and often they actually contradict one another. The main reason lies in the fact that the authors are often pursuing divergent objectives: some want to describe and explain whereas others wish to change the world in their own fashion; they start with different sets of assumptions— or, as these are frequently called, 'paradigms'—diverging on such fundamentals as the primacy of the state or the international system; they focus on different phenomena—war, conflict, strategy, diplomacy, power, economic relations, human rights; they look at the world from different ideological, cultural, and national perspectives. To add to the complexities of choice, they generally claim or imply that their approach alone is correct and often spend an inordinate amount of effort in 'proving' that the competitors are not.

The fact that there is no general agreement does not conclusively prove that one of the contending approaches is not superior to the others but it does cast grave doubts about any claims to exclusive truth. In fact many approaches can make a contribution, often an important one, to the general understanding of the subject, but only if we can fit them into a coherent general framework. The objective of this volume is to provide such a framework. It purports neither to develop a theory nor to support one, as many analytical writers do, nor to deal with the detailed 'reality' of international relations, which is the aim of the historians. It offers what is, I hope, a commonsensical 'model'—a way of looking at reality—readily intelligible to the beginner or to a reader with only partial knowledge of the field. The model is completely open-ended: it allows for and tries to accommodate the employment of other approaches. It has helped the author and several generations of users all over the world to absorb not only the historical events but also the currents and counter-currents of theory in the last quarter of the twentieth century.

The scope and contents of the volume have been completely revised to take account of these developments, but there has been no need to alter the basic approach. It is analytical, with a variety of mainly recent historical examples introduced for illustration purposes and not as 'proofs' of the arguments. As the passing of behaviourism has shown, my contention made in 1964 that 'scientific', especially quantitative, methods were not suited to the analysis of many *major* elements of international relations stands good, although this is not to deny their usefulness for the analysis of many specific problems. The underlying philosophy regarding the nature of 'truth' remains unchanged. To put it simply, on the one hand it emphasizes the importance of any theory being related to empirical evidence; on the other, it assumes that there are deeper truths to be reached under the surface of events although we can never attain a complete insight into them. It thus leaves full room for the exercise of the imagination by readers in the formulation and pursuit of questions which stimulate their curiosity and appear to them important.

Consequently, although my treatment of the subject can be regarded as fundamentally conventional, I can quote with approval the well-known radical anti-nuclear campaigner E. P. Thompson when citing Shelley: 'We must imagine what we know'—although with the important qualification that we must make a real effort to 'know' first. This does not imply that anybody could be expected to become omniscient, which is palpably impossible, but merely that he should aspire to the ideal of the educated man outlined by Dame Veronica Wedgwood: he should know not only everything about something but also something about everything.

Lockinge, 1987   JOSEPH FRANKEL

Contents

List of abbreviations

CIA	Central Intelligence Agency
CMEA or COMECON	Council for Mutual Economic Assistance
COMINFORM	Communist Information Bureau
EC	European Community
ECSC	European Coal and Steel Community
ETA	Euzkadi ta Azkatasuna
EURATOM	European Atomic Energy Community
FAO	Food and Agriculture Organization
GATT	General Agreement on Trade and Tariffs
GDP	Gross Domestic Product
GNP	Gross National Product
ILO	International Labour Office
IMF	International Monetary Fund
IRA	Irish Republican Army
NATO	North Atlantic Treaty Organization
OAS	Organization of American States
OAU	Organization for African Unity
OECD	Organization for Economic Co-operation and Development
OPEC	Organization of Petroleum Exporting Countries
PLO	Palestine Liberation Organization
SALT	Strategic Arms Limitation Talks
SDI	Strategic Defense Initiative
START	Strategic Arms Reduction Talks
UN	United Nations
UNESCO	United Nations Educational, Scientific, and Cultural Organization
WHO	World Health Organization

1

Thinking about international relations

Thinking about international relations shares to a high degree the problems of thinking about any other area of social life. The intention of the author is to avoid an exposition of the methods of the social sciences which would be, by necessity, both lengthy and controversial, and instead merely to refer to some useful categories of thinking.

By their very nature, all social phenomena exhibit both some general characteristics which they share with other phenomena, opening opportunities for classification and categorization, and some specific characteristics which are unique to them. This book, like all political scientific analyses, stresses the general, but no full understanding of any single phenomenon can be complete without the knowledge also of its unique characteristics, which are the focus of interest of the historian. Furthermore, as social life is a seamless robe, one has to define both the boundaries of the subject and its linkage with the context. Social reality is characterized by conflicting characteristics: conflict runs parallel with co-operation, strength with weakness, idealism with realism, concern with the past with visions of the future; any analysis which excludes either element is incomplete. While the statement of the opposites is analytically useful, real-life situations are usually more realistically regarded as placeable within a 'spectrum' of situations between the two extremes.

We should at least occasionally abandon the modern obsession with the 'scientific explanation' of social phenomena—through discovering causal links—in favour of the widespread common-sensical desire to make sense of the totality of phenomena which defies precision. All causal explanations of social phenomena are bound to be misleading, not only because of the great complexity of the latter but also because they ignore the fact that man possesses and exercises the faculty of choice. There is no parallel in the social sciences with the 'necessitating causes' of the natural sciences: the statements that wars start through the expansionism of states, competition for territory and resources, or in the minds of men, are no equivalent to the statement that the fall of a stone is caused by gravity; the very fact that so many conflicting theories are simultaneously advanced clearly indicates that none is likely to be totally correct. All we can discover by scientific enquiry is a probabilistic estimate of conditions in which certain decisions will be taken—or, as the social scientists rather inelegantly tend to say, the 'parameters of action'. Obviously it is crucial to analyse these parameters as precisely as possible, but neither those who claim that some conditions are bound to lead to wars nor those who claim that others are bound to prevent them can be trusted. In fact the best way out is to face the uncertainty by abandoning the notion of 'causality' altogether and thinking instead of probabilities and correlations.

It is essential to be clear about our time-scale. On the one hand we should undoubtedly bear in mind that while the earth was formed some 4,700 billion years ago, *homo sapiens* in his present form has a history of a mere 50,000 years and settled to agriculture only some 10,000 years ago. On the other hand, if our main concern is with the present and the future, with the political, economic, ecological, and nuclear problems of our age, our immediate terms of reference have to be much shorter—the modern international political system formed in the seventeenth century, the post-Napoleonic Concert of Europe, and, for many purposes, only the post-1945 period. We draw entirely different 'lessons of history' from the different time-scales. The further back we go in history, the more do historical events appear to have been inevitable, as the record of the uncertainties and anxieties in the minds of the participants gradually disappears. It is a useful corrective to the widespread post-war obsession with the uniqueness of our present-day problems to engage in occasional exercises in 'counterfactual history', an attempt to investigate systematically the possible different outcomes in the past. There exists no firm theoretical basis for a dynamic model which would combine the past with the present and future and, despite valiant attempts at world models, it is beyond the capacity of the human mind. Hence a basically static model is here adopted, representing the state of affairs in the late 1980s, but indicating both its roots in the past and its dynamism. It means that the main concern will be with the 'structure' of the international system—that is, with the characteristic relations between actors across time—rather than the 'process'—the more ephemeral forms and modes of interaction.

A fully articulated theory of international relations incorporating all the relevant elements and meeting all the above-mentioned criteria is clearly unattainable as we could not possibly decide about the priorities and the relationships between the different categories; even if it were possible, it would be much too complex to be really useful. It is none the less important that we state as clearly as possible the reasons why we select some questions as being major and seek to answer them, while others are regarded as major but as defying an answer and yet others, though frequently regarded as major, are omitted altogether. If, as often happens, analysis were limited to what is fully explicable, particularly in precise quantified terms, the resulting analysis would defy commonsense perceptions of reality. This often happens, for instance, with attempts to explain the phenomenon of 'power' in terms of concrete 'capabilities' while the elusive psychological elements involved are omitted, as discussed in Chapter 6.

This brings us to the issue of methodology which, as may well be expected, is highly controversial. The choice of methodology—although often argued in terms of the rational advantages of one methodology over its rivals—is, up to a point, no more than a matter of individual preference dictated by personal history, temperament, and similar idiosyncratic elements. To my mind, all our judgements on broad social issues are subjective and, on the whole, intuitive; when based on sound observation and analysis and clearly articulated, however, they become intelligible to others and thus interpersonal. Contrary to the behaviourist school, I think that only minor phenomena are amenable to 'scientific' analysis, paralleling that employed in the natural sciences. Hence all that follows does not aspire to the status of scientifically established, objective 'truth'. It is no more than a statement of subjective perceptions of reality by the author, aspiring to come as close as possible to the preceptions of many actual participants in the processes of international relations, such as diplomats, politicians, international civil servants, the military, and business men engaged in international transactions. The basic guide is common sense.

Writers show a fair degree of agreement about what phenomena are sufficiently important to warrant discussion but not about their relative importance. Nobody, for instance, is likely to deny that geography is a constant factor in determining events, or that the accumulation of collective experience embodied in history plays a part in determining both national values and processes. The treatment of these two constants nevertheless varies enormously from book to book, and the same is true of such generally accepted important variables as power and capabilities, perceptions, values and interests, etc. On basic methodological issues there is general agreement. We should make a distinction between and be careful to separate the various levels of analysis, always making clear whether one is talking about the 'micro-level'—states and other actors—or the 'macro-level'—the international system as a whole. This is the basis of the division of this book into two parts: Chapters 2–7 and 8–11. It is necessary to distinguish also a third, and frequently neglected, level—of individuals. These are not only the major decision-makers, as discussed in Chapter 5, but also the five billion individual human beings whose basic needs, most of us feel, have to be met and whose human rights have to be satisfied. The latter are mentioned in the concluding chapter.

We must also come to grips with the issue of the delimitation of domestic politics—politics within individual states—and international politics—politics among states—and the relationship between the two, however difficult it frequently is to draw a clear boundary. Indeed, the most important issues, whether predominantly domestic or international, are not entirely either. Defence expenditure, for example, hinges largely on international insecurity but also on the funds available at home; wage policies affect primarily the pockets of the individual but have important repercussions on export prices and hence on the country's foreign trade. As in life the two domains overlap, understandably people try to comprehend international affairs, of which they have no direct experience or thorough knowledge, by resorting to analogies from domestic politics. Here everybody is to some extent an expert: however uneducated he may be, he has some knowledge of the life and traditions of his own country; he can reasonably guess the thoughts and reactions of his countrymen; through the mere possession of voting rights he participates in the political process. Unfortunately these analogies are usually wrong: all this domestic expertise is of little use when applied to international affairs—in fact it can be downright misleading.

To start with, the study of the politics of other states presents considerable problems. We are all culture-bound, and persons quite well-versed in the politics of their own country do not necessarily understand the politics of others, based as they are on distinct cultures, traditions, and historical experiences and differing also in their political concerns and priorities and their conceptions of right and wrong; in fact they often disregard the differences or consider them as unnatural deviations from their own national norms. Even residents in a foreign country, who are more intimately acquainted with it, are often prone to misjudgements due to their different cultural background, as can be amply demonstrated by the frequently mistaken view of many expatriates, the 'old hands', on the countries of their sojourn. Moreover, it is easy to forget how much points of view differ according to whether one is inside or outside the country. Citizens are naturally interested mainly in the domestic affairs of their country while foreigners are equally naturally interested mainly in its foreign policy. It does not require much effort to imagine how different the resulting images are. Both the American 'capitalist' and the Soviet 'communist' societies appear peace-loving to their own citizens, who are impressed by domestic policies aiming at the attainment of economic and social goals; both appear aggressive to the citizens of the opposite number, who think primarily of their foreign and military policies which are much less peaceful.

If it is hard to understand other states, it is even harder to understand *international society* as a whole. To start with, this society does not consist of individuals but of states and other group-actors. However sophisticated our approach may be, we still tend to be misled by linguistic usage and to consider states not as mental constructs, which they are, but as real entities. We *speak* about the relations between Britain and the United States as if they were relations between two persons, and we therefore tend to *think* about them in the same way, even employing the simplified graphic images of John Bull and Uncle Sam. It is just as easy to slip into the error of considering the two countries as personified in their representatives, the President and the Prime Minister, or the Secretaries of State and of Foreign Affairs. The briefest reflection will indicate the dangers of forgetting the full implications of the artificial, conventional nature of states and other group-actors and of the important differences between persons acting in their official capacities and as private individuals.

Since the language of politics has been coined within the domestic sphere, its extension to international relations easily leads to analogies which are not fully warranted. We speak of international society and of international organizations as if they were groupings of people; we discuss the international equivalents of law and morality; we discern the rights and duties of states; we analyse the organs of international institutions in terms analogous to the traditional three branches of government. Needless to say, all these analogies are defective. To the professional lawyer, international law is a very peculiar type of law; the application to the behaviour of states of moral codes developed for the individual constantly breaks down; the ambiguities of the concept of group rights are best demonstrated in the dangerous effects of the principle of 'national self-determination', the international equivalent of the 'freedom of the individual'; the comparison of the General Assembly of the United Nations (UN) with a legislature, or of the Security Council with a government, makes little sense, and even the less far-fetched analogies between the UN Secretariat and a national civil service, or between the International Court of Justice and national courts, should be approached very cautiously.

These difficulties of institutional analysis are repeated in the theory and philosophy of politics. From the earliest traditions of ancient Greece, thinkers have been concerned mainly with state governments, with the relations between the individual and authority. Theories and philosophies have been devised for a society of men which can be advanced either through the improvement of its members, or of the social order, or of both, and to which the concepts of 'order' and of 'justice' can be meaningfully applied. They have only limited application to a society of states where each member constantly confronts other intractable members, and hence is concerned primarily with its own survival and is subject to the dictates of necessity. Many continental thinkers, from Machiavelli onwards, have noted this fundamental difference but, with their long-standing preoccupation with national security and the 'moral opportunity' arising from it, many British and American thinkers have tended to neglect international relations. Only the growing interdependence of states since the Second World War has made the linkage between domestic and international politics obvious.

Somewhat independently of the mainstream of political thought, diplomats and international lawyers have developed a common language, a set of common traditions with a specifically international content: such concepts as 'balance of power' for example, belong fully to the international sphere. Unfortunately, although these traditions are still cherished by Western diplomats and lawyers, their application is rather limited. International society as we know it today has come into being only in the post-war years; the majority of its members, the Afro-Asian states, are newcomers to the international stage, while the two superpowers, the United States and the Soviet Union, are relative newcomers to their exalted status. Clearly categories and norms developed within the predominantly European context of the international society of the nineteenth century could scarcely be of general application today. Adaptation through the formulation of universal standards, such as 'human rights', has so far been very limited.

Consequently, the popular metaphor of 'steering the ship of the state' requires a modern re-interpretation. Nowadays it is no longer a question of skilful construction of the trireme, organization of the rowers, and navigation along the coasts of the Mediterranean, as in ancient Greece. Modern equipment has greatly reduced the required navigational skills. The two new needs—and also opportunities—for the modern 'ship of state' are to learn to modify and control the environment and to control the frequently unruly crew.

In our century, the growing popular interest in the relations between states has led to the development of a new specialized branch of knowledge, usually described by the name earlier coined by Jeremy Bentham as 'international relations'. This new discipline is more than a combination of the studies of the foreign affairs of the various countries and of international history; it includes also the study of international society as a whole and of its institutions and processes. It is increasingly concerned not only with the different states and their interactions but also with the web of transnational politics. In a way, the term 'world politics', employed by some writers, describes its contents more truthfully than the traditional name 'international relations'.

No general theory of international relations commands widespread acceptance, nor is the subsequent discussion based on any individual theory. However, in order to generalize about the relations of over 160 states, all different in size, power, and other attributes, and all acting against the backgrounds of their individual national traditions, it is necessary to have at least some working general hypothesis or model. The difficulty lies in accommodating the conflicting patterns of international politics: it is impossible to deal with the subject without emphasizing the role either of states or of the transnational processes or of the international systems; either of conflict or of co-operation; either of the clear but disappearing patterns of the past or of the vague and merely hypothetical trends for the future.

The pattern of the past is still prominent. We are living in a loosely organized international society of states which are formally entitled to complete sovereignty over their territories and to complete independence in their external relations. The traditional patterns of state behaviour relying largely on power continue even though they are now being challenged by a variety of domestic and international disruptions and by a growing awareness of the need for international co-operation, both on fundamental strategic and ecological issues and in numerous functional fields. The states are represented by individuals holding certain official positions who determine state policies under the complex, often conflicting, influences and pressures from their domestic and international environments. Inevitably this international society is subject to repeated crises and to the recurrent danger of a major conflict. However, the fear of a nuclear war, the growing awareness of the pressing need for international co-operation, and the volume of transnational activities, give some hope for an advance towards a degree of international order.

This model is neither particularly original nor profound, but it is useful and flexible. It not only provides a realistic approach to the study of the 'behaviour of states' through that of the behaviour of their representatives, but it also accommodates both the facts of the world of sovereign states governed mainly by power politics and the many phenomena of the contemporary world which cannot be fitted into this mould. It allows full scope for the co-operative trends which encourage hope for the order of tomorrow. Any reasonable treatment must be able to do that in order to do justice to our confused period of transition.[1]

2
States I

The structure of international society

Writers on international relations agree that the structure of international society is becoming increasingly complex, but they violently disagree about the most helpful way of looking at it. The traditional way was to concentrate upon the states as the historically prominent units, and to ignore other agents (or, as they are now often called, actors) which lack the basic characteristics of states—their sovereignty and their territoriality, on which more later. The influence of the post-war evolution of the behavioural sciences has led to a greater or lesser acceptance of a behavioural analysis of the international system as consisting of numerous, more or less autonomous interacting actors. In order to make up for the omissions of the traditionalists, many innovators have been concentrating excessively upon the crisis of the traditional states and/or upon the newly arisen non-state actors.

In order to restore the balance, it seems advisable to combine the two modes of analysis. We should think of the international system as one combining several kinds of actors of varying degrees of autonomy in their international behaviour, with the states among them retaining a leading but by no means exclusive or uniform role. The difficulties of analysing such a multi-actor system are, however, immense, and in practice authors tend to concentrate either upon state or upon non-state actors. Concentration upon either class inevitably precludes a balanced analysis of the international system as a whole; an attempt will therefore be made here to avoid such restriction and to do justice to both types. The non-state actors are, however, given much less prominence than the states, for two connected reasons: first, they are behaviourally less significant and, second, their analysis has not been developed nearly as adequately as that of states. Some factual information about them is, however, included because it may not otherwise be readily accessible.

To start with, it seems useful to attempt a common framework for looking at all the actors, both states and non-states, from the angle of their positions in the international system. In order to achieve this it is necessary to bear in mind at least the following four basic dimensions, developed in the analysis of states but equally applicable to other actors:

1. *Orientation towards participation* in the international system. There is a wide spectrum of possible policies between the extremes of full participation in the web of world politics, characterizing the United States, and the relative isolationism of contemporary Burma; a similar spectrum could be developed for multinational corporations or terrorist movements.

2. *Scope*, which can be understood as a geographical dimension, with actors dividing into those with mainly global, regional, subregional, and more local scope, and a functional dimension according to the fields of international interaction in which they participate. While non-state actors have, as a rule, a limited functional scope, states have a potentially fully comprehensive multifunctional scope. Individual states do not, however, necessarily exercise it: they sometimes withdraw both from security and trade interactions by deliberate policies of neutrality or isolationism, as Japan, China, Burma, and Cambodia have all in turn done.

3. *Power*, which must be clearly defined both in functional and in relative terms specifying what the power purports to achieve and in relations with whom. This merges into the somewhat overlapping category of *influence*—the ability to achieve the desired ends. The best way to clarify the confused relationship between these two concepts is to regard power as a potential for influence.

4. *Domestic structures* relevant for international interaction. One element is readily discernible—the decision-making institutions. There are, however, other, less clear-cut but very important aspects: stability and capacity for adaptation to change,

taking into account the nature of challenges at home and abroad;
legitimacy—manifesting itself in the loyalty of the members of
the organizations and their outside friends and allies.

The development of the state system

Modern states and modern international society are only a very
recent phenomenon: the three or four centuries of their history
are a small fraction of the more than seven thousand years of the
recorded history of man and a proportionately smaller fraction
of his very much longer biological history. Yet international relations were foreshadowed a long time ago.

In its broadest historical perspective, the present state system
is best explained by Aristotle's celebrated observation that man is
by nature a political animal. At all stages of development, people
have needs and wants which they cannot realize alone; hence they
form social groups. Such groups differ greatly in their nature and
scope, according to circumstances, but they invariably strike a
host of organizational problems pertaining to the structure of the
group, and also to its relationships with other groups, the equivalent of modern international relations. One fundamental problem here is that of delimitation, of finding the size best suited for
the purposes of the group. Plato and Aristotle discuss it in their
analyses of the Greek city-states; modern social scientists are
concerned with the same question: is the existence of a system of
heterogeneous states tenable or will the smallest units prove to be
non-viable or the largest ones ungovernable? Will the states
amalgamate into larger units or will they decentralize, or both?
For the comfort of the citizens, the sovereign political units
should be as small as possible, but for the preservation of peace
and the protection of the environment, only a global organization would ultimately do; is the logical consequence that states
should be replaced by a variety of organizations sized according
to their functions politically feasible? The major theoretical
approaches are those of social communication, of areas of
loyalty, and of relations between 'ingroups' and 'outgroups'.
Economists, too, are concerned with the economics of size and,
recently, with the question of whether 'small is beautiful'.

Something approaching international relations can in fact be read into the social behaviour of animals, which has been re-interpreted by zoologists since the Second World War. Groupings of animals are now seen as being determined by considerations of biological survival; they must secure food and breeding grounds and hence are capable of fierce intra-species conflicts which generally revolve around the exclusive use of territory for breeding and feeding and the exclusion of trespassers likely to compete for its use. Maybe the bare structure of human relations is the same, however much more complex they may be.

Most analyses of human organization start with an assumption about the original state of nature, describing it either as a state of innocence, a Golden Age, or as a Hobbesian war of all against all. For the purposes of this discussion it is unnecessary to decide in favour of either view. Whether man was originally motivated by sentiments of sympathy or of hostility, or by a mixture of both, he soon discovered that co-operation within a group provided benefits, and also that the contacts of his own group with other groups affected his interests, either positively or negatively, or, confusingly, both. We can only speculate about the development of relations among primitive groups. Possibly, while they were few, men simply avoided contacts, but it is plausible to assume that, with growing numbers and increasing sophistication, such contacts soon grew. If an analogy with the animal world suggests that the first contacts may have been hostile, already in prehistory some non-violent forms of inter-group relations were established and institutionalized (heralds, for example, were endowed with immunity) and mutually advantageous trade exchanges took place. Once such relations had reached a certain frequency and intensity, they became an important incentive to establish an efficient central government within each group to control them.

They required also some minimum conditions for intercourse between groups—some degree of linguistic understanding and probably also of religious community, sufficient at least to enable them to trust the oaths sworn by the other side. The perennial dilemma of international relations thus already faced man in pre-history. When a group is no longer self-sufficient, when some of its vital needs can be satisfied only from the outside, is it preferable to ensure their satisfaction through the subjugation of the other groups involved or through some form of inter-group co-operation and exchange? The choice between war and peaceful coexistence is painful, since both carry their risks. Military conquest is the simpler method; indeed, it seems to have been the rule throughout history—although we must allow for the likely tendency of the scanty early records to refer to the spectacular military feats of rulers rather than to the unspectacular flow of peaceful intercourse such as international trade.

It is possible to interpret the political history of mankind as an age-long series of attempts to determine the size of supreme social groupings suitable for the circumstances of the time and the place. While unifying forces led to empires based upon conquest or to confederations based upon consent, separatist forces invariably reasserted themselves, causing the disintegration of the larger units. In many vital respects the whole globe has now undoubtedly become one area of activity, but it does not necessarily follow that the forces of unity will inevitably score a permanent victory. Few people today would accept Sir Halford Mackinder's thesis of geographical compulsion that 'the grouping of lands and seas, and of fertility and natural pathways, is such as to lend itself to the growth of empires, and in the end of a single World Empire'.[1] The nuclear menace, modern communications, and economic interdependence *could* lead to the integration of the world either by conquest or by growing co-operation, but there is nothing inevitable about the process nor any assurance that, even if it succeeds, unity would remain permanent; the problems of governing the whole globe are likely to prove to be insuperable.

The first large-scale political organizations, states, and state systems of which we possess records developed about 5000 BC in the Tigris-Euphrates and Nile valleys and somewhat later in the valleys of the great rivers of China. Their location was not due to accident but to a social need common to all these areas. They all required strong centralized organizations capable of constructing and maintaining irrigation systems which were indispensable for food production. Karl Wittfogel has developed a plausible theory about the resulting despotic character of these societies which he called 'hydraulic'.[2]

Growing numbers and sophistication constantly increased the range of human needs and led, although jerkily, to larger human groupings. First in the valleys of the great rivers and then in larger areas, states became enmeshed in networks of interstate relations alternating between the two patterns of separate warring and co-operating units, and of great empires imposed upon them. These political systems, usually called civilizations, were fluctuating in their boundaries, but were geographically fairly segregated from one another; each developed a degree of cultural and political coherence. On the whole, contacts between them were sporadic although some were of great cultural importance. The intrepid scholars, missionaries, and travellers who crossed the formidable Gobi desert in the early centuries of our era brought Buddhism from India to China; oriental influences introduced by Alexander the Great altered the character of Greek civilization; the 'barbarians' who harried the Chinese and the Roman Empires were not only enemies of these civilizations but also creative elements which became assimilated into the former and rebuilt the latter in the form of the medieval Christian Commonwealth; in our century, anthropological studies of primitive people have opened our eyes to many problems of our own.

In the eastern Mediterranean, civilizations interacted more intensely and occasionally came into dramatic conflict. From the unfortunate position of their small buffer-state between the Assyrians and the Egyptians, the Hebrew prophets recorded the clash between the two empires which began in the fourteenth century BC; in the fifth century BC the Persians invaded Greece, and in the following century Alexander invaded the Orient; the Middle Ages witnessed a prolonged conflict between the Christians and the Muslims. Until the second half of the fifteenth century AD, however, Europe and the Middle East remained almost wholly separated from the large organized civilizations in China and India as well as from the other, less organized continents.

Our image of the international society of today as having arisen mainly from the background of Western history is partly

culture-bound in its origins, but is, nevertheless, of general validity. It is a historical fact that, owing to its superior technology
and political organization, from the fifteenth century onwards
European civilization gradually extended its rule all over the
globe. Today, when other civilizations and continents have successfully asserted themselves against Europe, their own histories
and traditions have assumed an obvious importance, but only as
additions and corrections to the existing system. Throughout the
world, science and technology, political institutions, culture-
bearing languages, the very idea of a society of sovereign interacting states—all have their origins in Europe.[3]

Being conducted within an international society or system,
international relations imply a multitude of units separate in
some respects but constituting a whole in others—the result of an
interplay between unitary and particularist forces. This interplay
can be taken as the focus for the study of the rich and varied
Western heritage; the subsequent few paragraphs will indicate a
way in which this can be done.

The Greeks, who devised the vocabulary of domestic politics,
were less inventive for international relations, although they
clearly distinguished some features which are characteristic of the
modern state system, such as bipolarity and balance of power
among sovereign states. While jealously preserving the independence of their city-states, they recognized a degree of unity in
Greece as a whole and developed such common institutions as the
Amphictyonic Council and the Olympic Games; they distinguished between conflicts within their own system (*stasis*) and
wars with outsiders (*polemos*). The Romans epitomized the idea
of unity in the ingenious institutions of their empire which toler-
ated cultural divergencies as long as they were not politically
dangerous. The medieval Christian Commonwealth successfully
preserved the *idea* of unity through the institutions of the
Church, the Empire, and the Universities, while a chaotic multitude of local political units gradually combined into several hierarchically arranged loose feudal systems. The medieval order
eventually crumbled under the impact of the Renaissance and the
Reformation.

With the disappearance of religious unity, particularist forces reasserted themselves. For a while both the Catholic and the Reformed Churches clung to the idea of medieval unity based on a common faith and endeavoured to impose their respective creeds on the whole of Europe. The local princes who rose to political importance through the acquisition of territory, whether by marriage or by ruthless use of power, became immersed in religious wars, both fighting for their creeds abroad and trying to ensure their complete sway at home. As Machiavelli rightly observed, modern states are based on power; however, their religious origin must not be neglected. Religious forces did not disappear from politics completely but, in the form of national churches, generally adapted themselves to the new units.

The resulting system of sovereign territorial states, which was formally established by the Peace Treaty of Westphalia in 1648, was at first limited to Europe. Gradually, however, European states extended their rule over other continents which they considered fair game for their expansion. On the one hand, by including overseas territories within their empires, they spread the diversity of the European state system over the whole globe. On the other hand, they united the world physically, by opening communications, and culturally, by spreading European culture.

Early in the twentieth century the system faced challenges from several different directions. The empire-building process which was essential for the functioning of the European community came to an end when there were no more continents to annex or people to subjugate; great powers—the United States and Japan —arose outside Europe; under the impact of nationalism, non-European peoples began to act more independently. Although still predominantly European, the inter-war international organization, the League of Nations, was, at least in concept, universal. The final blow to unity was caused by the gradual dissociation of the system from its Christian origins and by the split between the three offspring of Western tradition—liberal democracy, Communism, and Fascism.

During its course, the Second World War was generally thought to be the defence of the system against its most dangerous adversary, and, for some time afterwards the forces for unity appeared to be on the march, admittedly not in favour of

world-wide but rather of bloc integration. It seemed likely that
the smaller states would become gradually absorbed into the
orbits of the United States and the Soviet Union, the two superpowers which had arisen in the wake of the war. The envisaged
bipolar world has not, however, materialized. The nuclear stale-
mate has partly neutralized the two superpowers and has thus
enabled other states to assert themselves, whether they are
uncommitted and neutral or dependent. Instead of a bipolarity
based upon blocs integrated around the two superpowers, a
world-wide polycentric system has been gradually shaping, a
system subdivided into Western, Communist, and Third World
subsystems within which the separate state-units can act with a
degree of independence.   While the forces of unity have not
prevailed within the blocs, they are operating, although in a very
attenuated form, in the United Nations, which is world-wide.
Simultaneously transnational forces have continued to assert
themselves and important non-state actors have begun to appear.

In the last few decades, particularly since 1945, international
society has undergone important changes, but its basic structure
has remained the same since 1648, especially in its theoretical
foundations; it is a society of sovereign territorial states. Consequently it is necessary to start with the analysis of the 'classical'
international society and its member states and to postpone the
discussion of the changes in this century. This approach emphasizes diversity, which is embodied in these states and has been
prominent for the last three centuries. The forces of unity have
never fully disappeared, however, and will be discussed in
Chapters 8–11.

A word may be added about the implications of the highly
dynamic nature of international society. Social forces operating
within it change all the time in their nature but not in the mode of
their operation. The metaphor of the swing of the pendulum is
here quite illuminating, provided we accept that the swing
changes from beat to beat, both in its extent and in its speed. If we
apply this metaphor to the interaction between the forces of unity
and of particularism, the unity achieved under the Roman
Empire meant that the pendulum reached one extreme position
and then slowly, but in the last stages with catastrophic speed,

swung to the particularism of the Dark Ages. The Holy Roman Empire constituted merely a feeble swing towards unity, and was again followed by the extreme particularism established at Westphalia. There is little doubt that the forces of unity have been building up since then, but the extent of the swing and its present momentum are ambiguous and uncertain.

Elements of statehood

At the outset the fact must be stressed that states, being the most extensive and comprehensive units of human organization, are extremely complex. Hence they show quite different features when considered in their different capacities, either as political organizations of governmental authority in their relations with the citizens, or as economic, social, or cultural structures. By necessity the discussion of states here focuses around the role they play in international society; consequently many of their otherwise important characteristics can be barely touched upon or even mentioned and only the elements of the state structure directly relevant for relations with other states are discussed. A convenient starting point may be found in the formal legal approach. According to the British authority on international law, L. Oppenheim, a state 'is in existence when a people is settled in a country under its own sovereign government'.[4] This definition includes four distinct elements: a people, a territory, a government, and the attribute of sovereignty.

The people

Since states are a form of social organization, this is obviously an essential element. The people are an aggregate of both sexes living in a community which need not be homogeneous. The size of the group is not fixed: there are over a billion (1,000 million) people in China while the people of the smallest states are counted in thousands. Most jurists used to agree that there is some lower limit to the size of a people and they had doubts about the statehood of such tiny groups as Liechtenstein or Andorra, and denied the existence of conditions for a separate statehood of the smallest surviving colonial territories; however, nearly all of them have gained full statehood. Of course all these small groups are generally poorly equipped in other essential elements of statehood, too.

The territory

Perhaps the most important characteristic of the modern state, distinguishing it from the medieval order, is its territoriality. This feature, sometimes described as impermeability or impenetrability, can be considered as the basic ingredient of the modern state: its strategic aspects are usually included in the analysis of state power, the political aspects are described as independence, and the legal ones as sovereignty.

The origin of the territorial state lies in the 'gunpowder revolution' which destroyed the security of the medieval castles and cities and resulted in a shift of the 'hard shell' of impenetrability from walls and moats to the broader confines of state boundaries. When neither local defences nor the popes and emperors could provide security, the princes, the rulers of larger territories, became its best guarantors and their states became the basic units. We can consider the rise of the modern territorial state both as a triumph of particularism over medieval unity and as a partial victory of unity over the anarchy and disorder of the Middle Ages. On either interpretation, the modern territorial state is based on the twin elements of internal pacification and external defensibility.

Territories of states vary in size as much as do their populations. The largest state in existence, the Soviet Union, covers an area of approximately 13.5 million square kilometres but some states measure only a few thousand or even a few hundred square kilometres.

The government and sovereignty

The government consists of one or more persons who represent the people and rule according to the law of the land. Since all states conduct their foreign affairs through their governments, an anarchist community, even if it could exist on a sufficiently large scale, would not qualify as a state. After the October Revolution in 1917, the Bolshevik rulers tried to do away with their foreign ministry and to replace intergovernmental relations with direct relations with other peoples, but they soon gave up their futile attempt and their Utopian expectation of the 'withering away' of the state has not materialized. Governments play a crucial part in the making of foreign policy on behalf of their states; their structures and mode of operation are therefore discussed in some detail in Chapter 4.

Theoretically, sovereign governments are in full control both of the domestic and of the foreign affairs of their countries, but here, as on some other issues, a sharp distinction must be drawn between the two. As long as a government is recognized as such by other governments, it remains the legal representative of its country, even if its control over it is severely challenged or completely lost. Thus, for a long period, the Nationalist Government of China remained recognized by the United States and by several other states as the government of the whole of China despite the fact that, from 1949, its rule was limited to Taiwan and a few small islands; during the Second World War, the governments-in-exile in London retained the recognition of Britain and the United States although they were temporarily divorced from the other elements of statehood. Juridical sovereignty, the fact that they are recognized as sovereign states, is the main reason why some weak African states which lack most of the elements of empirical sovereignty do not disintegrate: breakaway entities face the insuperable hurdle of being refused recognition. Inevitably a discrepancy between recognition and actual control leads to difficulties in international intercourse but it may persist for years, as in the case of Southern Rhodesia. Naturally entities which constitutionally are not autonomous in the conduct of their foreign affairs can lay no claim to sovereignty—hence the glaring empirical anomaly that even the most populous state of the United States, California, which commands the seventh largest economy in the world, enjoys no international status.

The basic meaning of sovereignty has remained unchanged ever since its formulation in 1576 by the French lawyer Jean Bodin as 'the supreme power over citizens and subjects unrestrained by law', even though Bodin's sovereign absolutist rulers have now been replaced by wider bodies politic. Both state practice and legal and other scholarly analysis show, however, great confusion about the application of the concept. There are several ambiguities. The first is the confusion between the formal legal status and actual independence, that is, the capacity to operate without control by another entity: there are hosts of 'sovereign' states whose freedom of action is substantially limited but this does not deprive them of the status. This is the case with the small, isolated South-west Pacific communities or with countries under foreign military occupation like Afghanistan or Kampuchea. Sometimes the formal status is denied to entities which are in fact fully independent—like Southern Rhodesia during its brief existence under this name following the unilateral declaration of independence in 1965 or the Democratic Republic of China on Taiwan.

The second confusion regards recognition. States are under no legal obligation to recognize other entities and often situations arise when state practice is not uniform, especially when new units emerge and declare their independence, for example, Israel, Biafra, Bangladesh, the Turkish Cypriot Republic. The outcome, whether or not they are generally accorded sovereign status, depends upon the interplay of international politics and not on conformity with a fixed legal formula. The obverse is likewise true: small, emancipated colonial territories have been accorded sovereign status by being accepted as members of the United Nations—which is the most convincing hallmark of the legal status—although the entities utterly lack the conditions for independent foreign policy. One should also clearly distinguish between the issue of recognition of a state and of its government (see pp. 29–31).

'Sovereignty' gives rise to different problems in the domestic and the international spheres. The classical problems of internal sovereignty such as the source and justification of the supreme power, its relation with the citizens, its location, and the question of whether it can be divided, need not detain us. In international relations, sovereignty is accepted as a fact and governments are considered as representatives of their states, wherever political scientists and jurists may locate the ultimate sovereign power. External sovereignty can be divided, as shown by the historical cases of such 'semi-sovereignties' as protectorates, or the Free City of Danzig in the inter-war period, or the Free Territory of Trieste between 1945 and 1954, or by the still existing case of Monaco. In substance, however, in all these instances the semi-sovereign state has no supreme authority to conduct its foreign affairs, and hence is not really sovereign at all.

External sovereignty implies a basic contradiction to any notion of a normative international order. An international society of fully sovereign states is just as unthinkable as a domestic anarchist society of fully free individuals. Since law is the formal expression of social order, this contradiction shows most clearly in the relations between the institutions of the sovereign state and of international law.

International law establishes norms of social behaviour in the same way as does law within a state—or, as the lawyers call it, municipal law—but it is a much weaker kind of law precisely because its subjects, the states, are sovereign. International law is based on two apparently contradictory assumptions: first, that the states, being sovereign, are basically not subject to any legal restraint; second, that international law does impose such restraints. Obviously neither assumption is fully tenable: neither can the state's external authority be quite unlimited, otherwise there would be no law at all, nor can we expect the legal order to be centralized and strong. The principle of 'consent' enables us to reconcile this basic contradiction, at least in theory: in the exercise of their sovereignty, states can and do bind themselves to observe certain rules and contract certain obligations. Thus the rules of international law which they have accepted, explicitly or implicitly, do not derive from a superior authority above states—which would contradict their sovereign character—but are made by the states themselves. Consequently, international law is a law among states and not above them. Specifically, the states often agree to limit their sovereignty through the conclusion of innumerable international agreements and through their membership of international institutions.

To sum up, however confused the concept of 'sovereignty' may be, it expresses an important political reality and it evokes strong emotional responses. It has been rightly described as the

supreme legal formula of international society. Those who blame
its allegedly obsolete nature for the major ills of this society are,
in fact, criticizing the very institution of states.

Social coherence, nationalism, and legitimacy

Some lawyers argue that a state exists as soon as the four formal
elements can be found in it, and that recognition by other states
merely recognizes this social fact. Others argue that such recognition is constitutive; that it is only through receiving such
recognition that the state assumes its identity as a member of
international society. On the former theory, the formal elements
are deemed sufficient; on the latter, recognition is required in
addition, and is in fact the most important element since it can be
granted even if the formal elements are defective or refused when
they do exist. A sociological investigation of the issue of the
state's 'legitimacy' offers a convenient tool for analysing both
the domestic and the international aspects of recognition.

To start with the domestic angle, we must try to explain how
the formal elements of statehood are fused, what endows the
government with legitimacy in the eyes of its people and ensures
its domestic sovereignty, what holds society together. The government's primary task is to organize the political life of the
country; hence it concentrates political power. Some of the newly
established states have been recognized as such on the basis of
this political organization alone, although the social, economic,
and cultural ties characterizing older states simply do not exist in
them. It is, however, a historical fact that all states within the
classical political system have either started with or achieved such
ties and that modern governments wield a considerable amount
not only of political but also of economic and social power.
Deficiencies in these non-political bonds must be taken into
account when assessing the position and the prospects of the new
states.

Even political power, which is the very basis of the recognition
of the government by other states, cannot be taken for granted.
The concentration of political power in the hands of the government is the rule, but not a rule without exceptions: it may be

challenged by separatist forces, insurgents may arise and take over part of the state's territory, aggressors may occupy it, regional and minority allegiances may prevail against loyalty to the state. Even without any specific opposition, the citizens' loyalty to the government can become eroded by persistent failure in economic performance or in the provision of a minimum degree of order. Especially with new states, we must check in every case the extent of the actual political powers of the government; there are many examples of such powers being highly deficient.

Ever since the French Revolution nationalism has been the main spiritual and emotional force cementing all the elements of statehood in nation-states, and these have become the classical type of unit. Wherever the nation-state was a reality, nationalism buttressed and reinforced the state; where it remained an aspiration, nationalism endangered the existing multinational units. Hence the relations between the state and the nation require careful consideration. The close historical links between the two concepts date back only just over a century and a half and we would not be justified in considering them as perennial; they vary greatly over time and place. Sometimes states precede nations, as in Western Europe, sometimes nations precede states, as in Central and Eastern Europe. At present, states of vastly different nature are multinational, for instance the Soviet Union, Switzerland, and Yugoslavia; other states have large national minorities; some nations are divided into separate states, for instance the Germans and the Koreans. Relations between the state and the nation cannot be equated with those between the state and society because in no state is this society limited to the members of one nation alone, nor is any nation limited to society within a single state.

If by a community we understand a social group within which men live all their lives, as distinct from associations within which they satisfy only some of their needs, a nation is a community. It differs from other communities first of all in size: the smaller communities, the family and the village, are small face-to-face groups, whereas a nation encompasses millions or at least many thousands. Second, the nation commands the supreme loyalty of its members; third, it has become closely connected with the institution of the state.

A nation can be defined either through the objective characteristics common to its individual members or through the subjective sentiments of those members, or through a combination of both. In most, though not all, nations the prominent common features are: the idea of a common government; a territory; common distinguishing characteristics, especially a language; certain interests common to all members; a certain degree of communal national feeling or will. The last, psychological element is sometimes regarded as decisive; in fact some definitions limit themselves to it, regarding nationalism purely as a state of mind. Thus in his *Representative Government* (1861), John Stuart Mill stressed common sympathies among members of a nation which 'make them co-operate with each other more willingly than with other people, desire to be under the same government, and desire that it should be government by themselves or portion of themselves, exclusively'. In 1882, in an oft-quoted passage, Renan spoke of the nation as a 'soul, a spiritual principle', whose existence is a 'daily plebiscite'.

Nations do not emerge from these definitions as clear-cut entities, nor are they clear-cut entities in life. Even in Western Europe where nation-state relations are of the longest standing, large national minorities have not been fully assimilated, for example the Irish, Scots and Welsh in Britain, the Basques in Spain, the Bretons in France. In Central Europe the situation is even more precarious and fluctuating. The separation of the Austrians from the German nation has been a complicated process—even in the inter-war period many Austrians considered themselves as Germans; the post-war division of Germany into the Federal Republic and the Democratic Republic of Germany has resulted in an ambiguous and potentially explosive conflict between the desire for re-unification and the gradual crystallization of two ideologically and socially distinct communities which are not quite clear about the shape of the future they desire. There are great tensions between the constituent nationalities of Yugoslavia, while the condition of the Hungarians in Transylvania remains the subject of a bitter dispute between Hungary and Romania.

Outside Europe the situation differs from continent to continent. In North America, Australasia, and, despite lingering racial friction, in Latin America also, modern nation-states have had sufficient time to become consolidated. In Asia, with its long tradition of native states, the pattern of stable national and multi-national states has become quite firmly established. In the Middle East, Africa, and the small islands of the Caribbean and the South Pacific, local traditions offer no promise of stability. The mosaic of nationalities, religions, and sects in the Middle East does not fit either into the pattern of the individual states arbitrarily carved out of the remnants of the Ottoman Empire in the inter-war years nor into one of a single Arab nation, the ideal professed although not actively pursued by the vast majority of the Muslim and the Christian Arabs. The situation is further bedevilled by the establishment, in 1947, of Israel, the only national state on the Western pattern in the region. This has led to painful population shifts—of Arabs from Palestine and of Jews from Arab states—and to an acute and apparently insoluble conflict, accentuated by four major armed confrontations. Moreover, as Israel includes a large Arab minority, especially while it retains control of the West Bank occupied during the 1967 war, it is not a homogeneous national state either. In Africa states were formed within the boundaries of European empires, arbitrarily drawn in the last century without any regard to tribal divisions. Hence the new states are beset by tribal rivalries leading to alternating patterns of repression and rebellion; their strenuous efforts at nation-building have been generally ineffective. Racial friction on the small islands of the Caribbean and the South Pacific occasionally leads to political upheavals.

To sum up, there is sound reason for considering international society as 'multilayered' rather than composed of nation-states. Nationalism has served as a powerful stabilizing force in Western European states, and in other continents too; it has been a powerful factor in disrupting colonial empires but ineffective in consolidating the successor states. It is likely that from the Western European perspective we tend somewhat to exaggerate its political impact. Nationalism is, however, a spiritual force also, motivating human behaviour or, at the very least, used for what is generally regarded as a legitimate rationalization of such behaviour. Many thinkers consider it to be the modern replacement of religious faith: it provides the main basis for governments to claim legitimacy and demand loyalty from their citizens. It is in the name of nationalism that the major wars of this century have been fought, and the unresolved territorial conflicts continue. If, as has been stated, the Europeans tend to exaggerate the importance of nationalism, it is partly because they accept that there exists a basic human need to believe in something and no effective rival or successor to nationalism has arisen. Class loyalty, as proposed by Marx, has not been vindicated by history: in the two World Wars the proletarians of all countries did not unite as he had envisaged but rallied on the sides of their respective national states.

In all likelihood the lingering force of nationalism stems largely from its association with states; it remains highly influential, at least negatively, by bolstering opposition to alien domination through the appeals of anti-imperialism. Hence it becomes necessary for all those seeking state power and control over citizens to ally themselves with it. A fusion between nationalism and Fascism took place in inter-war Italy, Germany, and Japan; during the Nazi invasion Stalin rallied the citizens of the Soviet Union by appeals to great Russian patriotism; in new states modernizers bent on development try to buttress their efforts by nation-building; even the fundamentalist religious revivalists do not replace nationalism but ally themselves with it, as has been dramatically demonstrated in Iran.

With the single exception of Japan, no state comes anywhere close to the ideal nation-state—that is, the population consisting almost exclusively of the members of the nation and nearly all the members of the nation being resident in the state; many states are distinctly multinational. The deviations from the nation-state ideal are potentially disruptive in themselves, but the stability of the individual states depends primarily on the satisfaction of the citizens' economic needs, both in very poor countries where people struggle for survival and in affluent countries gripped by the philosophy of consumerism. The spiritual reaction against this materialism tends to take the form of religious, fundamentalist revivals, and nationalism comes into play only when the material or spiritual dissatisfaction leads to open opposition to the institution of the state. It seems clear, for instance, that the future of Yugoslavia, a multinational state which, since the death of Tito, has been affected by increasingly acute nationalist tensions, will be ultimately determined by the success or failure of the Yugoslav economy: nationalist antagonisms are created by economic failure as attempts at equalization fail to satisfy the poorer constituents while they create resentment among the more affluent ones. This analysis of the stability of states in terms of economic performance is not disproved by the fact that, as has been mentioned, some acute purely nationalist tensions have remained with us.

If the issue of the internal legitimacy of governments is complex and unclear, the issue of their external legitimacy is even more confused. Again for analytical purposes, it is important to distinguish whether the legitimacy of a government or, more fundamentally, of the very state is in question. International law has never been a decisive arbiter of recognition—the United States practice has always been openly political, granting or refusing recognition of states and governments according to the decisions of the President, whereas the British have tended to grant recognition following the actual exercise of authority over territory. Naturally the practical results have differed greatly: in 1947, for example, the United States immediately recognized the newly established state of Israel whereas Britain was much slower; by contrast, the British recognized the Central People's Government in China a short time after its final consolidation on the mainland, whereas the Americans continued to recognize the Government of the Democratic Republic of China on Taiwan until 1979.

The best example of the confusion surrounding the issue of recognition can be found in the different attitudes to the recognition of the governments of Afghanistan and Kampuchea. In both cases the Western governments and China strongly disapprove of the existing governments, owing to their dependence on occupation troops—the Russians in Afghanistan and the Vietnamese in Kampuchea. The government of Afghanistan does, however, have a tenuous claim to continuity with previous governments and is opposed by disunited opposition groups which seem unable to unite into a single front. In Kampuchea on the other hand, there does exist an opposition government with claims to legal continuity, but it is also morally reprehensible and rather ineffective in the field. In this legally and politically confused situation, outsiders are unable to formulate rational policies; hence they seem to be generally governed by the desire to avoid the need for action. The status quo therefore prevails: recognition of the Afghan government in Kabul and of the rebel government in Kampuchea.

Since 1945, it is no longer Britain and United States but the ideological blocs and the General Assembly of the United Nations (UN) that have become the purveyors of legitimacy. The separate parts of the nation-states split by ideological divisions after 1945 commanded recognition according to the ideology of the other states: Western Germany, Southern Korea, and, while it remained in separate existence, South Vietnam were recognized by the Western bloc while their Communist counterparts were recognized by the Communist bloc. The Third World established fairly clear rules about the legitimacy of the successor-states after decolonization: the states were recognized within their existing colonial boundaries and breakaway units were recognized only exceptionally. In most cases they were refused such recognition, especially if support from the ex-colonial ruler or racial minority rule were involved. Thus Ruanda and Burundi were allowed to separate into two states but not Eastern Indonesia or the Katanga (Shaba) province of the Congo.

The case of Southern Rhodesia is the most prominent example of the central importance of legitimacy. After its unilateral declaration of independence in 1965, the government of Southern Rhodesia was universally denied legitimacy not only because of its illegal breakaway origins but increasingly also as an oppressive, racist minority government. This led to the declaration of mandatory sanctions against it by the United Nations and to widespread support for the independence fighters challenging it, resulting in its gradual decline.

This was by no means an isolated case. The international

system was gradually moving towards a situation in which governments generally regarded as reprehensible would be denied legitimacy—and not only at their inception: in the late seventies, under Chinese pressure, recognition was gradually withdrawn from the Democratic Republic of China on Taiwan; South Africa came under an increasing threat of international sanctions for its racist policy of apartheid; the Arabs, powerful as oil exporters, were pressing hard against Israel, although their original denial of the legitimacy of the state had been generally replaced by a less far-reaching demand that Israel should abandon the territories occupied in the aftermath of the 1967 war, the return of which has been persistently demanded by the General Assembly but refused by the Israelis. A new category, sometimes called 'pariah states', has thus come into being, of states whose recognition has been withdrawn or is threatened. Although this does not preclude their continuation as states—Taiwan, for example, remains stable and prosperous—it greatly impedes their international relations. By the late eighties international pressure on South Africa had become so intensive that the government could no longer simply rely on suppressing black opposition, for which it had adequate forces and determination.

To conclude, one cannot deny a degree of common sense, even occasionally wisdom, to the radicals who dismiss politics and power as pernicious and conventional thinking about them as illusory or even dangerously misleading. How can we continue to think in terms of an international system of states evolved in Europe several centuries ago when Europe no longer dominates the world? How can we think adequately about all the baffling problems of the contemporary world mainly using concepts evolved in the tiny Greek city-states? And yet it would be grossly mistaken to consider the radical approaches—whether they focus on a world order or community, the global eco-system, some form of Marxist analysis, human rights, or ontological needs—as representing the future whereas the suggested power-political model represents only the past. Only the future will tell how much, if at all, these radical approaches correspond with historical developments and how much will remain of the traditional power structures. For the time being, at least, the radical approaches constitute no more than normative attempts which are to a limited extent influencing power-political structures and therefore require notice. They do not, however, offer a valid substitute for the conventional model.

3
States II

Classification of states

In the second half of the nineteenth century it was possible for a politician concerned with foreign policy, a diplomat, or a scholar to become well acquainted with the foreign policies of all the states that mattered—the five great European powers—and to acquire a reasonable knowledge of any specific trouble or danger spots arising in the world. In the inter-war world this became much more difficult as the number of states had grown greatly and international politics had become more global. The difficulty has become further accentuated since 1945, when the United Nations, with its nembership of 160, has long surpassed the maximum League of Nations membership of fifty, and issues of international politics have grown in number and complexity. This is the basic justification for an analytical approach to international relations, as the detailed encyclopaedic knowledge open to a nineteenth-century practitioner or scholar is no longer feasible. It is possible, and intellectually attractive, to generalize about the behaviour of all states and, indeed, some quite meaningful generalizations can be made about it, summing up all the behavioural characteristics arising from their position as states. Clearly, however, the behaviour of individual states is not only similar to that of other states but also different in many significant respects. We should try to avoid the necessity of studying all the details of each particular state, and the danger that we may do so in a manner which would make comparisons with other states difficult. Hence the importance of establishing a clear and articulate general framework of analysis which will allow us a certain degree of generalization about all states, and also of distinguishing sub-classes of states which show similarities going beyond the characteristics common to all states, thus reducing the area requiring detailed specific study for each individual case.

The simplest and justifiably most popular method of classification is by geographical regions, which is the basis of area expertise. Clearly not only a range of common problems but also of behavioural similarities peculiar to the states in the region exist in the European Community (EC—now generally used rather than European Economic Community—EEC) area, Eastern Europe, Latin America—and, within it, Central America—the Middle East and Africa and, although to a lesser extent, also in the Far East and South-east Asia. Regional similarities can be found in different forms: some may take an institutional form, as with the members of the European Community channelling certain foreign policy issues through the institution; some are the outcome of sharing a common foreign policy problem of overriding importance, like relations with the adjoining superpower; some may be largely attributed to greater intensity of interaction and to the evolution of historically established customs, as with the Latin American styles of diplomacy and doctrines of international law. A similar process may be slowly taking place within the Organization for African Unity (OAU).

Area similarities apply, however, primarily to area politics; in the context of global politics, other sources of similarity are generally sought, primarily in terms of power. The traditional division used to be into the 'great powers' and other states, occasionally subdivided into small and middle powers. Post-war literature has been increasingly less concerned with the issues of this simple classification, which used to take up an inordinate amount of space and energy without ever resolving the crucial issue of the yardsticks for delimitation. The basic idea of classifying states according to power and status has nevertheless survived, and new, more sophisticated attempts have been made in the post-war period—adding, however, complexity rather than precision to the old-fashioned classification. One well-known attempt is that of James N. Rosenau, proposed in his 'pre-theory' of foreign policy, first publicly discussed in 1964. It is based on the plausible assumption that some domestic attributes of states can be regarded as conducive to certain characteristics of foreign policy behaviour and should therefore be used as the basis for the classification of such behaviour. He proposed three such attributes of states as being impressionistically the most important ones: geography and physical resources (large and small), state of economy (developed and underdeveloped), and state of polity (open and closed). This classification was widely discussed, criticized, refined, and applied for a number of years without producing satisfactory results. No reasonable empirical indicators could be agreed upon; several experimental applications of the three attributes to the analysis of the behaviour of states showed that, with the exception of 'size', the attributes, whether singly or in combination, had no significant influence. However, no new attributes have been suggested as being more significant.

After more than a decade of analysis of the attributes of states, attempts at a better classification have not advanced much beyond the old-fashioned one into great, middle, and small powers, although post-1945 events have created the additional category of the two superpowers and also one of the smallest units, 'micro-states'. All these categories are based on various combinations of power and status, on which more in Chapter 7. As there is no general agreement on the criteria, there is considerable confusion about the boundaries of each class. There is, nevertheless, a considerable amount of agreement too. Nobody would disagree with the contention that, say, Tuvalu, with its 9,000 inhabitants, is a very small or micro-state, and that a state like Brazil is not a very small state, although we may disagree about whether it is a middle or a great power, as this depends on the nature of the definition. All agree, however, that the United States and the Soviet Union should be singled out as two superpowers, and the vast majority limit this category to these two states.

The most realistic model seems to consist of a spectrum of states based upon power and status, with the two superpowers at one extreme and the micro-states at the other, leaving open the question as to where precisely an individual state may fit in between but recognizing that broad agreement is possible about the zone of the spectrum into which it would fit, and often about ranking; thus Brazil is clearly closer to the 'superpower' end of the spectrum than a small Central American republic. It does not seem to be worthwhile to break up this spectrum into clear-cut sections, nor does it seem possible to illustrate them by analysing a representative state as none could be considered as really typical for a class. Chapter 5 on decision-making will therefore be limited to the general categories of the process, while the substance of foreign policies will be indicated only in the subsequent analysis of the two superpowers. Although by no means fully characteristic of other states, these are, of course, particularly important in themselves: they not only pursue their national foreign policies on a fully global scale, as no other states do, but they also play a central role in the operation of the international system.

It is important to note that the role of the superpowers in this respect is quite unique: even at the height of her imperial power Britain was not automatically enmeshed in everything that happened all around the globe. This can be attributed to the conflation of two elements: ideology and technology. In other states national ties are specifically national—involving ethnicity and historical experience. Only in the two superpowers do they incorporate ideology as a major element—the liberal creed in the United States and the Communist one in the Soviet Union. Although in both states these ideologies are now in crisis, they are so closely linked with national interests that it has become impossible to be clear about their actual role: one can argue with an equal degree of plausibility that, by endeavouring to spread their creeds, the two superpowers merely serve their respective national interests or the reverse, that their national interests (narrowly defined as being separate from the ideologies) are subordinated to ideology.

The existence of the superpowers is also an entirely new phenomenon. It has arisen primarily through the United States acquiring military and economic preponderance during the Second World War and through the Soviet Union then attaining a rough equality in military and political, though not economic, capabilities. To a significant extent the two superpowers have gradually lost their ability to control events around them and their predominance has come under challenge from several quarters; the starkest manifestations of this phenomenon have been their setbacks at the hands of small nations—the Vietnamese and Afghans. In 1986, moreover, they both experienced significant technological setbacks and domestic problems. The Americans lost the space shuttle *Challenger* and became embroiled in the political scandal of the arms sale to Iran; the Russians experienced the catastrophic accident at the nuclear power station at Chernobyl and embarked on the uncertain course of fundamental economic and political reform. Both inevitably lost much confidence and inclination to intervene outside their boundaries —excluding only counter-moves to the moves of the other superpower. Nevertheless, the superpower position remains unique: what they do and what happens within their territories can fundamentally affect the international system; specifically they remain militarily predominant and the sole possessors of full-scale nuclear arsenals and space technology. Their relative diminution of power does not mean that they are likely to be replaced by others, as they replaced the dominant Western European great powers, but merely that their power and influence may be gradually matched by others who could join them and constitute a new international order.

If such a new global order did arise, in all likelihood it would signal the final passing of the European era. The most frequent guess is that it would be a pentagonal order, including two Asian states, Japan and China, and only one European entity, the Economic Community, incorporating the Western European states. To sum up briefly their potentials: Japan has grown to be the third largest economy in the world and, by 1986, the largest international investor; while her economic growth has retained much of its dynamism, she has very slowly been assuming a correspondingly increased political/strategic role. China has a formidable human potential of over a billion technologically gifted people but remains in the throes of a painfully slow economic development and subject to periodic crises of political authority. She has developed nuclear weapons and space technology, but by the late eighties was playing only a marginal role in global politics despite the strategic position she could obviously occupy in the Sino–American–Soviet triangle. The European Community has a unique human, economic, and technological potential but the constituent states are historically entrenched as autonomous units and it remains uncertain whether the organization will ever integrate them into a fully coherent political entity (Chapter 4).

Next in order of importance are the large Western European states: the Federal Republic of Germany, France, and Great Britain, all of which have a high degree of global importance owing to their economic and military strength; all have gross national products (GNPs) over $500 billion and populations over 50 million, and are substantial international traders. Germany, although still burdened by the memory of Hitler's period and facing the insoluble problem of national division, has by far the strongest economy of the three and contributes the most substantial contingent of conventional forces to the North Atlantic Treaty Organization (NATO). Both France and Great Britain retain a degree of influence within and through their previous colonial empires and both possess nuclear weapons. Outside Europe, India is the most important power of the middle rank; by the mid-eighties her population was around 700 million and, although poor, she was developing healthily; she has the technological potential for producing nuclear weapons. The most populous and powerful countries in other continents, Brazil in South America and Nigeria in Africa, are only of regional importance.

Before passing to the discussion of individual states, it is necessary to repeat and elaborate the warning against their personification. The comparison of states to persons is fundamentally unwarranted because states signally lack certain basic characteristics of persons who, whatever we think of them, are clearly delimited and integrated entities. States are not solid communities; hence their governments cannot, as is sometimes erroneously assumed, try to carry out the will of their people through foreign policy—there exists no underlying consensus and will about this policy. Moreover, the governments themselves are not monolithic; analysis of decision-making (see Chapter 5) clearly reveals that there can be no greater fallacy than the conventional view, which prevailed until the Second World War, that governments rationally formulate and implement policies. All this suggests that the traditional delimitation of the powers of states and governments goes far beyond the actual capabilities— governments in fact being incapable of controlling not only their own bodies politic but even their own organizations. If the mistaken analogy to a person were pursued, it would lie with a person whose nervous system (the equivalent of government) is disorganized and who suffers from a succession of disorders in his body (the equivalent of the body politic). On this argument, it does not really make sense to discuss the characteristics of states as if we could identify such constants—whether states are immoral or aggressive or oppressive. This, of course, is not to deny the usefulness of analysing the institutions and behaviour of states, because it enables us to guess at the probability of certain outcomes. Despite attempts at arguing their demise, states remain powerful and influential.

Although there is no general agreement about the most suitable framework for the analysis and comparison of foreign policies, a fair degree of agreement exists about what are likely to be the most significant factors. A strong argument can be made in favour of an explicit scheme; hence one is offered here, without claiming special theoretical virtues for it. The significant factors are arranged in five groups:

1. capabilities and salient characteristics, especially those deriving from geography and from historical tradition;
2. major features of the decision-making machinery;
3. major issues of foreign policy and the means to meet commitments;
4. attitudes to the most important states and blocs;
5. attitudes to international order.

The subsequent brief outlines of the policies of the two superpowers are arranged according to this scheme.

The United States

1. The United States has a territory of approaching eight million square kilometres and in the mid-1980s its population was reaching 240 million. In so far as they reflect isolation from

Europe, American traditions resemble those of the British. Protected by the whole width of the Atlantic, which was then under the control of the benevolent British Navy, throughout the nineteenth century the Americans practised 'splendid isolation' and concentrated upon their own continent. They conquered and colonized a large part of it, pushed forward 'the frontier of civilization', and evolved the 'Monroe Doctrine' which aimed at the exclusion of rivals from the remainder. They rapidly developed the great natural riches of their country and built up industry on a scale hitherto unequalled.

The Americans had only one outside interest—to avoid an imperious incursion from Europe. Here they relied upon Britain to maintain the balance of power and to prevent the rise of a European state with dangerous imperial ambitions. Consequently they had scarcely any foreign policy, so their traditions in this field are relatively new. This preoccupation with domestic and continental affairs engendered the American conviction that the domestic and foreign spheres could be permanently separated, and also what some writers call the 'myth of omnipotence' —the belief that the unparalleled American domestic successes could be repeated in international relations also.

At the turn of the century, having straddled the North American continent, the United States embarked on a policy of territorial expansion in the Pacific and the Far East. Its aims were not very clear: by and large they were to keep China independent—as a counterbalance to the rising might of Japan—and open—as a market for American trade.

The great open spaces of North America were almost empty and required labour for their development. First, slaves were imported from Africa; their emancipated descendants amount to over 10 per cent of the American population today and, owing to the racial difference, have not been fully assimilated. Then many millions of European immigrants of various nationalities flocked into the United States. Finally, millions of 'Hispanics' from Latin America, Vietnamese, and Filipinos have entered the country since 1945. Thus, in complete contrast to the fairly homogeneous states of Western Europe, American society has incorporated many different elements in quite recent times. The original common mould was largely shaped by British traditions, but the vast spaces, the persistence of the individual identities of the separate colonies, and the 'melting pot' of the various national and racial strains, have produced a highly decentralized system characterized by a federal constitution, by a lack of discipline within the two great national political parties, and by the prevalence of regional and particular interests. Nor is it political power alone that is decentralized: until recently, there have been no national mass media, excepting the syndicated columns in the press and the occasional national hook-ups of television networks.

In the 1960s the political system entered a period of crisis. The racial problems became increasingly acute and public opinion split over the American involvement in Vietnam; urban violence increased, culminating in recurrent summer riots and in the assassinations of one president and one presidential candidate. In the next decade this was followed by the Watergate affair, a political scandal which forced President Richard Nixon to resign. By the end of the seventies, however, the American political system had regained its stability. Its most acute and unresolved problems were economic—how to cope with the chronic weakness of the dollar induced mainly by large foreign trade deficits due to the massive imports of oil, the price of which quadrupled in 1973, and by the successful rivalry in industrial production on the part of Japan and the Federal Republic of Germany. Although the American economy recovered and unemployment was greatly reduced under President Reagan, elected in 1980, by 1986 the persistent balance of payments deficits had turned the country from the largest creditor to a debtor nation and the enormous budgetary deficits could not be controlled.

The basis of United States power lies in its great natural resources, in its highly evolved industrial system, and its spectacular technological advance, unparalleled until the late seventies. In the mid-eighties its GNP was estimated at $3,000 billion, of which some 7 per cent was spent on defence. It continued to enjoy one of the highest per capita income and consumption levels.

2. The nature of American democracy, particularly decentralization, the division of constitutional powers, and the impact

of public opinion, are gravely prejudicial to an efficient foreign policy. De Tocqueville's famous remarks made over a century ago are still fully pertinent:

Foreign politics demand scarcely any of these qualities which are peculiar to democracy; they require, on the contrary, the perfect use of almost all those in which it is deficient . . . a democracy can only with great difficulties regulate the details of an important undertaking, persevere in a fixed design, and work out its execution in spite of serious obstacles. It cannot combine its measures with secrecy or await their consequences with patience.

American governmental machinery is extremely cumbersome. The President is undoubtedly the chief decision-maker within the Executive, but under him some fifty agencies deal with foreign affairs. The Congress, on the basis of the 'checks and balances' doctrine, has co-ordinate powers; it interferes in foreign affairs and, in the absence of party discipline, the President is unable to control the regional and sectional interests within it. Moreover, as national congressional elections take place every two years, the volatile opinions of the electorate at large incessantly intrude.

Until 1945 American diplomacy was relatively undeveloped; it suffered from inadequate apparatus and insufficient professionalism, and was generally ill equipped to cope with the difficult post-war tasks. Since then the Americans have built up the largest diplomatic service in the world with missions in nearly all other states. This service lacks long tradition and is gravely handicapped by the activities of a poorly controlled intelligence service as well as by the constant intrusion of domestic politics. Its shortcomings and occasional blunders must, however, be viewed against the background of a generally successful development.

3. Within the first half of this century the Americans, who had formerly had little or no foreign policy, suddenly became one of the two superpowers, and their world-wide commitments required from them a complete mental reorientation. In spite of occasional disturbances, they were on the whole successful in their adjustments. When their security was menaced by the prospect of a German victory, they reluctantly took part in the First

World War; they entered the Second World War equally unwillingly in 1941; but in both wars they fought with will and determination. When Britain was unable to continue her task of containing Communism, the United States stepped in in March 1947 with the 'Truman Doctrine', thus taking on the role of protagonist in the 'cold war'. With the Marshall Plan and NATO it stabilized the situation in Europe, but its interventions in Asia were less uniformly successful. The Americans enabled Japan, Taiwan, and South Korea to rehabilitate themselves and prosper, but were unsuccessful in their attempts to ward off the establishment of a Communist regime in China. They became involved in a prolonged, massive military intervention in Vietnam, which was extremely costly in terms of manpower and economic losses, as well as of opprobrium at home and abroad, and ended in failure.

Undoubtedly the major issues of United States foreign policy today—military, political, economic, and ideological—all stem from its position as a superpower balancing the power of the Soviet Union. American foreign policy requires great expenditure of money, constant vigilance, and alert diplomacy. The Americans have scored successes but have also suffered defeats, and the rising—and occasionally clashing—demands of their world-wide commitments often confront them with apparently insoluble dilemmas. Political will, presidential authority, and defence expenditure, all of which are closely linked, have been widely fluctuating. The greatly increased military expenditure for the Vietnam intervention was covered by borrowing but subsequently, under the Democratic President Carter, presidential authority, and the political will to match the Soviet expansion of armaments and Soviet expansion into Africa, weakened. Reaction set in at the end of the seventies, however, and led to the election of the Republican President Reagan for two terms. He restored presidential authority and engaged once more in a massive military build-up, until his authority was weakened by a new political scandal and the massive budgetary and balance of payments deficits threatened continued American prosperity.

In the order of their historical evolution, the major direct American foreign policy interests lie in the Western hemisphere;

the somewhat less direct interest in Europe is of equal age, whereas interest in Asia stems from the end of the last century only. The direct interests in the Western hemisphere persists but, with the rapid growth in the population centres on the Pacific seaboard and the increased importance of Japan and China, Asia and the Pacific have become rivals to Europe and the North Atlantic. Only since 1945 have the Americans developed an intensive political interest in other regions, eventually covering the whole globe and seriously stretching the conception of what constitutes vital American national interests.

4. Ever since its rise to the position of a superpower, the United States' foreign relations with the Soviet Union, its fellow superpower, have become centrally important, including, as they do, the element of nuclear rivalry. In the cold war, the main objective of the United States was to deter a direct nuclear attack on the territory of the United States or its allies, and to contain Communist expansion, the danger of which had gradually spread from Europe and the Far East to all other continents and regions. In spite of the loose proclamation of a more active policy of 'liberation' of Eastern Europe in 1952, the American attitude to the Soviet Union remained fundamentally passive, as expressed in the formula of 'containment', coined by the influential diplomat, George F. Kennan. The United States pursued this policy by accumulating a massive stockpile of armaments, by concluding a series of alliances, and by establishing foreign bases. It furnished lavish aid, both military and economic, to its allies and also to neutrals. The Communists scored a victory in China in 1949 but elsewhere the Americans generally succeeded in containing them —in Korea through a full-scale war fought with conventional weapons. Only in Vietnam were they unsuccessful, despite their large-scale involvement.

Stalin's death in 1953 ended the era of crude Soviet military menace. Thereafter the conflict began to shift to economic and ideological competition to win the sympathy of the non-committed, neutral states of Asia and Africa. Gradually the two superpowers began to find accommodation on several important issues, including those of nuclear strategy and some of their respective spheres of interest. After having been brought to the brink of a direct clash during the Cuban missile crisis in October 1962, the cold war gradually changed into what the Americans usually call a '*détente*' and the Russians 'peaceful coexistence'. Tensions continued, however, and the Soviet military intervention in Czechoslovakia in August 1968 disrupted progress. At the beginning of the seventies, serious new attempts started to limit the nuclear armaments race, leading to the partially successful Strategic Arms Limitation Talks (SALT) and the more successful stabilization of the division of Germany and of the status of Berlin. *Détente* did not, however, become firmly established and its peak, the Helsinki Conference on European Security and Co-operation in 1975, led not only to increased economic exchanges but also to acrimonious disputes about human rights while the security results were not very promising, especially as the Russians were rapidly improving their armaments.

American relations with China were much slower to improve. After a direct armed clash in Korea, the Americans remained entrenched in their bases on Okinawa and Taiwan, and became gradually involved in a massive military intervention in support of the anti-Communist regime in South Vietnam. Chinese success in developing nuclear weapons exacerbated the antagonism. A *détente* with China did, however, follow the gradual American withdrawal from Vietnam in 1970 and 1971 and was firmly established by President Nixon's visit to Peking in February 1972. The Americans did not fully meet the Chinese desire to secure support against the Soviet Union, to which they had become increasingly hostile, and the issue of continuing American support and recognition of Taiwan delayed the re-establishment of full diplomatic relations till 1979, but relations between the two countries have been improving quite steadily since then.

American relations with other regions and states have to a very large extent reflected their relations with the Communist powers; sometimes, to the detriment of American interests, they were excessively governed by the dictates of the cold war. This applied even to allies: in the Western hemisphere the Americans tried unavailingly to transform the Organization of American States (OAS) into an effective anti-Communist alliance, but since 1961 they have been compelled to endure the pro-Communist

Government of Fidel Castro in Cuba; even their most successful coalition, NATO, has lost much of its urgency of purpose and has proved incapable of resolving some serious problems of co-operation.

During the seventies economics moved towards the centre of American international concerns, especially the massive imbalance in the trade with Japan. In the eighties the economy became chronically unbalanced through a bout of armaments spending accompanied by lowered taxes, resulting in massive budgetary and balance of payments deficits.

5. Through traditions held in common with Britain, the Americans felt identified with the international order of the nineteenth century more than any other non-European state. They contributed to the evolution of some international norms, especially to the law of neutrality; throughout their early history, although concerned mainly with their own continent and pursuing a policy of 'isolationism', they remained intensely interested in the maintenance of the balance of power in Europe, even though they preferred not to play an active part in it. When the balance was seriously threatened by the Germans in the two World Wars and by the Russians since, reluctantly but effectively they stepped into the breach.

The American attitude to a new international order embodied in the international institutions of the twentieth century has been inconsistent. Although the League of Nations was President Wilson's brain-child, American public opinion did not share his internationalism and the Senate refused to ratify the Peace Treaty of Versailles and to join the League. During the Second World War, the Americans were determined to set up a new order and were the initiators and main proponents of the United Nations as the comprehensive institution as well as of the important 'specialized agencies' dealing with economics. This was a manifestation both of their conviction that this would be in their own national interest and of their idealistic convictions. Indeed, at first the United Nations seemed very much an instrument for imposing a *pax Americana* upon the world: with the support of the Latin American states (twenty out of the original membership of fifty) and of the Western European allies, the Americans

commanded crushing anti-Russian majorities on all controversial matters which came up before the General Assembly.
They greatly benefited from UN sponsorship of what was in fact
an American intervention in Korea. But even in the sixties and
seventies, after the easy majorities had disappeared as the membership had more than tripled, the Americans retained a positive
attitude to the United Nations and remained by far the most
important contributor to its finances. Being located in New York
and thus providing local news, the United Nations figured in the
American mass media much more frequently than in any other
country. In the late seventies, however, tensions arising from its
new minority position and from the violently anti-Israeli and
anti-capitalist policies of the majorities began to tell, resulting in
the refusal of the United States to pay its full contribution to
the United Nations and its withdrawal from membership of the
International Labour Organization (ILO) and the United
Nations Educational, Scientific, and Cultural Organization
(UNESCO).

It may be added that these ecumenical ideas have not fully
eliminated all narrower ideas of an international order. The
Americans have officially abandoned the traditional Monroe
Doctrine, embodying their aspirations to control the Western
hemisphere, but have continued to intervene in the politics of
their neighbours, even using military force in the Dominican
Republic in 1965 and in Grenada in 1984. They maintain a primary interest in maintaining order within the Americas, which
means preventing the rise of new Communist regimes, although
tolerating Castro's on Cuba, after attempts to remove it had
failed. They have extended this notion of a regional order to
what they sometimes call 'the free world', meaning all anti-
Communist countries which, at least in theory, subscribe to the
ideas of liberal democracy and a free market economy. Again in
theory, it is conceivable that—in concert with the Soviet Union—
the United States could introduce a world order based on the
drawing of boundaries between their respective spheres of interests. Such an order is unlikely, however. The Communist world is
split; Communist expansion into the Western hemisphere milit-
ates against such accommodation; moreover, the Americans feel a

fundamental antagonism to Communism and could not accept Communist rule over a third of mankind even as a factor of stability. There are in fact no signs that either superpower is willing to become a custodian of a universal world order (see Chapter 8).

The Soviet Union

1. Any analysis of Soviet affairs must inevitably include a discussion of Communist ideology. All countries are governed by systems of values and beliefs which we now call ideologies, but, whereas in the United States or in any other established non-Communist country ideologies have developed organically together with other political and social traditions, in the Soviet Union the Communist ideology was imposed upon the country in 1917 and its exact relation to the Tsarist heritage remains ambiguous.

Although most Marxists emphatically deny that the geographical position of a country may have a determining effect on its foreign policy, this is more clearly the case with Russia than with many other countries. Russia is by far the largest state on earth, embracing over 22 million square kilometres, fully half of the Eurasian continent and two and a half times the size of the United States. No 'natural frontiers' exist to which Russia could aspire since no physical features delimit her from the Central European plain. The country is clearly indefensible, the fluctuating nature of Russian frontiers reflecting the strength or weakness of the central government; for three centuries Russia was under the Tartar yoke and as late as the seventeenth century she had temporarily a Polish ruler.

While the indeterminate nature of Russian frontiers made the country an easy prey for attacks, it also encouraged the Russians to seek security through expansion. They expanded in all directions, reaching the physical limits of the Arctic and Pacific Oceans and clashing with neighbouring countries everywhere else. In contrast to the relative isolation of the United States, Russia has always been in constant interaction with her neighbours—when she was weak and disunited she was subject to depredations; when strong and united, she expanded as far as possible. The traditional aims of Russian foreign policy are to absorb or truncate weak neighbours and to exercise as much control as possible over those unwilling to yield and able to resist. Her specific territorial objectives are sea outlets, ice-free ports, the object of the historical drives towards the Straits, the Gulf, and the Yellow Sea.

The imperious demands of foreign policy set such a premium upon unity and centralization that Russia has achieved a fair degree of both despite her enormous area and her large population, divided into some 150 ethnic and linguistic groups which differ greatly in many important characteristics. Although her constitution is federal in form, the Soviet Union perpetuates the Tsarist tradition of centralized control which is now exercised by the Communist Party.

The October Revolution in 1917 brought into power the Bolsheviks, whose Marxist ideology not only prescribed a new central objective of world revolution but also a new system of knowledge and new strategies of foreign policy. During the twenties the break with the past seemed to be complete: the Soviet rulers were pursuing their goal of world revolution in a ruthless and unprecedented fashion. When, however, in the late twenties this goal was replaced by that of 'building socialism in one country', and when various traditional Russian policies and ways of behaviour were revived, the question of the interrelation between ideology and national tradition was re-opened. While some Western experts contend that Soviet foreign policy is still rigidly controlled by ideology, others claim that this is merely a thin disguise for traditional Tsarist policies which are no more than the obvious reaction to the challenges arising in Russia's environment. Others again try to combine both approaches and to study the changes in ideology in actual Soviet practice.

The Soviet regime gained full control over the country and industrialized it, won the Second World War and recovered from its colossal destruction, but only through the exercise of a strict and ruthless totalitarian regime, extremely oppressive to the citizens. By the end of the Second World War, the Soviet Union had secured the position of a superpower. The problem of her different ethnic and linguistic groups remained unresolved, however, and, especially since the death of Stalin in 1953, the Soviet rulers have been facing increasingly insistent demands for greater political liberty and more consumer goods.

The Soviet Union possesses tremendous natural resources, but much of them in the inaccessible wastes of Siberia. The industrial system is unevenly developed: although in some respects her nuclear weapons and some of her heavy armaments equal or even surpass in their sophistication those manufactured in the United States, she is quite backward as regards most consumer goods nor can she master the organization of agriculture, in which collective and state farms have proved quite inadequate. In the mid-eighties the population of the Soviet Union was around 270 million; after a period of very rapid post-war growth, which slowed down in the seventies, her gross domestic product (GDP)—which is very hard to estimate—had reached about $2,000 billion, of which some 12–17 per cent was spent on defence. Consequently her per capita income remained very low compared with that of the United States.

2. As in all single-party totalitarian states, the making of foreign policy in the Soviet Union is characterized by complete control by the Communist Party of the Soviet Union; the governmental apparatus, including the Foreign Ministry, merely executes the policies decided by it. Within the Party, power was formerly rigidly concentrated in the hands of Stalin, but under the 'collective leadership' which succeeded him it was vested in the Praesidium or Politburo, numbering eleven to fifteen. Between 1956 and 1963 the First Secretary of the Party, Nikita Khrushchev, dominated Soviet politics and was internationally the only prominent figure. He was not, however, a dictator with unlimited powers; he depended upon the other members of the Praesidium, and also, to a much smaller extent, on the members of the larger Central Committee of the Party. Until the selection of Mikhail Gorbachev, no other individual became fully predominant in Soviet leadership—not even the long-lasting Leonid Brezhnev.

Soviet diplomacy is unorthodox; it engages in widespread espionage and propaganda and is therefore generally distrusted.

Moreover, it is rigid and slavishly dependent upon central orders. Consequently, in spite of the large funds at its disposal and the great pool of ability from which it can draw, it is not particularly successful. The position did not change after Stalin's death: the blundering treatment of the Czechoslovak crisis in 1968, and of the human rights issue after 1975, indicate that it remained essentially similar. The first serious attempts at reforms were undertaken only in 1986 by Gorbachev.

3. Soviet foreign policy cannot be evaluated with any degree of certainty because we cannot be sure to which of their objectives the Russians give priority; in fact the Soviet leaders themselves are divided, or unclear, or both. The Soviet Union is a rapidly developing country in which the standard of living of the citizens is still very low. Although it is still expanding, the Soviet economy remains highly inefficient and cannot provide enough for the growing needs of consumption, the mounting military expenditure, and minimal foreign aid. In the sixties, and even more so when economic growth slowed down in the late seventies, it became obvious that, although in possession of all the elements of power, the Soviet Union was feeling the strain rather acutely.

It is not a case of the proverbial choice between guns and butter; all Soviet rulers choose and are likely to go on choosing guns as long as they deem these essential for national security. The question is to what extent they feel that they must still work with all the means at their disposal for a world revolution which, according to Marxist doctrine, is in any case inevitable. Moreover, having rebuilt the country after the ravages of the Second World War and secured a fair degree of economic and social advancement, they are chary of jeopardizing their achievements and also badly in need of Western technology. Gorbachev's attempts at reform both at home and in foreign policy indicate clearly that all this may have, at least to some extent, transformed their ideology. Finally, although at the moment this is highly speculative, in view of the difficulties arising from their relations with Communist China, the Russians may find the prospect of an all-Communist world much less attractive; some of their interests in the Third World now coincide with those of the capitalist, highly industrialized countries and the remainder of the white race.

These are, of course, Western interpretations of the major issues of Soviet foreign policy. It is quite likely that many, perhaps most, of the Soviet leaders genuinely believe their own protestations that Soviet foreign policy is defensive, that the Soviet Union is threatened from all directions by the United States, which has established a ring of alliances and military bases all around her, and which conducts a strongly anti-Communist policy. The future development of Soviet foreign policy is bound to revolve around these two fundamental issues; priority of domestic or foreign commitments, and evaluation of American intentions.

4. Soviet relations with the United States thus clearly dominate the whole of Soviet foreign policy. It is difficult to appreciate from the outside exactly what the Russians mean by their slogan of 'peaceful coexistence' with the capitalist world. Although crude military expansionism ceased with Stalin's death, a fundamental hostility and distrust persists. In all probability, many Soviet Communists still think in terms of the ultimately inevitable war between the United States and the Soviet Union. Even Khrushchev, the main architect of peaceful coexistence, repeatedly made it clear that it meant to him not the abandonment of hostility but merely a shift of the conflict from the military to other fields. To some extent, Soviet-American relations are bound to depend on what the Americans do and on how they behave, but in all likelihood they depend very much more on the evolution of Soviet society and of Communist ideology.

Soviet relations with other Communist states give rise to problems which are much more complex and independent of the cold war than similar problems confronting the United States in relations with its allies. Until 1945 these countries had been neither Communist nor under Russian rule. In conformity both with Tsarist tradition and with the goal of world revolution, the Soviet Union imposed Communist regimes wherever the Red Army marched: local Communists seized power by themselves only in Yugoslavia and later in China. It proved difficult for the Soviet

Union to control the new Communist governments as they had habitually done with Communist parties abroad: in 1947-8 they tried in vain to squash nationalist opposition in Yugoslavia; in 1956 Poland and Hungary asserted their independence.

Of greatest importance, however, was the Sino–Soviet rift which came out into the open in the late fifties and gradually grew until China became a dangerous and outspoken opponent of the Soviet Union, threatening her long frontier by her claims for the return of lost territories, and rivalling her as a more radical leader of international Communism—admittedly with only limited success. In the late sixties, the Communist bloc further loosened, with Albania coming out firmly on the side of China, with Romania asserting herself through an independent foreign policy, and, in 1968, with Czechoslovakia rapidly liberalizing her regime. With the assistance of similarly apprehensive regimes in East Germany, Poland, Hungary, and Bulgaria, the Russians first threatened the liberalizers and then had to resort to a large-scale military intervention in Czechoslovakia, thus showing how brittle the solidarity of the bloc had become. Patriotism united the Czechs and the Slovaks against the occupiers. In the late seventies the 'Eurocommunism' of the Western European countries went out of control. In the early eighties dissent in Poland broke out. Instead of being monolithic, the Communist bloc is now clearly polycentric: the various Communist governments and parties are dependent on the Soviet Union militarily and economically and cannot effectively defend themselves. Nevertheless, they are able to exercise a degree of independence, according to their individual strength and determination. In a military conflict with the West their forces could prove unreliable.

In their relations with the non-committed countries, the Soviet leaders came up against a contradiction between their support for world revolution and for foreign Communists and their interest in alignment with 'bourgeois-nationalist' governments which were willing to stay out of American alliances. They were inconsistent and vacillating. After initial opposition to the post-colonial governments, they unsuccessfully attempted to cajole them into an anti-Western 'camp of peace' which would embrace the Communist and the non-committed blocs. In the early sixties they abandoned this policy as unpromising. At first, the Russians scored diplomatic successes in Asia, Africa, and Latin America owing to two important assets which were effective in spite of their contradictory diplomacy: the imperialist taint of the Western powers and the prestige of the Communist formula for 'pulling oneself up by one's own boot straps', of economic growth through central planning. Although the continuing racial problems in Southern Africa tended to ensure sympathy among the Africans, by the late seventies the Western imperialist excesses and exploitation were otherwise a matter of the past and the Russian model of economic growth had become tarnished by its shortcomings everywhere it had been applied and even in the Soviet Union itself. Furthermore, for some time the Russians had been suffering from Chinese competition, both in ideology and in aid-giving and, moreover, could scarcely afford substantial economic aid, except to a few selected countries. Nevertheless, when new opportunities for intervention in Africa appeared in the late seventies as a result of inter-African struggles, the Russians intervened in great strength both in Angola and on the Horn of Africa, although only through Cuban proxies. In 1981 they intervened directly in considerable strength in Afghanistan. The involvement was costly and condemned throughout the world. In the reform movement under Gorbachev in the later eighties, the Russians began to show signs of wishing to withdraw, despite the continuing weakness of their protégés, and to shift away from their general reliance on military means and support for revolutions in the Third World.

5. Although in many respects the Soviet rulers have reverted to Tsarist traditions, it was obviously impossible for them to build upon the traditional Russian attitudes to international order. As one of the major powers, the Tsarist regime had participated in the Concert of Europe and even wished to transform it into a kind of world government which would intervene whenever necessary to preserve the status quo. The Communist regime pursued a policy which was the very opposite of this: instead of being whole-heartedly conservative, it was revolutionary; instead of wishing to preserve the existing order, it aimed at its complete

overthrow. As long as the final goal of world revolution persists—and the Soviet rulers cannot abandon it because it is the crux of their ideological legitimacy both at home and among Communist parties abroad—they cannot take part in international transactions on the same footing as other, non-revolutionary states. They reject the existing order as undesirable and untenable, even if possibly they no longer consider the task of abolishing it as very urgent or even feasible. In all probability 'peaceful coexistence' with non-Communist states is merely a question of tactics, though probably quite long-range tactics.

Soviet attitudes to the institutions serving international order shape accordingly. The Russian leaders believe in one type of internationalism alone—the proletarian, through the solidarity of the working classes with the Communist governments. Their relations with non-Communist governments are fundamentally inimical if not actively hostile. Their diplomacy is less a way of arriving at an agreement with other states than a method of conducting hostile propaganda. To them, international law which expresses and buttresses the existing order is as undesirable as the order itself; international institutions are seen as controlled by and serving the ends of capitalist states.

All these declared attitudes and intentions are certainly not fully reflected in Soviet diplomatic practice, which frequently deviates from them and increasingly resembles the orthodox diplomacy of Western powers. When interested in the conclusion of a specific treaty, the Russians thus stress their habit of faithful adherence to agreements: in the mid-thirties, when afraid of Hitler, they tried to bring to life the moribund collective security system of the League; in 1950, when confronted with UN support for the American action in South Korea, they immediately resumed participation in the organs of the institution which they had been boycotting for several months; as the membership of the United Nations expanded, they began to represent themselves as defenders of the non-committed countries against imperialism and cashed in on the anti-colonial and hence anti-Western sentiments of the latter to harass the Western powers in the General Assembly. At the same time, wishing to avoid the possibility of an independent, that is, potentially anti-Communist, grouping, they tried to induce the neutrals to support the Soviet proposals for the splitting of the central position of the Secretary-General into a 'troika'—a three-man directorate, one of whom would represent the uncommitted states—and thus paralyse the organization.

Until Stalin's death the fundamental hostility of the Soviet Union to the existing international order could not be doubted, but one cannot reject the possibility that the Soviet Union then began to shed her aggressively revolutionary character and is slowly but gradually becoming more conservative, more ready to participate in the preservation of the existing order within which she has secured herself a leading position. The new dynamic young General Secretary of the Communist Party, Mikhail Gorbachev, who came to power in 1985, engaged on a thorough reform of the economy at home as well as of foreign policy. There were powerful reasons for him to do so. The Russian economy was becoming increasingly sluggish and the burden of armaments crippling, particularly in view of the need to match the developing American 'star wars' technology. The disaster at the nuclear power station at Chernobyl in 1986 sapped Soviet confidence in her technological self-sufficiency and underscored the need to avoid the possibility of a nuclear war. Better relations with the United States seemed imperative in order to reduce the arms race, buttress the chances of peace, and secure increased trade and technological co-operation. Moreover, the opportunities for Soviet-supported revolutions in the Third World had dwindled, and the burden of support for the faithful adherents, Vietnam and Cuba, remained heavy; China, the rival to be matched in ideological appeals, was engaged on an inward-looking course of modernization and had become less antagonistic.

At the time of writing it still remained uncertain whether the pronouncements and tentative moves towards what the Russians called a 'mature *détente*' would consolidate into a fundamental change from a revisionist, revolutionary position to a conservative, status quo attitude to the international order. The previous *détente* in the early seventies ended in a resurgence of the cold war but this was, to some extent, due to American policies; these may become the decisive factor this time too.

4

Non-state actors

The crisis of the territorial state

After the final consolidation of the major states in Europe in modern times, states were considered stable, permanent units. To contemporaries, the elimination of Venice during the Napoleonic Wars appeared to be daemonic; the disappearance of Poland as a result of three partitions at the end of the eighteenth century left an explosive issue of her restoration which repeatedly disturbed international relations; other cases were few and of little importance. The First World War shook this stability of states. It destroyed two large empires, the Austro-Hungarian and the Ottoman, and replaced them with a number of new states established on the principle of 'national self-determination', which could not be realized with the complex mixture of nationalities in Europe. The Second World War seemingly weakened stability even further. The two new superpowers, the United States and the Soviet Union, which shouldered the primary responsibility for maintaining international order, were both relatively inexperienced in diplomacy; all other nation-states emerged from the war in a shattered condition. Moreover, there soon proliferated a multitude of new states arising from the break-up of colonial empires, which were not only inexperienced in the European traditions of international society but generally unwilling to accept them.

In the first decade after the war the issue of the precarious nature of international stability was often conveniently summed up in terms of the 'viability' of states. According to the cogent analysis of John Herz,[1] we were facing a situation closely resembling that of the sixteenth and seventeenth centuries when the small medieval units were merging into modern states. As the gunpowder revolution had made the former inadequate for the

needs of the day, so the technological revolution of the war and
the post-war period rendered the territorial states obsolete. For
some time the frontiers had been losing their meaning as lines
delineating a territory under the complete sovereignty of its government. The first challenges were economic and psychological.
Industrialized and hence no longer fully self-supporting states
became extremely vulnerable to severance from external sources
of supplies and markets. Psychological warfare was already
in evidence during the French Revolution, and during the
Napoleonic Wars blockades proved quite effective. Then industrialization greatly increased economic vulnerability, and, after
its invention, radio became extensively utilized for propaganda
by all states. The main challenge, however, came from the recent
technological developments in warfare, from the bombers, and,
even more so, from the nuclear weapons and long-range ballistic
missiles. The interiors of states, even of the superpowers, suddenly became 'soft', since they could be effectively struck from
the outside.

While the erosion of the impenetrability of states weakened the
external roots of their sovereign existence, they became seriously
threatened also by explosive domestic forces. In the post-war
world they were called upon to satisfy a rapidly growing variety
of social needs and demands at a time when their capacity to do so
had been seriously diminished. Independently of the nature of
the political and socio-economic regimes, all states faced the
same fundamental problem of having turned into extremely complex multi-functional social organizations while becoming
increasingly less capable of fulfilling all their functions: for security and for many major economic purposes, they were too small
but, at the same time, for a variety of domestic issues, they were
much too big, as the citizens, especially some minorities, violently objected to the lack of grass-roots influence on national
policies. Thus states in their traditional form faced disruptive
forces from two directions: defence and some major economic
needs called for merger in larger units whereas dissatisfactions at
home required greater pluralism, recognition of the interests of
groups, the granting of autonomous powers below governmental
levels, and, in the case of really dissatisfied national minorities,

even full devolution. The two groups of demands were often incompatible; both threatened the very continuation of states.

Nevertheless, the survival powers of states have proved to be unexpectedly great. Since the end of the seventies, when the scattered residual remains of colonial empires were still achieving statehood and adding new, ostensibly even less 'viable' new members to the family of nations, no cases of disintegration or disappearance of a legitimate state have been recorded. It requires a longer historical perspective to arrive at a balanced assessment of the causes for the tough durability of states; some likely major factors are listed below but they clearly do not apply to all cases and do not add up to more than a fairly impressionistic checklist:

1. States generally retain their international legitimacy, however deficient their domestic legitimacy may become.

2. They remain the largest-scale meaningful communities and command the supreme loyalty of the vast majority of their citizens, particularly as political representatives of nations and as guardians of national cultures.

3. They retain the monopoly of sovereign control of territory and the near-monopoly of large-scale legitimate force.

4. They remain the only truly comprehensive large-scale multi-functional organizations with great built-in powers of inertia due both to the variety of the social needs for which they cater and to the built-in bureaucratic and other sectional interests which have a stake in their survival.

5. Negatively, they have not been generally faced with really serious rivals.

6. Perhaps most importantly, as the discontinuation of any state could undermine the stability of the international system as a whole and threaten others with a possibility of a major war, disastrous to all, everybody has now a substantial stake in the continuation of the status quo.

At the same time, however, the membership of the international system is decisively broadening beyond states alone, although the latter have, at least so far, retained their dominant position. In order to meet the new challenges they have developed new institutional devices—coalitions, blocs, international organizations. In one way all these serve the purpose of buttressing the sovereignty of their members; but in another, they are further undermining it by becoming actors in international society in their own right and by pursuing their own interests or those of international society as a whole, as distinct from the individual interests of their members.

Interstate governmental organizations

There are three main types of these new groupings of states—regional, functional, and comprehensive. The regional groupings are of shorter standing but became conspicuous in the post-war years when the Communist and the anti-Communist blocs gave the appearance of developing into two rival empires which would eventually divide the whole globe. Although the bipolarization did not fully materialize, institutions of great moment grew within the two blocs.

NATO is concerned with the defence of Western Europe and the Atlantic; it includes the United States, Canada, and their thirteen European allies. NATO constituted a departure from the traditional patterns of international military co-operation in that it was the first alliance to establish in peacetime a permanent integrated force under joint command. This force neatly solved the problem of German rearmament by including all the German armed forces and thus preventing the re-establishment of an exclusively national German force. Other members, however, retained some of their forces under their individual, national control. Moreover, the strategic nuclear forces and the members' commitments outside Europe were excluded from the scope of NATO. Thus NATO does not override the sovereignty of its members in defence matters though it circumscribes it to a considerable extent. The Supreme Commander of the integrated force, invariably an American, is in direct command of some of their troops and they are committed in advance to a range of strategic decisions. Moreover, the national defence programmes are negotiated with NATO at an early stage of their formulation and come up for discussion at the North Atlantic Council in

December each year, thus influencing their national parliaments. Finally, NATO serves the purpose of debate and adjustment of the foreign policies of its members towards the Soviet Union. Members do, however, often persist with their individual views and policies in the face of NATO pressures; the ultimate decision is theirs and NATO has no provision for majority voting.

The evolution of NATO was slow and uneasy. The members' dedication was directly related to their fears of the Soviet Union; NATO therefore thrived under the impact of the Korean crisis but began to wilt when the cold war abated. Its strategic provisions were never fully adequate for the defence of Europe, as its members did not provide the minimum forces necessary for this defence in a conventional war, while its place in the nuclear strategy became somewhat doubtful when the United States replaced its 'massive retaliation' doctrine by that of 'graduated deterrence'. There is no satisfactory doctrine for the employment of tactical nuclear weapons assigned to NATO by the United States and remaining under American control, nor has any institutional form been found for incorporating a strategic nuclear component. In the early eighties NATO was violently disturbed by domestic opposition in the European countries which had agreed to the stationing on their territories of United States intermediate-range missiles. Politically, NATO has not managed to resolve the problems of the preponderance of the United States within the alliance, to arbitrate in the feuds between individual members such as between Britain and Iceland over fisheries or between Greece and Turkey over Cyprus, or to cope with the issues arising from the American, British, and French interests outside Europe, as manifested in the Suez Crisis in 1956 or the Vietnam issue.

As the political *détente* between the Americans and the Russians weakened the basis of the alliance, by the mid-sixties NATO had entered a period of crisis which culminated in President de Gaulle's withdrawal in 1966 from all its military organs, although not from the political alliance. NATO's original sense of purpose was, however, revived by the Soviet military intervention in Czechoslovakia in 1968 and by continuing Soviet incursions into the Middle East and Africa, and the alliance has survived the succession of internal crises due to technological developments, differences over strategy and other issues among members, economic stringencies, and the continuing direct bilateral negotiations between the Americans and the Russians on strategic nuclear arms control.

The institutions of the European Community—the European Economic Community (the EEC or the Common Market—recently increasingly the European Community or EC), the European Coal and Steel Community (ECSC), and the European Atomic Energy Community (EURATOM), incorporated in it—are, in a way, even further-reaching. Its original membership of six—France, the Federal Republic of Germany, Italy, and the smaller Benelux countries (the Netherlands, Belgium, and Luxembourg)—was enlarged by the adhesion of Great Britain, Denmark, and Ireland in 1973, and then of Greece, Portugal, and Spain by the mid-eighties.

The European Community bears a limited 'supranational' character, which means that within its sphere of activities it can actually make decisions which are binding upon members. Its central organs act on behalf of the Community, but must obtain for important decisions the concurrence of the individual members represented at the Council of Ministers, although not all decisions require unanimity. Consequently a member can be overruled, can be obliged even unwillingly to pursue a policy decided upon by the Community, although not on an issue it regards as vital. Finally, in contrast to the customary time limitation of treaties or the provisions for withdrawal, after an initial brief period membership of the European Community is permanent. The Community is meant to be a step towards the political integration of Western Europe, which, however, has not progressed very far in other fields.

At first, the progress of European integration was slow and halting. The ECSC was established in 1951 as an avowed first step towards a European federation, but its proposed successors, the European Defence and Political Communities, had come to grief by 1954. The favourable market conditions and the great efforts of the dedicated European 'integrationists' were the only reasons why the ECSC not only survived but was followed by the establishment in 1957 of EURATOM and the European Economic Community. They went initially from strength to strength, attracting Britain and other reluctant outsiders to make unsuccessful attempts to join them. By the mid-sixties, however, they had reached a crisis. The boom was over and economic growth had slowed down; the three Communities became institutionally amalgamated but increasingly cluttered up by their own bureaucracies. Most importantly, grave political difficulties arose between France and the other members owing to de Gaulle's opposition to further progress towards supranational controls as well as to accepting Britain as a member. Like NATO, the European Community reached a stage of acute crisis.

In the seventies these trends were reversed, although not very conspicuously or decisively. The expansion of membership strengthened the Community politically but further obstructed its decision-making processes by introducing additional national interests and styles. At the same time, however, as the world's largest international trader, the European Community began to play an increasing role in co-ordinating the members' international trade policies and, gradually, to a limited extent, other foreign policies also. Thus the European Community spoke on behalf of its members in the General Agreement on Trade and Tariffs (GATT) negotiations, on agricultural and fisheries policies, and at the Helsinki Conference on European Security and Co-operation and its sequels. It fully co-ordinated its members' attitudes, and secured recognition and attracted diplomatic representation as an important international actor by the vast majority of states, including, after initial hesitation, the Soviet Union.

After a series of unsuccessful attempts, in 1978 the European Community made another, more serious move towards stabilizing the members' currencies, and a form of democratic control was introduced by implementing a decision to elect the European Parliament directly. It was clear that the full political integration originally envisaged would not succeed in the face of rooted attachments to individual national interests, especially in France and Britain, but also that the Community would be increasingly called upon to act on behalf of all its members whenever these proved incapable of acting individually, especially when facing intractable problems following the energy crisis of 1973, inflation, recession, and massive unemployment.

Within the Communist bloc, the regional institutions have never been more than pale counterparts of the Western institutions. The Soviet Union had separate bilateral arrangements with Communist China which had broken down entirely by 1962. In Eastern Europe, they established the Council for Mutual Economic Assistance (CMEA or COMECON) as a counter to the Marshall Plan and the European Community, and the Warsaw Pact to meet the challenge of NATO. Both organizations served merely to institutionalize Soviet hegemony and neither proved really effective. From 1962 the Russians began to plan to endow the CMEA with supranational powers in order to prevail against the persistent economic nationalism of its members and to discourage their individual attempts to improve their economic links with the West. This was not, however, successful and during the seventies a rapidly increasing proportion of the CMEA members' trade was diverted to the West.

The Warsaw Pact has been mobilized only once, in August 1968, not for its avowed purpose of defence against NATO but to subdue and occupy one of its own members, Czechoslovakia, and to prevent her from developing an individual style—of a liberalized socialist regime—that was unacceptable to the Russians. In contrast to the CMEA, however, the Pact effectively organizes the military forces of the Communist bloc, ensuring a much greater unity of strategy and organization than that of the opposing NATO. Since the disbanding of the Communist Information Bureau (COMINFORM) in 1954, there is no permanent institution in charge of the ideological direction of Communist parties and states, but periodical international conferences of Communist parties take care of that. Their stress upon Soviet leadership has occasionally been challenged by 'polycentrism', the idea that the national paths to Communism may legitimately differ. In the early sixties they became a battlefield for the ideological struggle between the Soviet Union and China; in the seventies, when China absented herself from these conferences, new ideological struggles arose over the issue of 'Euro-communism', especially in the Italian Communist Party. By the eighties the differences precluded the convention of further conferences.

Other regional and subregional organizations came into being in the post-war period. Their historical predecessor, the OAS, was not very effective in buttressing US influence over the continent, but it became a significant factor in Western hemisphere diplomacy. The OAU became an important international actor in representing the struggle against colonialism and racism by the African states and helped to stabilize continental affairs. Similarly, the Arab League became instrumental in co-ordinating Arab anti-Israeli policies. These organizations could not, however, fully control their members even on their main issue of interest; they were completely ineffective in the recurrent outbreaks of violent conflict among members. Other regional organizations took longer to become established, such as the Association of East Asian Nations, or were merely attempted.

Governments combine not only on a regional and/or ideological basis but also for specific functional purposes, whenever an activity transcends national boundaries, traditionally in the fields of international communications and in the control of international rivers. Although, on the whole, politically less important than the regional organizations so far discussed, the functional ones are much more numerous; they constitute the overwhelming majority of the hundreds of intergovernmental organizations which exist. Some of them deal with technologies which are clearly of central importance, for example telecommunications, aviation, outer space, and nuclear energy. Although for the convenience, sometimes approaching necessity, of smooth international co-operation these organizations tend to operate without much publicity, the complex politics underlying their operation occasionally breaks out.

Owing to the central importance of oil for the economies of the world, one of the best-known and politically most significant of these organizations is the Organization of Petroleum Exporting Countries (OPEC). OPEC is sometimes referred to as a successful cartel of oil producers but this ignores its important characteristic of being an organization of governments and not of oil companies. Admittedly its original and basic aims were concerned with oil as a commercial commodity, with the regulation of its flow and its pricing. Owing to a growing oil scarcity in the early seventies, OPEC made use of the new round of the Arab–Israeli wars to quadruple the price of oil; in the subsequent lingering world recession in which oil demand slumped, its solidarity was greatly weakened. OPEC, especially its Arab subsection, AOPEC, also has an explicitly political significance. The Arab oil producers used the 'oil weapon' in 1973 to exercise pressure against Israel and could conceivably do so again. Moreover, OPEC had the potential for developing a common policy on really substantial aid to the poorer countries and on North–South issues in general. By the mid-eighties, however, OPEC's position had greatly weakened: oil production outside the Middle East had grown and, owing to energy conservation and the sluggish international economy, the world's consumption of oil was reduced. In 1986 the solidarity of the members crumpled and the price of oil slumped to less than one-third of its peak. Consolidation at the end of 1986 was only partial and seemed to be precarious.

All these intergovernmental organizations, both regional and functional, are in essence extensions of nation-states which enable them to pursue their interests and to exercise influence. To some extent they infringe, of course, on the sovereignty of their members, especially when they become the instruments of the foreign policies of their leaders and most powerful participants. Universal international organizations, the United Nations and its specialized agencies, are more than that. They are agencies which act on behalf of the international system as a whole, and will therefore be more appropriately discussed in the latter context in Chapter 8. The United Nations and its collective security system does not, however, try to do away with the system of sovereign states. On the contrary, it can be considered as an attempt—admittedly not a particularly promising one—to perpetuate this system through a collective guarantee for all the member-states. Within the UN system, the individual states are still most powerful. They try desperately hard to preserve their own sovereign positions, although they are often much less careful regarding the sovereign positions of others. It is unnecessary for our purposes to identify all the voting blocs operating in the General Assembly and to discuss their performance. It suffices to mention the existence of these blocs and the fact that, on many issues, states no longer take an individual stand but are governed rather by bloc considerations.

The element that is least concrete, but nevertheless important, in the United Nations is that of an international community. Although intergovernmental in form and relying mainly on the support and actions of its member-states, the United Nations has occasionally acted on behalf of this community, notably when pressing for decolonization and for universal declarations of human rights. Since, however, the greater part of international relations still hinges around the actions of individual states, the machinery through which these states operate will have to be analysed first.

Interstate non-governmental actors

There is a basic physical reason for the dominance of states in international relations: they are in control of the whole habitable surface of the earth and, since any other organization must operate somewhere, it must either acquire the control of a state or become subject to one. Indeed, the history of mankind is full of examples of such mergers and often it is not quite clear whether the state or the other grouping is predominant. It is thus possible to consider Communism as an instrument of state policy of the Soviet Union, but also the Soviet Union as an instrument of Communism; the Catholic Church may be subject to the state, but again the state may be subject to the Church. Without deciding on the merits of either interpretation, it is possible to agree that in many situations internationally important organizations and groupings tend to merge with states. Moreover, among non-state actors resistance movements which aspire to the control of states rank high; they are discussed in the following section.

In the post-war period the interdependence of the world has

greatly increased and there have arisen numerous powerful cross-national (sometimes called transnational) actors and forces. State boundaries have begun to lose their traditional significance as being of ultimate political importance so that it is possible to consider them also as discontinuities in the flow of transnational transactions, often obstructing the meeting of some human needs. The traditional state-centric view of the international system has come under sustained attack, a large part of which is based upon the identification of non-state actors and the analysis of their role.

Some of these have been in existence for a long time and among them churches are the oldest and best known, especially the Church of Rome, often referred to as the Vatican or the Holy See. Traditionally the Vatican has been treated as a sovereign state, although its present territory is scarcely 80 hectares, and for a while it had no territory at all. The Vatican maintains diplomatic relations with well over forty states, not all of which are Christian, and hierarchical relations with many hundreds of millions of Catholics scattered all over the world. By virtue of its spiritual supremacy over the faithful, the Vatican can exercise political influence over states in which these are a majority or a substantial minority. Needless to say, difficulties sometimes arise, especially in relations with Communist states, in which Catholics are treated with great suspicion; notably the Church plays a central part in the national politics of Poland. It is also politically important in Latin America, where some priests adopt the cause of radical rebels.

The non-Catholic Christian churches, organized since 1954 into the World Council of Churches, play a much less significant political role but participate in the anti-apartheid movements. Islam has no central organization since the abolition of the Caliphate in 1923 but in the post-war years the new Organization of the Islamic Conference has played a limited part in supporting Arab opposition to Israel and in rather ineffectively dealing with conflicts among Muslim states. Islam is an essentially political religion which purports to control the whole of social life. Its fundamentalist variety has been playing an increasingly significant role in most Muslim countries, notably in Iran where a fundamentalist government was established by Ayatollah Khomeini after the 1978 revolution. In contrast to Christianity and Islam, the other world religions—Buddhism, the religion with the largest number of believers, and Judaism—have no proselytizing ambitions and no international organization. Although Judaism has its religious as well as political centre in Israel, where its fundamentalist faction plays a part in domestic politics, the world Zionist Congress is a secular organization; its political role is limited to support for the state of Israel to opposition to major manifestations of anti-Semitism.

The new interstate non-governmental organizations rarely reach real political importance but have been extremely rapidly growing in numbers. Leaving apart multinational corporations and terrorist and revolutionary groups, on which more later, *The Yearbook of International Organisations* lists several thousands of such organizations. Many of these play the role of fairly independent actors in their individuals fields of endeavour. It is likely, however, that the degree of their autonomy is directly related to the relative political unimportance of their field of activities—chess players or folklorists, for example, are bound to enjoy much greater independence from governmental interference than organizations active in the field of telecommunications.

The really important transnational elements are economic. The first great trading organizations, like the English and the Dutch East India Companies, started as purely commercial ventures. They could not, however, conduct their trade without a degree of political control over their sources of supply, and so their activities became increasingly political and military. After they had reached sufficient importance, the state invariably stepped in. The financial interests of the eighteenth and nineteenth centuries are epitomized in the fabulous Rothschild family. Between 1811 and 1816 the five sons of Amschel Rothschild established themselves as important bankers in five European financial capitals. While maintaining close links among themselves, they became providers of finance for their respective governments and, despite severe competition, their near-monopoly remained unimpaired for some three generations.

There then arose the great industrial empires and corporations. Their interests extended beyond state boundaries and became intermingled with state policies. In the nineteenth century they could and sometimes did ask their national governments to acquire territory which they needed for supplies of raw materials or as markets. It is, however, a fallacy to attribute all imperialism to this factor, as Marxists do. In fact on many, perhaps most, occasions, it was the reverse: the governments used economic interests in order to promote national expansion. The corporations had the alternative of straight competition with their foreign rivals, but this was hindered by governmental restrictions on free trade and was often not very profitable. The usual solution was found in co-operation through international cartels, but these again were sometimes used by states for political purposes. The cartel arrangements between German and American firms in the inter-war period in the chemical, light metals, and plastics industries, for example, succeeded in preventing the production of strategically essential materials in the United States because they were more profitably obtained in Germany. Only when the Second World War broke out did the Americans realize to what extent their military potential had thus been weakened.

Giant multinational corporations today maintain direct relations with foreign governments through their equivalents of foreign ministries and ambassadors. Especially prominent are IBM, the oldest and by far the largest computer manufacturer; the seven giant international oil companies, including Royal Dutch Shell and British Petroleum; Unilever; car manufacturers, especially General Motors and Ford; some chemical giants; and the companies representing American interests in copper in Chile, in sugar in the Dominican Republic, and in fruit in the so-called 'banana republics'. In the seventies they were joined by several Japanese concerns. In contrast to their predecessors in previous centuries, on the whole these corporations operate independently and do not seek government protection, except in the cases of nationalization of their foreign establishments which have become frequent since 1945. Government protection is not, indeed, of much avail, as is shown by the gradual nationalization of Western oil interests in the Middle East in the post-war period, despite the fact that they belong to the most powerful corporations domiciled in the most powerful states, especially the United States. Sometimes governments intervene in the policies of the corporations, and, having the ultimate power, are obeyed. Thus American administrations successfully restricted trade with Nazi Germany in 1940–1 and prevailed on the American oil companies to refrain from purchasing or carrying nationalized Persian oil in 1952. The industrial empires, however, are not fully subservient. Even in wartime some trade with enemy states has continued, and the trade restrictions directed against Communist countries and against Rhodesia were widely avoided.

The question to what extent the economic powers of multinational corporations encroach upon the political sovereignty of states is controversial but need not be discussed here as it cannot be decided in the abstract. There exist no generally accepted criteria for classifying what constitutes a multinational corporation and individual authors disagree about these. Useful analytical categories include the concepts of the states involved in their activities, the 'home state' and the 'host state'; the degree and nature of the control exercised by the two; the basic type of enterprise (extractive, agricultural, manufacturing, service, financial, or conglomerate); the ownership of the subsidiaries; and the degree of autonomy of the subsidiaries in relation to the parent firm, which has been aptly classified into the ethnocentric, polycentric, and geocentric types.

The most prominent is, however, the economic dimension— the strength of the corporation. Sometimes this is very crudely measured by comparing the average sales of the giant corporations with the GDPs of states, revealing the staggering fact that in the early seventies eight giant corporations (General Motors, Ford, Standard Oil of New Jersey, Royal Dutch Shell, General Electric, Chrysler, Unilever, and Mobil Oil) were among the forty economically largest entities of the world; the leading giants had average sales some hundred times larger than the GDPs of small poor new states. Different and somewhat more sophisticated indicators are found in equally staggering figures for the added values accrued in the operations of these corporations.

As in the inconclusive debate about the power of states, these indicators of the economic strength of the corporations are meaningful not in absolute terms but only in their relative contexts. It is important to ascertain the political influence of the corporation both in the home and in the host state—how central are its operations for the economy and how much political influence can it wield? What are the countervailing powers? We have on record the saying that 'what is good for General Motors is good for the United States' which, in a limited sense, is incontrovertible. In relations with host states relying upon one major item of exports, be it in mining or agriculture, the position of a multinational corporation yielding monopoly powers in the state's trade in this article is economically strong, but states have now become increasingly less helpless in their relationships through a combination of external forces favourable to them, especially the support of anti-capitalist states of the Third World organized for the purposes of such matters into the so-called Group of Seventy-seven, the existence of the General Assembly as a forum for complaints, and the sensitivity of public opinion in the home countries of the major multinationals.

For a while Marxists expected that the clarion call for the proletarians of all countries to unite would spell the end of national boundaries, but the First World War, in which the majority of the socialists in the various countries rallied behind their national governments, ended this illusion. The several successive Socialist Internationals did not have much impact on interstate relations. Their Communist successors were international only in form; the inter-war Comintern, which organized the Communist parties throughout the world, was under the Russian thumb and served as an instrument of Russian national policy; even more so was its more limited post-war successor, the Cominform, which was formally disbanded in 1954. Other political internationals such as the liberal one, or organizations of Eastern European Exiles, have no great political significance.

International trade union federations are another offspring of the Marxist idea of the international solidarity of workers, although, especially in Britain, Germany, and the United States, trade unions have become fully nationalized and are mainly concerned with obtaining bigger slices of the respective national cakes. The two mammoth international organizations which have come into being since the war, the Communist-dominated World Federation of Trade Unions and the Western-dominated International Confederation of Free Trade Unions, are engaged less in asserting internationally distinctive trade unionist interests than in supporting their respective sides in the cold war, particularly in competing for influence over the politically important trade unions in the new states.

Intranational actors

It is characteristic of the blurring of the traditional division lines between domestic and international politics that non-governmental groups and even individuals located primarily within a single state can attain the position of international actors. *Potentially* any issue of domestic politics can assume a sufficiently important international dimension to become conducive to a foreign policy objective, and hence any group or individual with a foreign policy objective can become such an international actor. This is a fairly new factor in international politics to which must be added the traditional factor that all interest groups of any importance are relevant to the stability of and changes in government and hence relevant, although only indirectly, to foreign policy. An explanation of how such domestic groups become international actors, that is fairly autonomous elements within international politics, is best provided by examples.

Take, for instance, a consumer protection group aiming at a far-reaching improvement in the safety standards of cars, like that of Ralph Nader, an individual who organized one in the United States. It would generally start operating as an orthodox domestic pressure group, trying to influence the government to introduce suitable domestic legislation to enforce the desired standards with the home producers and to exclude imports falling below them. Inevitably such domestic arrangements have international repercussions as the interests of the producers of the car imports are affected and, if the country is itself a car exporter, also its external markets, as long as the foreign competitors in them are free to observe lower safety standards and hence enjoy lower production costs. All these international activities, although induced by the group, have been governmental and hence the group cannot be regarded as an international actor.

However, as happens in an increasing number of fields, the government may be unwilling or incapable of attaining the objectives of the consumer group, and this can logically lead it to seek the support of similar forces outside, especially among the major importers and exporters of cars; it would then help to organize similar groups in other states and link forces with those already in existence. This may finally lead to complete internationalization —the establishment of an international association of consumer protection groups which could operate quite autonomously. One can thus think of a spectrum of consumer protection groups according to their degree of internationalization.

Potentially the most important of these groups are the ecologists or the greens. They started as pressure groups within individual countries, striving to influence their governments to deal with the environmental problems which were worrying public opinion, such as nuclear dangers, industrial pollution, contamination of water and air, and protection of endangered species. They have become influential in all Western industrialized countries, and in the Federal Republic of Germany they have even formed a separate party, which won the support of over 9 per cent of the electorate in 1987. The activities spilled over from the national to the international forum mainly through the operation of Greenpeace, an organization which has engaged in numerous spectacular activities aimed at the prevention—or at the very least disruption—of what they found objectionable. Greenpeace became involved in nuclear affairs when a ship sent by it to disrupt proposed French nuclear tests in the South-west Pacific was sabotaged by French agents with the loss of life. The tests took place but the adverse publicity made their repetition much more costly.

The issues are somewhat different with ethnic, racial, religious, or ideological minority organizations, the starting point for which is found not in the international extension of their functional objectives but in their original link with a foreign country. The degree of their internationalization can again be regarded as constituting a spectrum. At one end is activity as a traditional domestic pressure group trying to influence the policies of the home government in a direction favourable to the outside state with which they are linked. For instance, like other ethnic groups, the Jews in the United States have generally operated as what is sometimes called the 'Zionist lobby', a pressure group aiming at making American foreign policy more favourable to the state of Israel. At times, however, the target changes and, especially in the late seventies, the 'Zionist lobby' was trying to induce the Israeli government to become more accommodating in negotiations with Egypt. Likewise, Western Communist parties which operate primarily as domestic political parties generally endeavour to influence the policies of their respective domestic governments in favour of the Soviet Union. In the late seventies, however, the Soviet Government also became their target, when they came out in favour of greater respect for the protection of human rights, as provided by the Final Acts of the Helsinki Conference of 1975. A similar analysis can be applied to human rights protection groups in their national and international activities.

Classifying the activities of subnational groups according to their target thus offers a convenient focus for the analysis of their activities—according to whether they operate more on the home or on another government. It is, however, no yardstick for the classification of the groups themselves which, as the examples have shown, often aim at both targets. It seems best to abide by the criterion that an international actor must be a fairly autonomous agent in international politics and hence to consider groups whose target is limited to their home government merely as potential international actors.

There is, however, one type of subnational group which is of special importance even if its target is so limited—comprising those organized to remove the government. Such an organized group, when capable of replacing the government, be it through the electoral processes or force, is clearly significant as it may become the government; even if not fully successful, it may disturb governmental activities. The nomenclature of the groups relying on force is confused and confusing because it is extremely difficult to find an emotionally neutral name which would free it from ideological connotations. What is 'freedom fighters' or 'independence fighters' or 'resistance movement' to the supporters of change, becomes 'terrorists' to the supporters of the status quo. In a spirit of neutrality they will be called 'resistance movements' or 'fighters'. Again an example will best serve the purpose of elucidating the international role of such groups, especially the history of the Palestine resistance movement, which in its confusing evolution demonstrates the meaning and significance of the dimensions suggested and has been, moreover, the most important international actor in this category.

Widespread Arab opposition to the settlement of Jews in Palestine under an international mandate in the inter-war period formed the background of a Palestinian resistance movement after the establishment of the state of Israel following a war in 1948 and the subsequent mass exodus of Arabs from Palestine. Although unity of purpose among the movement was ensured by their common goal—opposition to Israel—unity of organization remained an unattainable but constantly pursued goal. The physical dispersion of the refugees and the dependence of each group on one of Israel's close neighbours, allied with the conflicts among the Arab states and their rulers, obstructed such unity. The first of the major organizations, Al Fatah, which was formed in 1956–7, was largely dependent upon Syria, whereas the Palestine Liberation Organization (PLO) was established in Cairo to provide the Egyptians with some leverage. The 1967 'Six Days War', which ended in a crushing Arab defeat and in a new exodus of refugees, invigorated the resistance movement, ensuring the strengthening of its political objective and a great supply of manpower and equipment, while guerrilla successes in other parts of the world, especially Algeria and Vietnam, provided encouragement. At the same time, however, the proliferation of uncontrollable terrorist groups made the forging of organizational unity even more difficult. Against the background of intrigues and manoeuvres the momentum towards unity reached its peak in 1968 in a formal reconciliation effected at a Palestinian National Assembly at Cairo. Soon, however, the PLO was faced by a military mutiny of some of its supporters and, in the following year, Fatah began to dominate it, having its leader, Arafat, elected as the chairman of the PLO. This ensured no unity, as even the united organization could not exercise control over the more radical elements of the movement or over the national commando groups formed in the individual Arab countries. The latter inevitably became the primary concern of each individual host country, leading to violent conflicts and even civil wars, exemplified in the crushing of the Palestine resistance movement by Jordan in 1971 and the Civil War in the Lebanon in 1976.

The resistance movement obtained a great degree of publicity, largely as the result of spectacular terrorist activities in the sixties, and, despite all the intra-Arab conflicts which helped to deprive it of unity, also a high degree of *legitimacy* in principle. A meeting of the Arab League in Cairo in 1969 declared the PLO to be representative of the Palestine Arabs, blocking for some time the possibility of local peace arrangements between Israel and her neighbours, Jordan and Egypt. A degree of broader international recognition followed—the General Assembly invited Arafat to address its meeting, and the Arab delegation to the abortive Geneva Peace Conference in 1973 included PLO representatives. The PLO thus became a widely recognized international actor. It was, however, subsequently outflanked by uncontrollable radical splinter movements and thus weakened by continuing feuds between Arab states, giving rise to a dramatic bilateral peace initiative between Egypt and Israel in 1977-9.

As is the case with the conception of national interest in sovereign states, the *objectives* and *strategies* of the PLO have changed following changes in circumstances. Starting with a programme for the elimination of Israel and the return of the Palestinian refugees to their original homes, the PLO gradually shifted to a demand for statehood for the Palestinian Arabs, merely restricting Israel to her pre-1967 boundaries; its strategy gradually shifted from terrorism to diplomacy and from seeking support primarily in the Communist bloc to seeking legitimacy in the eyes of other states. As the Israelis understandably argued, however, the change of emphasis towards much greater moderation may have been merely a matter of convenient tactics; it also remains vulnerable to a sudden change of leadership which could be caused by the assassination of Arafat.

Finally, the Palestinian resistance movement has generally had really substantial capabilities, including not only small arms but even short-range rockets. The supply of equipment from Soviet sources, whether directly or indirectly, and of money from rich Arab sympathizers, has always been ample. Moreover, the PLO has developed a broad international network with other radical fighter groups whose personnel have occasionally participated in its paramilitary operations and who in turn have been offered training facilities and equipment in PLO centres. All these facilities were destroyed during the Israeli military invasion of the Lebanon in 1983, but substantial PLO forces had been re-formed by 1987.

In sum, although in its original form the Palestine resistance movement can best be regarded as a subnational group with ramifications in neighbouring countries, in the seventies it became a very important regional and even global actor which played a much more significant role in international politics than many a sovereign state. Although none of the many other nationalist movements (for example, the Ulster Irish Republican Army (IRA) or the Basque Euzkadi ta Azkatasuna (ETA)) have attained the degree of international recognition accorded to the PLO, they share many organizational characteristics—including the tendency to break up into warring sections and the resort to terrorism. Terrorism, which may be briefly defined as intimidation through thuggery, is, to the true 'independence fighter', a means to a political end; it is the only strategy of warfare available to him. Invariably, however, the movements also attract elements to whom thuggery is an end in itself, be it out of liking for violence or search for loot. As a means to political ends terrorism has been partially effective: it does not achieve its political ends because modern states cannot be decapitated by the elimination of a despotic ruler and only rarely yield to blackmail and to the taking of hostages. It does, nevertheless, keep these ends on the political agenda, greatly aided by the publicity value of acts of violence in the modern mass media. From the point of view of the international system, the terrorists are actors in their own right as, although to some extent aided and manipulated by governments, they cannot be controlled by them and remain basically autonomous. Nor can the men who resort to terror for its own sake be controlled; the sophistication of modern means of destruction runs ahead of the capacity to preserve order. Despite elaborate—and very costly—efforts to stamp out terrorism, bomb outrages, hijacking of aeroplanes, and the taking of hostages persist.

Finally, regarding the role of individuals in international politics, one must remember that international actors are defined by their relative autonomy. One source of confusion about the role of individuals in such a capacity, similar to one found in international law, is that individuals have traditionally been the objects and not the subjects of both; the growing concern with human rights since 1945 does not alter this situation. The second reason for confusion is that an individual often becomes an important international actor by virtue of the organizational role he plays. Naturally the personality of the incumbent of such prominent positions as the President of the United States or the Secretary-General of the United Nations is important; even more clearly so is the personality of a leader of a smaller state whose autonomy and influence may be entirely out of proportion to the relative unimportance of his state—Nasser of Egypt or Tito of Yugoslavia were striking examples. As it is difficult to unravel the amount of personal and institutional significance in such cases, it seems advisable to limit this category of international actors to individuals who are occasionally able to behave autonomously in their purely private capacity, although they could generally be expected to attract some organizational support. To choose among the diverse though few cases, one may mention the Norwegian explorer Fritjof Nansen, who originated international protection for refugees, the American Andrew Carnegie who endowed a peace research institution, the Swede Count Gustaf van Rosen who organized the rebel air force during the Nigerian Civil War, the Argentinian revolutionary Ché Guevara, and also

the pop singer Bob Geldof who single-handedly launched a massive aid campaign for the victims of famine in Ethiopia. All these
individuals acted in relatively limited fields, and not many significantly active individuals could be added to this list. The ineffective attempts by the well-known British philosopher,
Bertrand Russell, to act as an intermediary between the Russian
and the American leaders of his day show how limited is the scope
in the mainstream of international politics.

5

The making of foreign policy[1]

The process and the constitutional machinery

It is customary to personify states and to speak of 'British foreign policy' or 'British decisions', but in fact these are not made by the state but by single individuals and groups who act on its behalf. Theirs, like all other human activities, can be considered in terms of interaction between the decision-makers and their environment.

Most human needs and desires cannot be satisfied without some form of action, and this is generally preceded by a decision, meaning an act of will determining in one's mind the course of action to be taken. Decisions and the resulting actions are the product of a confrontation in the minds of the decision-makers between their wants and desires and what they know about their environment. It is this psychological environment, the *image* (or perception) of reality that people hold, which plays a part in their decisions, however much such an image may deviate from the environment as it really is.

The fundamentals are identical, but decisions taken on foreign policy differ from those taken in other fields in that they are subject to a unique interplay between domestic and foreign environments. The persons involved usually occupy certain official positions of trust and importance empowering them to act on behalf of their society in its external relations. It is the values of this society which they are to uphold; it is the interest of this society which they represent. When, however, they engage in their jobs, they are confronted by statesmen and officials belonging to other domestic societies and pursuing their own values and interests. Thus the international environment often proves intractable; statesmen sometimes face insuperable obstacles when pursuing the interests of their respective countries and they are constantly subject to pressures which are at variance with domestic demands. The traditional image of foreign policy-making is that it consists of a rational assessment of the best means to attain certain established goals and objectives, over-coming the obstacles and using the opportunities offering in the external environment. Detailed analysis of some outstanding cases of decision-making, especially of crisis situations in the United States, has shown that many aspects of the process are determined by its inner dynamics and by political rather than by rational processes. Especially since Graham T. Allison ana-lysed the Cuban missile crisis of 1962 in these terms, many treat-ments have concentrated upon his alternative models: the 'organizational process' model, which centres upon the inter-action between loosely co-ordinated semi-independent groups within the government, and the 'bureaucratic politics' model, which centres upon the political manoeuvring of individuals. These somewhat overlapping models for studying decision-making processes have proved popular in many subsequent ana-lyses and can be regarded as an extremely useful complement to, although by no means a substitute for, the traditional 'rational' model.

Political life does not invariably conform to legal rules determining competence, but in the making of foreign policy the *formal* decision-makers are particularly important. On the whole governments fully monopolize the control of foreign policy. This is partly due to historical traditions dating from the absolutist period, and partly to the logic of the present situation, in which, as a rule, governments alone deal with other govern-ments, command the best sources of information, and have the monopoly of legitimate, and a near-monopoly of physical force. Any influence on foreign policy coming from other sources must be exercised through governments.

Although domestic political systems vary greatly from country to country and from period to period, certain uniformities do exist. The head of state does not usually play an effective part in foreign policy and his participation is mainly ceremonial. Exceptions can be found only in countries where the head of state combines executive functions with his office—as do the

Presidents of the United States or of the Fifth French Republic. Powers are concentrated in the hands of the government, or, as the Americans call it, the Executive, and within it, in the hands of its head and of the minister of foreign affairs (in Britain called the Secretary of State for Foreign Affairs or Foreign Secretary for short; in the United States called the Secretary of State). Other elements which should be taken into account are legislatures; the civil servants in the foreign ministry and in certain other, for the purposes of foreign policy, subsidiary departments; and public opinion. All these will be considered in turn.

The head of government and his foreign minister

The head of government usually plays a decisive role. In the United States the members of the President's Cabinet are merely his advisers; although this is somewhat over-simplified, it is fundamentally true, as President Truman remarked, that 'the President makes foreign policy'. In Britain major policy decisions are generally taken by the Cabinet as a whole, but the Prime Minister is fairly free in the choice of its members and leads its deliberations. Moreover, we have on record several important instances when the Prime Minister did not consult the Cabinet as a whole on major foreign policy moves, for example on the Suez expedition in 1956 or the modernization of the Polaris warheads in the seventies. He is normally sure of the loyalty of his Cabinet colleagues and of the support of his party members in Parliament; provided his parliamentary majority is reasonable, his power is secure. This is not so with coalition governments, such as that headed by Winston Churchill during the Second World War.

The head of government generally chooses a foreign minister to his liking but he may be restricted by party priorities or coalition requirements. The minister is subordinate, but when the head of government lacks any special interest in foreign policy and fully trusts him his may be the decisive voice. In the post-war period this was to some extent the case with Ernest Bevin in the Attlee Governments in Britain and with John Foster Dulles in the Eisenhower Administrations in the United States. The modern tendency, however, is for the heads of government to assume personal responsibility for major foreign policy decisions; very occasionally they combine the two offices, despite the crippling amount of work involved. In any case, they are personally involved in the increasingly more frequent 'summit meetings' which have been made possible by modern communications.

Even when personally conducting foreign policy, the head of government cannot help leaving large areas of activity to his minister. When the views of the two are closely related, no serious problems of co-ordination arise, but where they diverge, in time the head of government would tend to remove the minister from office or bypass him by using other ministers or personal agents.

In the Soviet Union and in other Communist states, real power is vested in the Communist parties rather than in the traditional governmental machineries which they all possess, though it is possible to exaggerate the unimportance of the latter. Undoubtedly the General Secretary of the Communist Party is the key figure, even if he does not combine his office with that of the President of the Council of Ministers, as, for a while, both Stalin and Khrushchev did. While Stalin was omnipotent within the Party, his successors have to tolerate opponents and depend on decisions taken by their colleagues—admittedly those in the Politburo and not in the Council of Ministers. Their position thus differs in degree rather than in kind from that of the heads of government elsewhere.

The developing states are governed by a variety of governments which fall into a wide spectrum; at the one extreme are those that are completely autocratic, with the head of government often being a military figure; at the other, those which are democratic in the sense that the government can be removed through the electoral process. In all cases, however, there is a strong tendency for a much greater concentration of power in the hands of the top leader and for a much less articulated political system below them than we find in longer established countries.

Legislatures

Discussion here must be limited mainly to the Western democracies since, with the partial exception of India, parliamentary institutions, when they exist elsewhere, do not wield real powers.

Parliamentary powers are generally smaller in foreign than in domestic affairs, but even so they can be important. They vary from country to country and they are determined by an interplay between fairly stable constitutional arrangements and such more ephemeral elements as the political climate, the strength of the parties, and the characters of the leading personalities. One extreme can be found in the United States, where the principle of 'checks and balances' and the absence of party discipline ensure the Congress a role co-ordinate with that of the Executive; the other in the Soviet Union, where the Supreme Soviet lacks any effective powers; other systems lie somewhere in between.

Being large and clumsy bodies, parliaments cannot effectively initiate foreign policy and are limited to the exercise of the power of veto over policies proposed by governments. Their main legal power usually lies in the ratification of treaties. In a particularly stiff form, the American Constitution requires the concurrence of a two-thirds majority of the Senate. This led to occasional rejections of treaties, notably the Peace Treaty of Versailles in 1919, but since then improved methods of consultation, bipartisanship, and the employment of 'Executive Agreements' which do not require ratification have rendered the Senate's powers much less formidable. In the post-war period the power relationship between the President and the Congress has been fluctuating: when successive presidents involved the USA in Vietnam, the Congress reasserted its control, leading to near-paralysis of foreign policy under President Carter; in turn presidential leadership was reasserted under Reagan in the early eighties. In a multi-party system also refusal of ratification can have serious effects: in the Fourth French Republic, for example, parliament threw out the European Defence Community Treaty in August 1954. The British House of Commons lacks legal powers of ratification, although it has the opportunity to debate important treaties which, under the convention of the so-called 'Ponsonby Rule', lie on the table for three weeks before their ratification by the government.

All legislatures which exercise real power hold the purse-strings and governments depend upon them to allocate the funds required for foreign policy. This is a telling power today when defence expenditure usually constitutes one of the main items of the budget and foreign aid is widely given. It is one of the major reasons why the House of Representatives is becoming increasingly important in the making of American foreign policy. Parliaments are also required to pass any laws which may be necessary to implement international treaties.

Legislatures can go beyond that and continuously control foreign policy through their standing committees. This has happened particularly in the United States, where such committees employ staff independent of the Executive, are constantly consulted by the State Department, and conduct investigations and hearings. The Chairman of the Senate Committee on Foreign Relations occupies a key position which, at times, may be more important than that of the Secretary of State. In other parliamentary democracies (for example, Britain, France, Germany, or Japan), legislatures play only an intermittent, though occasionally important, role. Reflecting rather than leading public opinion, they concentrate on domestic affairs but deal also with the few issues of defence and foreign policy which—apart from personal scandals—really interest the public; these are usually related to nuclear weapons, defence costs, and ecology.

Civil service

An important distinction is usually drawn between policy-making and administration. In theory, the ministers make the policy while the officials merely execute it, but the bureaucratic machinery is extremely important. Its members preserve the continuity of policy, while foreign ministers of different parties and views come and go. Moreover, these ministers—and also heads of governments—usually rise to power on the basis of their achievements in the field of domestic politics; when they assume their responsibilities for foreign affairs, they naturally become dependent on expert advice.

It is difficult and somewhat futile to decide to what extent a minister makes decisions or merely confirms decisions made by his officials. This is only of academic interest when they do not differ in their views; when they do, the politicians generally prevail, though only in the long run. Both in Fascist Italy and in Nazi

Germany the permanent officials who rejected or only half-heartedly accepted the policies of their masters were bypassed and eventually removed; in Britain, when Neville Chamberlain clashed with the Foreign Office over his policy of appeasement, he removed Lord Vansittart from his powerful position of Permanent Under-Secretary and continually bypassed diplomatic channels, using for the purpose his personal agent, Sir Horace Wilson.

Nevertheless, where policies are less firm and clashes less pronounced, the advice of the officials carries much weight, and, if it is ignored, the implementation of policies contrary to their views may be slowed down or even actively obstructed. The ingrained attitudes of the permanent officials should be neither minimized nor exaggerated. On the one hand, it is unlikely that a British Foreign Secretary would succeed with a pronouncedly pro-Israeli policy against the pro-Arab traditions of the Middle Eastern Department; the Foreign Office traditions of giving only lukewarm support to international organization and, until the late fifties, of lack of sympathy with European integration, may have strongly contributed to British policies in these fields. On the other hand, the French Foreign Ministry must have gone through a fundamental reappraisal before embarking on the policy of integration with Germany. Bureaucracy is particularly prominent in France, where it provided the main element of continuity in the constant change of constitutions and governments; it remains powerful in the Fifth Republic. In the Federal Republic of Germany, it has survived the Second World War as one of the least affected centres of power and has been confirmed in its traditional importance by the occupation authorities, but apparently the average German official remains indifferent to politics beyond his narrow specialist domain.

Little information is available about the secretive workings of Soviet bureaucracy. In terms of power, the Soviet equivalent of Western foreign ministries is probably the Foreign Department of the Central Committee of the Communist Party, the various sections of which maintain close relations with the corresponding sections of the Foreign Ministry. Stalin's personal secretariat—the so-called 'technical cabinet'—an institution perpetuated by

Khrushchev and his successors, may still continue to play a central part in Soviet politics.

The enormous increase in the scope of international relations has led to the blurring of the traditional demarcation lines between domestic and foreign affairs in governmental machineries. Despite the fact that foreign ministries are now grossly overworked, most other departments are involved in many foreign issues, giving rise to grave problems of co-ordination. The situation is most acute in the United States, owing to its transition from the restrictions of isolationism to the expansion of world leadership. In 1949 no less than forty-five out of the identified fifty-nine departments, commissions, boards, and interdepartmental councils were involved in some aspects of foreign affairs. In Britain eight ministries were seriously and continuously concerned in the negotiations with the European Economic Community between 1956 and 1958; nearly all ministries are now to some degree involved in the working of the Community and many maintain direct links with Brussels.

While co-ordination in Britain is undertaken through informal contacts and through Cabinet Committees, in the United States it has led to a confusing proliferation of bodies and to the employment of various procedures, none of which has been really successful.

Soviet experience is characteristic of the problems involved. Until recently Soviet foreign policy, which is rigidly controlled by the Party, was much better co-ordinated than are foreign policies in the West. Since the Second World War, however, the Soviet Union has intensified and ramified its foreign relations—there are intimate links with other Communist governments as well as parties, foreign aid, delicate relations with the new, uncommitted countries, increased cultural and commercial exchanges with the West. Despite strict central control, difficulties of co-ordination at middle and lower levels are likely to arise. Most difficult of all, however, is the co-ordination of the frequently conflicting requirements of domestic and foreign policies, as exemplified in the continuing suppression of Soviet citizens concerned with the monitoring of human rights enshrined in the Final Acts of the 1975 Helsinki Conference. Although the Soviet leaders have suffered a great degree of opprobrium abroad to the detriment of their foreign policy, they apparently consider their policy necessary in order to keep domestic politics under control.

Inevitably the administration of foreign affairs is partly decentralized since states maintain diplomatic missions in the capitals of all other states with which they have relations of any intensity or importance. Before the development of modern communications, diplomats in charge of missions could not receive prompt instructions from their ministries and were often forced to make major decisions on their own responsibility. Today this is rarely necessary, but foreign envoys are much more than mere subordinates following instructions. They supply and interpret information from the country of their sojourn and can occasionally make an impact by the way they present the policies of their government.

Subsidiary services

Foreign policy is not conducted by diplomacy alone; it relies heavily on the military forces and on the scientists who supply them with up-to-date weapons, on economists, and also on intelligence and propaganda services. Absolutist rulers of the past could personally deal with all these matters, but now such integration is unthinkable and extensive specialized services have been developed. Theoretically these services are merely subsidiary to diplomacy, but in some circumstances they can exercise great influence upon the decision-making process—the military when it comes to securing strategic frontiers, or allies or bases; the scientists concerning the development of weapons; the intelligence services, especially when, like the Central Intelligence Agency (CIA) in the United States, they act without full government control or diplomatic guidance.

Of these, the military are by far the most important, although civilian control is the rule both in the West and in Communist countries. Of all the industrialized countries, it was only in Germany and Japan that the military developed fairly independently of civilian control, but in neither have they recovered their independence since the Second World War. In the Third World, however, they often replace ineffective civilian governments— sometimes for long periods.

Naturally, strategic and diplomatic considerations do sometimes clash, especially in wartime, but although the civilians can
ignore military advice only at their peril and hence do not reject it
lightly, they do so when it seems to them expedient. Matters are
further complicated today by the policy of deterrence, in which
the weapons are not supposed to be used, but only to deter.
Hence success depends on what weapons are available—and this
is in the hands of the scientists—and not simply on how they are
to be used, which is the traditional subject-matter of military
strategy. Ever since 1937, when the potential of nuclear energy
was finally ascertained, some nuclear scientists have indeed tried,
though unavailingly, to take part in politics, to prevent the use
of bombs against Japan and to bring them under international
control. Their advice on new weapons and on the likely achievements of the rival power—advice inevitably coloured by their
professional interests as well as political views—undoubtedly
affects policy decisions, especially in matters related to nuclear
strategy. It is conceivable that in a real crisis political direction
could be overwhelmed by the impact of the military and scientific
groups involved.

Aid-administering agencies play a relatively minor part in the
countries offering foreign aid, particularly in the United States,
where they have been partly but never fully subordinated to the
Department of State. Similarly subordinate are the propaganda
services, despite the great sums of money lavished upon them by
all major powers. More independent are the intelligence services,
which tend to engage in cloak-and-dagger activities and pursue
them beyond the mere collecting of information. The United
States CIA has been conducting a foreign policy of its own for a
number of years. It was responsible for the support of Chinese
nationalists in northern Burma, the U-2 reconnaissance flights
over Soviet territory, the invasion of Cuba in 1961, and the opposition to left-wing governments in Latin America. Repeated
presidential efforts to bring the CIA under central control have
not been fully effective. It is difficult to identify the impact of the
highly diversified Soviet intelligence services but undoubtedly
these, as well as the services of other major powers, operating

as they do in secret and with substantial funds, have ample opportunities for at least an occasional independent action.

Public opinion

It is unnecessary to postulate a democratic ideology or a theory of the 'general will' in order to acknowledge the ultimate importance of the people as a whole. As David Hume noted, 'It is . . . on opinion only that government is founded; and this maxim extends to the most despotic and most military governments as well as to the most free and most popular'. Public opinion comes to bear as an unorganized whole, in the form of a 'mood', which prescribes the limits within which policy can be shaped, and also through organized sectional interests and their leaders and intermediaries. Until 1914 public opinion was only marginally interested in foreign policy but, during the later stages of the First World War, the rapidly growing labour force began to insist on its popular control as a key to a liberal peace. This new labour force was vulnerable to outside influence and was appealed to both by Wilson and by the Bolsheviks; the internationalists regarded it as the great weapon which would ensure peace.

This new element in the conduct of foreign policy has given rise to a host of problems, most of which still remain unsolved. The people are generally poorly informed and, even if information is available to them, their judgement is often wrong. Here opinions vary—radicals tend to attribute some wisdom to the man in the street, while thinkers less radically inclined, especially practising diplomats, generally deprecate his powers of understanding. While the former favour more information for the public, the latter are inclined to withhold it on crucial matters and to manipulate it in the direction desired. This ties up with the problems of guidance. The idea of democracy does not imply that the leaders should rigidly follow public opinion, but it does imply— and sometimes even demand—that they should direct it.

It is not easy to know the reaction of public opinion to any given issue. This is so even in Western democracies where the people's views are generally fairly articulate and are frequently ascertained in free elections and through public opinion polls. On an issue as important as that of Britain joining the Common

Market, at the crucial moment in August 1961, when the government decided to apply for membership, the state of public opinion simply could not be guessed; the various sectional interests had not yet adopted a firm stand and the general public was completely ignorant of what was involved. Opinion became fully clarified as being favourable only during the second application in 1967, to some extent as a result of careful official manipulation.

In countries where political life has achieved a certain degree of sophistication, public opinion is structured and organized in political parties and pressure groups. Only a small proportion of the citizens may be interested, informed, and active in foreign policy matters, but those who are assume positions of leadership at various levels. Their opinions are indicative of the way in which public opinion is likely to react and they are the most promising people to be consulted and informed by governments. They are probably more influential than the popular press and other mass media, important as these are, in influencing public opinion.

In the rigidly governed Communist countries public opinion is not structured from below, as in the West, but organized from above, through a hierarchy of leadership. Here the extensive agitation/propaganda apparatus used for the purposes of discovering and manipulating public opinion has apparently been only partially successful.

In the well-integrated British and Western European societies, demagogic appeals by a Mosley or a Poujade find little hearing, but in the somewhat less integrated United States there exist deep undercurrents of instinctive right-wing orientation; these manifested themselves most acutely in the anti-Communist witch-hunt conducted by Senator Joseph McCarthy during the most acute phase of the cold war. In the many societies where political structures are rudimentary, the illiterate or semi-literate masses of unskilled and underemployed urban workers are unstable in their recent divorce from their rural origins and unhappy in their wretched living conditions, even if these do constitute an improvement on their previous lives. Moreover, the students, the first generation exposed to education, are acutely aware of the shortcomings of their societies but utterly inacapable of finding rational or practical remedies. Here demagogical radical nationalists, religious fundamentalists, and fanatical socialists of various brands find scope for stirring up urban mobs and for toppling governments.

National interest and national values

'National interest' is the key concept in foreign policy. In essence, it amounts to the sum total of all the national values—national in both meanings of the word, both pertaining to the nation and to the state. Inevitably this concept is rather vague. One common-sense definition describes it as the general and continuing ends for which the nation acts. It is thus characterized by its non-specific nature, by a degree of continuity, and by its connection with political action. A major ambiguity arises from the use of the concept in different contexts without sufficient clarification. National interest can describe the *aspirations* of the state; it can also be used *operationally*, in application to the specific policies and programmes pursued; it can be used *polemically* in political argument, to explain, rationalize, or criticize. The recurrent controversies on foreign policy often stem from these ambiguities and not only from the different ideas about the substance of the national interest.

National interest need not be so narrowly defined as to exclude moral, religious, and other altruistic considerations; indeed, to be politically effective, these must have been accepted as part of it. In actual practice it may not always make much difference whether a decision is made by a statesman who subscribes to the Hegelian theory that the state is the supreme good (which is the foundation of totalitarianism) or by another who believes that the state is merely an instrument to satisfy the needs of the citizens. As long as the state remains responsible for the welfare of its citizens in most avenues of life and the purveyor of many social needs, both would interpret national interest in a similar way. They may, however, disagree greatly in the future as increasingly more human needs have to be satisfied outside the confines of the state. A narrow interpretation of national interest, based upon the idea that the state and its sovereignty must be preserved at all costs, would indicate a different general attitude to international management than a liberal one based upon the idea that only such organization is capable of meeting some important needs.

All statemen are governed by their conceptions of national interests, but this does not mean that they can never agree on anything. On the contrary, they often do—although much more readily about what they do not want than about positive policies. Thus during the Second World War the Americans knew that they did not want the Nazis to win or the British to go under; soon after the war they knew they did not want Communist expansion. They found it very difficult to agree, however, about the exact shape of the post-war world they wanted; they were, for example, divided on the question of undermining the colonial empires of their allies, which could be regarded as bulwarks against Communism.

If a statesman agrees to concessions, he does so not only when he is convinced that it will bring some advantage to his state, directly or indirectly. The favourable treatment of the trade of another country, for instance, may secure not only trade openings but also friendship; support for a partly obnoxious international institution may be worthwhile in order to secure the continuation of its otherwise useful activities or to ensure international good-will. Co-operation is conditional upon the existence of a suitable framework, of a reasonably stable international order within which the actions of other states are predictable and therefore rational foreign policy is possible. From here stems the interest of all states in this international order, again according to their individual national advantage. If they find this order congenial, they support it and, if necessary, defend it; if uncongenial, they endeavour to alter it accordingly.

At least for the time being, no alternative to one's own national interest is conceivable. If a statesman were to give his allegiance to the national interest of another country, this would be treason, and is extremely rare at the very top level of authority. If his first loyalty were to international organization rather than to his own state, he would be unlikely to rise to a position in which foreign policy decisions are made. On a liberal interpretation of national interest, clashes between national and international loyalties can usually be avoided, but if one does occur, the statesman's first duty is to his state.

The notion of 'national interest' is based upon the values of the national community, values which can be regarded as the product of its culture and as the expression of its sense of cohesion, values which define for men what they believe to be right or just. The relationship between these values and concrete policy objectives requires some explanation.

Values are organized and systematically expressed in ideologies. All theorists, however divided over details of their definitions, distinguish between democratic ideologies based upon the principle of majority rule, freedom, and equality, and totalitarian ideologies which aspire to concentrate all political, economic, and spiritual power in the same hands; the latter differ in their objectives according to their left- or right-wing nature, but are similar in the means they employ. In fact the ideologies describe only aspirations: no society has ever become fully democratic or fully totalitarian.

Values belong to the realm of the 'ought' and may or may not be translated into concrete political objectives. To say that the rulers of the Soviet Union are adherents of the Communist ideology means that they believe that Communism ought to prevail throughout the world, but not necessarily that they are actually pursuing concrete objectives to achieve it. The historical fact that Communism has been expansionist throughout its existence indicates that the rulers actually do pursue such objectives, but a person wishing to analyse Soviet foreign policy should examine the question of whether these objectives have remained intact since Stalin's death. To say simply that, because according to Communist ideology the spread of Communism is desirable, therefore the Communist leaders automatically pursue appropriate expansionist goals, may debar us from noticing any change in these goals. With equal profit, the Communists could abandon their confusion between the United States' desire to get rid of Communism (which is, indeed, an important element in its ideology) and the aggressive strategic objectives which they impute to the Americans to achieve this in practice. The illusions during the *détente* period of the 'end of ideologies', which were influential among some thinkers in the West—though not in the East—were replaced in the late seventies by the realization that the clash of ideologies remains a central feature of the international system.

Usually value systems are loose, and they often include conflicting values; on any concrete issue the problem arises as to how to find out which values apply. A case in point is Western trade with Communist states. The Europeans think of it mainly in terms of achieving the maximum trade possible while the Americans are more concerned with the danger of strengthening a potential enemy; the issue is predominantly economic for the former but predominantly political for the latter. To make things worse, statesmen may be deliberately misleading in what they say; according to Freud, they may themselves be ignorant of their true motivations. Finally, different cultures do not attribute the same importance to the same values; there is, for instance, little meeting ground between citizens of developed countries who stress economic values and self-sufficient peasants in the Third World who refuse to do so.

Throughout the history of political thought man has been seeking a supreme value which could be used as a general yardstick. Unfortunately the very fact that so many conflicting theories have arisen casts some doubt on the general validity of any one of them. The popular yardstick of 'national interest' is too vague and that of 'power' is insufficient. Power has, in fact, been the necessary condition of self-preservation, and a state which ignores this condition persistently cannot escape the danger of disappearing. This does not mean that the yardstick is or can be persistently applied in all situations; indeed, it is sometimes ignored and even deliberately acted against.

Whenever two or more values clash, the relative importance of both must be weighed and established, even if there can be no agreement on the identity of a supreme value. This 'ranking' of values is not easy because intensity fluctuates from case to case and is often determined by emotions. A violation of national frontiers by a small detachment of an unfriendly neighbouring state may, for example, be considered as an unpleasant but purely local incident or it may be blown up to a symbolic issue warranting retaliation, even to the lengths of waging war. In short, it is quite impossible to develop a rational 'value calculus' and choices among values are bound to remain largely intuitive.

Values in their interaction with the environment

Values reach their full political significance only in action, when the statesman actively applies them. In the vaguest and most general form this leads to what may be described as a vision of the good life, an arrangement of the elements of reality—as perceived by the decision-maker—to approximate as closely as possible to the values he holds. Needless to say when it comes to actual action, the vision can never be fully realized because, at least to some degree, the environment is intractable. There is always some tension between the vision of the good life and life itself, even when the vision is so moderate that it can be easily translated into a concrete political programme. Some visions are quite Utopian, completely unrealizable, and most of them contain a sizeable Utopian element.

While the vision of the good life indicates only the general direction desirable for foreign policy, more specific principles of behaviour are deduced from it and, most importantly, also concrete political objectives—ends or goals—which the statesman decides to pursue. The decision as to how far they are prepared to go in their efforts to secure the values may be called the pitching of the level of aspirations. This level differs with the personality of the individuals and with national character. It can be either predominantly optimistic, determined, ready to take risks, or predominantly pessimistic, cautious, preferring to play safe. It fluctuates also according to how successful action proves to be.

To arrive at a political decision, a statesman must juxtapose his values and his environment; we must therefore investigate how he arrives at his knowledge of this environment. The major link here is information, assiduously collected by all foreign ministries and, within their specialized fields, military authorities also. However abundant, the open and legitimate sources of information are generally deficient in the most important matters and have therefore been traditionally supplemented by espionage.

Although by and large top-level statesmen have full access to the information available to their governments, they cannot possibly digest it all. By the time information reaches them it tends to have become condensed and separated from reality to the point of allowing complete misinterpretation. This being so, skilful politicians can and often successfully do use their intuition. Personalities differ immensely in this respect. In recent American history we may contrast President Eisenhower, who refused to become acquainted with the details directly and relied on John Foster Dulles to bring to his attention anything of real importance, with the voracious appetite for information and the extraordinary range of Presidents Franklin D. Roosevelt and John F. Kennedy.

In order to select what is relevant from the bewildering variety of facts and events, one must have some criteria of relevance. Every country develops interpretative rules in accordance with its national culture and traditions, but generally these rules are not articulated and hence it is hard to identify them and to change them, if necessary. It is difficult to understand the rules of one's own country, but even more so those employed by other national communities. Sometimes insufficient allowance is made for differences, for instance when the appeasers regarded Hitler as a politician of the same school as themselves, who would rationally accept a chance of satisfying his avowed and fairly legitimate ambitions, or when the Czechoslovak leaders were confronted with the cynicism of their Russian counterparts during their enforced negotiations in Moscow in August 1968. It is equally dangerous to proceed on the assumption that the rules which govern the behaviour of others are completely different from one's own, a belief held strongly by fanatics.

Interpretation is not fully rational but is often governed by emotions, by the tendency in people to develop 'blind spots' for what is unpleasant, and by wishful thinking. The underlying rational processes can also prove unreliable. We can no longer accept the notion of causality as a fully adequate link between events; Communist dialectical processes of reasoning lead to interpretations vastly different from those based on Western formal logic; the Chinese or the Africans may find either unacceptable.

What we find out about our environment is thus so remote from reality that instead of speaking about 'knowledge' we should employ rather the word 'perception' or 'image'. The important feature of a perception is its emphasis on the general outline rather than on detailed items of information. Once a statesman has formed a perception of an issue or of another state, this perception acts as an organizing device for further information and as a filter through which this information must pass. Perceptions, not detailed information, govern political behaviour. Voters tend to be swayed by the image of the party rather than by specific electoral issues; statesmen deal with another state on the basis of their image of that state rather than on the merits of the concrete problem on hand. The ingrained respective images of a hostile superpower govern the mutual relations of the Americans and the Russians much more than the details of their actual behaviour. Where this behaviour does not correspond with the image, it is simply ignored—the Russians took no notice of the elementary fact that the allegedly aggressive Americans did not destroy them when they had the monopoly of nuclear weapons, nor did the Americans acknowledge the conciliatory nature of some Soviet moves after Stalin's death or under Gorbachev.

One of the most significant relationships within the environment is the interaction between domestic and foreign affairs. On the basis of relative security and isolation from foreign affairs, it has been customary for British and American thinkers and statesmen to believe that the two domains are separable and that domestic affairs prevail. Very different is the tradition of the continental countries where such separation has never taken place. Even in powerful states like Napoleonic France or Bismarckian Germany, military requirements and foreign policy objectives invariably mingled with the basic issues of domestic politics. Small, weak states were always even more open to foreign influences. Hence the continental doctrine of necessity or *raison d'état*. Today, even in the West, there is no agreement about the interrelations between domestic and foreign affairs—some hold that all states can do is to react to the imperious dictates of foreign policy, especially the implications of the nuclear dilemma; others have retained the idea that statesmen have a freedom of choice, although within environmentally prescribed limits.

Human minds and energy being limited, excessive concentration on either domestic or foreign affairs must be at the expense of one or the other. At one extreme we can place the United States, which grossly neglected foreign policy throughout much of the inter-war period. The other extreme is described by George Orwell in *Nineteen Eighty-Four*: the suppression of the individual in a 'garrison state' concerned only with its own survival. When popular discontent at home reaches an acute stage, governments often resort to the expedient of diverting attention from domestic to foreign affairs, as recently shown by the Argentine invasion of the Falklands/Malvinas.

Often the domestic–foreign interrelation is blurred. Undoubtedly there was a close connection between Soviet policy in China in the later twenties and the dramatic struggle between Stalin and Trotsky at home, or between Soviet action in Hungary in 1956 and the relations between Khrushchev and his opponents. Nevertheless, it is an over-simplification to contend, as is sometimes done, that in both cases domestic considerations fully determined foreign policy, since in both cases the foreign reverses had, in turn, a profound effect on domestic policies. They rendered insecure the incumbents of office and impelled them to stress domestic change in order to divert attention from their failures abroad.

Particularly difficult are the problems of newly established states where political life at home is generally unsettled and domestic pressures often insuperable. Violent nationalism, which often brings these states into existence, dictates anti-imperialist and hence generally anti-Western policies, a situation which the Communists endeavour to exploit but which is unpalatable to those who prefer to preserve a more balanced policy and thus ensure access to Western trade and aid.

6

Interaction among states and state power

Core values and vital interests

So far states have been discussed singly, preparing the ground for the analysis of their interaction which constitutes the bulk of international relations. Here, the level of analysis employed must be constantly borne in mind: at the macro-political level (discussed later in Chapters 8–10), this interaction is considered primarily as a function of the coexistence of states in an historically established international system. First, however, we shall consider their interaction at the micro-political level, looking at states from their individual perspectives, as pursuing certain interests and meeting certain contingencies arising in the international environment.

Before tackling the issue of how states interact, it is important to investigate what they are doing it for. Among the amorphous category of values and interests, states regard some as most important, often referring to them as 'vital interests'; scholars tend to use also the somewhat overlapping category of 'core values'. Decision-makers disagree violently on ultimate, supreme values as much as do philosophers: some seek them primarily in the individuals served by the collectivity of the state and others primarily in the collective which is to be served by its members; some pursue narrow nationalistic and others broad ecumenical values, be they ideological, religious, racial, or regional. Whatever the substance of their beliefs, they are all concerned above all with the preservation of the essential features of the social organization of their respective states. Three preliminary observations must be made about these. First, the primary values of the states are thus domestic and are realized in the domestic sphere. This should be kept in mind when considering international relations since adjustments of domestic interests are constantly taking place and are complementary to international relations, and sometimes a full alternative to them. Second, the perceptions of the international environment held by the decision-makers are so crucial an element in their activities that academic conceptualization remote from their ways of thinking should never be imputed to them or perhaps even employed in the early stages of the analysis, although they can be extremely useful for precise analytical or normative purposes. A third point relates to our uncertainty about the basic nature of state interactions—are they mainly purposeful, rational acts, arising from the pursuit of certain objectives, or are they mere random actions and reactions arising from the historical configurations of the international and domestic systems? It is easy to agree that state interactions include an element of both but extremely hard to define how much of each category, especially in a concrete case.

Important as it is to state this question, it is possible to leave it open and to proceed with the analysis of the substance of the interactions—the meeting and clashes of interests among states. The clashes are particularly significant whenever they arise over vital interests, core values, so defined because people are attached to them to the point of being prepared to pay a very high cost for them, even to make ultimate sacrifices, and are not prepared to compromise. Traditionally the territorial integrity and political independence of a state have been regarded as such core values, at least in the last two centuries or so. In fact, however, as has been argued in Chapter 4, for some time we have been facing a crisis of the territorial state so that the traditional core values cannot be regarded as absolute because sovereignty is now never complete and boundaries are always to some extent penetrated. It is merely a matter of the degree to which these encroachments and penetrations are tolerable. The stark model of states confronting one another with conflicting and unmovable core values, however convincingly it seems to represent the situations leading to the two World Wars, does not therefore seem appropriate to the situation towards the end of the twentieth century, at least until and unless really violent conflicts break out. Core values are not absolute and rigid; hence it is necessary to think of categories useful for exploring their interpretation and trans-formation.

If we seek a modern redefinition of the traditional basic core values, we must first reduce them to what appears to be their common denominator, namely self-preservation. To repeat the point, in modern conditions such 'self-preservation' is defined no longer by a rigid adherence to the absolute concepts of territorial integrity and political independence, which have been eroded, but rather by more flexibly defined features, not only of the political but also of the socio-economic structure, making full allowance for ideological and cultural elements. In discussing the way in which states proceed, it is useful to apply the distinction made by Arnold Wolfers between 'possession goals', based upon the preservation of absolute control by the state—like sover-eignty over territory or power to conduct autonomously one's external relations—and 'milieu goals' concerned with the shaping of conditions in the international environment. If—as all the major advanced industrialized governments claim—it is a core value for each to preserve a national steel industry in the face of the threats to its continued existence by lower-costs rivals in newly industrialized states, the clash of interests with the vital inter-ests of the rivals can be met by an adjustment in the evaluation of the interest, an acceptance that effective competition is imposs-ible, and consolation with the resulting cheaper price of steel. An alternative is the preservation of domestic industry by the exercise of state sovereignty through the raising of tariff barriers—a policy now curbed by international agreements circumscribing this right. Another alternative is the elevation of the conflict to the category of milieu goals through arrange-ments made internationally, an expedient actually employed in the European Community in the late seventies.

Role, self-sufficiency, and interdependence

One important factor among those determining the international behaviour of a state is found in its position and function within the international system, often referred to as its 'role'. This concept, which is widely used and well defined in sociology, is much more diffuse in international relations; it coincides partly but not fully with the nineteenth-century concept of 'status', an important element in the ranking of states. By definition, the exact content of the 'role' is ambiguous: first, owing to the multifunctional nature of states, which allows us to use a wide variety of possible yardsticks, and second because the definition of the role by the state's own decision-makers cannot be expected to coincide fully with role definitions by other states. Although no satisfactory and generally acceptable definition of 'role' has been produced, most thinkers distinguish three major dimensions of state behaviour which cannot, however, be readily accommodated into a meaningful general scheme: a spectrum between satisfied and dissatisfied, active and passive, powerful and weak states.

The major distinction frequently noted is between the state's own role definition and definitions made by others. It is notorious that policies regarded as 'defensive' by the actor are the very reverse—'aggressive' or 'offensive'—to others. This is demonstrated by the continuous mutual accusations of the Americans and the Russians, when they support various friendly regimes and establish alliances and bases abroad or develop new weapons systems; the mutually conflicting role definitions of both differ from those produced by the Chinese. All these varying definitions refer, however, to the same phenomenon—the behaviour of states—which is variously interpreted, according to different yardsticks and priorities. This situation closely resembles differences in the perceptions of any other element of reality and requires the same kind of comparison not only of the various interpretations but also of their relationship to this reality.

A major underlying though poorly articulated and understood factor in international behaviour is the degree of self-sufficiency or dependence upon others. This concept has been somewhat blurred in the second part of the twentieth century owing to the rapid growth of what is often called 'interdependence' (on which more later). By interdependence is meant a dependence upon the international system which is now common to all states as a condition of their existence, especially to ensure their survival by preventing a major war and by preserving the minimum necessary of international trade and other exchanges. The situation used to be clearer in the past: a state with a large territory and ample natural resources could be regarded as capable of much more self-sufficiency than less well-endowed states. After 1945, however, only the two superpowers seemed to have the conditions for any great degree of self-sufficiency; China and the few small states trying to achieve it did so only at the cost of appallingly low living standards. Throughout the seventies, even the superpowers were losing their self-sufficiency; the United States was becoming dependent on oil imports and the Soviet Union upon the imports of Western grain and technology. Both could reverse the trends and survive the cutting off of supplies, but only at a rapidly increasing cost; dependence on the major suppliers has in both cases become so strong as to amount to an acceptance of the growing interdependence. It is a confirmation that the trend is general that, very soon after the issue of Mao's succession in China had been settled, the new leadership repudiated Mao's consistent philosophy of self-sufficiency.

Conflict, competition, and co-operation[1]

An important dimension of international relations is found in the dominant modes in which states conduct their international behaviour and engage in interaction. Relations between individuals can take shape according to a variety of patterns: at one extreme they are based upon pure love, as bestowed by the mother upon her child, and at the other upon unmitigated fear and hatred as felt by the caveman confronted with a stranger. Relations between human groups are similar, except that they are never based on pure love and only rarely on pure fear and hatred. The two extreme types of group relations are often called co-operation, where there is no conflict, and fight, where the conflict is so acute that it makes accommodation unthinkable and the elimination of the opponent the only worthwhile objective. The majority of situations fall between these two and may be called competition. There, conflict exists but is not absolute because it is tempered by some community of interest; it often ends in compromise.

Relations between states are governed both by the nature of states and by that of international society. The main characteristics of states may be recalled here—that they are the supreme form of human organization, that they recognize no superior, and that they are governed by self-interest. Accordingly, international society does not exercise authoritative power over them, although it does prescribe certain rules of behaviour. If social progress is measured by the evolution of co-operation and peaceful means for the resolution of conflicts, international society is still fairly primitive.

Interstate behaviour exhibits every type of conflict, from constant references to power politics and threats of violence to actual war which, in our century, has become increasingly more destructive. The logical conclusion of the present situation is that this Hobbesian starting point could lead to a form of social contract which would bring to an end this unbearable state of affairs.

The ferocious nature of the two World Wars led to several attempts to eliminate violence: the League of Nations Covenant, the Kellogg Pact, many agreements and declarations, and, most recently, the United Nations Charter. Although these approaches varied and were, moreover, open to differing interpretations, they did not, as a rule, constitute a departure from the fundamental structure of an international society of states governed by self-interest. The states have merely accepted the fact that they were so adversely affected by the danger of recurrent wars that this very self-interest demanded that violence should be eliminated, or, as became current in the language of international organization, that 'aggression' should be prevented. The attempts to outlaw violence have not, however, been successful; they did not prevent the Second World War nor have they decreased the danger of a third, nuclear war nearly as much as have common sense and prudential reasoning.

The new institutions and methods not only expressed the idea that a fight to the finish, to eliminate the opponent, was undesirable and therefore scarcely thinkable, but also reinforced this idea by institutionalizing it. During the Second World War, despite the fundamental nature of the Nazi menace, the Allies did not seriously contemplate the complete and perpetual elimination of Germany from the international scene; neither do the Americans and Russians necessarily aspire to mutual annihilation—they would be satisfied with a change in each other's social and political systems.

The first attempts to eliminate the use of force having failed, men have sought more effective methods of accommodation by analysing more thoroughly the nature of international conflicts. Especially in the late fifties and sixties the Americans developed ingenious though inconclusive studies based on the 'theory of games', and analysed the complexities of the policy of deterrence. The following paragraphs are based on the ideas of a prominent early theoretician of deterrence, the Harvard Professor Thomas C. Schelling, in *The Strategy of Conflict*.[2]

The starting point of his argument is that pure conflict, war to the finish, would be so mutually damaging that limiting warfare to minimize damage, or coercing the other side by threatening war rather than by waging it, has become expedient for both sides and has opened possibilities of accommodation. There is not only mutual opposition but also dependence. Victory in the conflict is not strictly competitive, not necessarily at the cost of the other side. Conflict situations are now essentially bargaining situations, since they combine a divergence of interests with the powerful common interest that the outcome should not be destructive to both sides; success for both sides means the avoidance of war. Hence the time-hallowed precept that the aim of policy is to enhance one's power no longer commands full validity. The long-term tendency seems to be towards complex mixed relationships: thus the post-war conflict between the Americans and the two major Communist states, which has taken the form of a 'cold war'—basic antagonism though without the direct use of force—has gradually and haltingly developed towards a *détente* which allows for separate and distinct agreements on an issue-to-issue basis. The old-fashioned alliances have remained a central feature of security policies but, if the East–West *détente* develops, strong fissiparous tendencies are likely to reshape them into much looser *ententes*.

In order to transcend the emotional difficulties of the cold war, Thomas Schelling recommends the study of conflict in other, less

emotionally charged and less complex relationships. Undoubtedly the combination of conflicting and common interests,
although in different proportions, occurs among non-enemies,
and deterrence has its place even among friends and allies. In
1956, when the Poles were standing up to the Russians, their
attitude was determined both by the physical threat from Russia
and by their interest in retaining Soviet support, which was indispensable for the maintenance of the Communist regime and of
the Western Territories acquired from the Germans. When the
Americans unsuccessfully tried to force the French to ratify
the European Defence Community in 1954, they stressed common
strategic interests but also hinted at the possibility of an
'agonizing reappraisal' in case of failure. Gang warfare offers an
interesting parallel. Like states in international relations, outlaws
lack enforceable legal systems, constantly invoke the threat of
violence, and ultimately engage in it although they have an interest in avoiding it. Hence they provide illustration for such
features of the international system as disarmament and disen-
gagement, surprise attack, retaliation and its threat, appeasement and loss of face, or the unreliability of the widespread
alliances and agreements.

The great advantage of this analysis lies in its realism; it takes
into account both the conflict and the community of interests, as
they exist together in life, while at the same time it shifts attention
to the more promising elements of community. Provided each
side acts rationally and fully understands the situation, not only
as it appears to itself but also as it appears to the other side, the
chances of accommodation greatly increase. The fact that the
Russians translated the major American analyses, and thus had
an opportunity to become acquainted with all the complexities of
American views, was an important, perhaps indispensable basis
for the subsequent *détente* in the seventies.

Finally, we speak of co-operation, where the problem lies not
only in the identification of common goals and the methods of
reaching them, but also in the achievement of these goals. This
interaction, in which no conflict is involved, does not, properly
speaking, come into the ambit of politics, which centres on conflict and power, but rather into that of administration. But

administration is not only the outcome of successful politics but also offers a method of resolving conflict situations, especially when they are not really acute.

If an international agreement about basic goals and methods were ever reached, it would be a sufficient foundation for the establishment of a world government. Obviously we are very remote from such a state of affairs today, but this does not prevent states from co-operating, in the narrower meaning of the word here employed, namely, interacting without conflict. From the establishment of the Geodetic Union in 1864, international organizations have multiplied to thousands, including many intergovernmental ones; important activities are carried out under the auspices of the United Nations and of its specialized agencies. The so-called 'functional co-operation' embraces wide areas of international life, but is completely successfully only when it does not affect power relations. Thus the peaceful progress of international postal administration through the Universal Postal Union strongly contrasts with the turbulent relations in the field of telecommunications. The reasons are not far to seek —they lie in the vastly different strategic importance of the two fields.

Although relatively unimportant from the angle of power relations, international functional co-operation is never fully divorced from them. It offers two interesting prospects. First, as institutions multiply and evolve highly complex methods of co-operation, the technical difficulties involved in implementing any political decision are being reduced and no agreement is likely to be wrecked by them. Even such a complex problem as phased disarmament, which would offer no sizeable advantage to either side during any phase, can be adequately solved, provided the political decision is made. Second, if the network of the slender ties of functional co-operation continues to increase at the present rate, it may eventually resemble the system of threads with which the Lilliputians tied down Gulliver: although each individual strand is weak and insignificant, if they are sufficiently numerous, their total strength may become substantial. It is conceivable that at some future time states will depend on functional international co-operation to satisfy so many minor human needs that eventually the disruption of such co-operation through violence will become unthinkable. This approach to peace need not exclude other approaches.

Moreover, co-operation can be substituted for conflict, even a central political one, in the interests of all the parties. This has been conceptualized by the theory of games in the so-called prisoners' dilemma, devised in 1950. In its basic version, it is the situation of two thieves in cahoots who are kept isolated in prison and are offered a deal by the prosecutor; if one confesses and implicates the other one, he will be set free; if neither confesses, in the absense of conclusive evidence, both will get away with a very light sentence; if both confess, they will get a somewhat mitigated sentence. The natural tendency of both thieves to seek the maximum personal advantage and to confess leads to the undesirable consequence of both receiving a mitigated sentence, whereas if they keep silence they both get away with a very light sentence. Much thought and experimental application in laboratory conditions have been applied to interactions in which the game is repeated. It is not only desirable but also possible to secure the co-operation of the opponent without giving him an opportunity for taking advantage. This can be done by applying some variant of a strategy named by its inventor Anatol Rapoport a 'tit-for-tat strategy'—co-operation together with limited retaliation if the opponent does not respond. Despite the obvious difficulties and dangers involved, in theory at least the strategy could be applied to the central political conflicts between the two superpowers.

The problem of power enters into all types of international relations. Wars, competition, and co-operation, all involve power—the first two military power, though in competition it is used only to deter. All three contain non-military elements—a state which is devoid of resources and organization can neither compete nor co-operate successfully with other states. Hence the logical next step is to discuss the meaning of state power.

The nature of national power

All politics, by definition, revolve around the exercise and pursuit of power, but in international politics power is considerably more in evidence and less circumscribed than in domestic politics; hence this field is often described as 'power politics'. The word 'power' is used in many connotations—we speak about great and small Powers, about the balance of power, etc. The conspicuous role played by power in international relations has led to a school of interpretation centring around it and also to a reaction in the form of a condemnation of power politics, based on the expectation that power could be eliminated and replaced by international institutions. Neither extreme approach is fully satisfactory. Although power does play a central role in international politics, it is fundamentally an instrument for the achievement of national values. International politics is determined not only by the power wielded by the various states but also by the values held by these states; the concept of 'national interest' which governs state behaviour is not limited to power considerations alone.

The school of thought seeking to eliminate power is even less realistic. It is based on the historical experiences of the Anglo-Saxon countries in the nineteenth century. In Britain, power relations at that time become obscured by the apparent divorce of economics from politics and by the temporary security of the country which led to the illusion of a rule of law in international society; in the United States aloofness from the game of European power politics was not only an aspiration but a tangible fact. The moralistic condemnation of power stemming from these experiences, and the exaggerated hope that international institutions would replace power politics, could not stand the test of the totalitarian challenge in the thirties.

A more balanced attitude prevails now. It is futile to attempt a moral evaluation of power in the abstract—it can serve both good and evil purposes. Power certainly cannot be done away with. Our problem is not how to try to eliminate it, which would be futile, but how to control it, to confine it within acceptable channels.

Not all the major problems of power in domestic politics require discussion within the international context. That states wield power is accepted as a fact independently of its possible justification through theories of sovereignty derived from God or from the people; in the international context, the theories explaining power in terms of its function or the ends it serves ultimately boil down to self-preservation.

It is not easy to explain the meaning of the word 'power'. In the first instance, a distinction must be made between the word as it is employed in various different spheres. In mathematics 'power' is a technical term meaning the product arising from the continued multiplication of a number by itself; in physics it means the rate of transfer of energy, as in work done by an engine; in human relations it is now generally understood as a relational phenomenon, not a thing that one possesses, it denotes *the capacity to produce intended effects*; specifically, political power is not power over nature, a material, or oneself, but *over the minds and actions of other men*.

The concept of 'power' in human relations is too complex to permit the precision with which it can be used in other domains. Even in interpersonal relations many interconnected elements must be taken into account. Cleopatra's nose is one famous example of the exercise of power—the argument being that, had it not been for Cleopatra's beauty, Antony could have rallied himself and successfully opposed Octavian. But beauty apart, Cleopatra was also endowed with mental and emotional attributes, and her power cannot possibly be understood without an analysis of the whole complex relationship between her and Antony.

In international relations the concept of 'power' tends to be befogged by two fallacies. It is often understood in a predominantly or even exclusively military sense, as power to wage war. This may have been roughly true about the pre-nuclear era, but the definition is obviously inappropriate to our own age when, against the background of mutual deterrence, other, non-military elements of power are increasingly significant. Moreover, whereas military power remains extremely important in relations between *governments*, it is not much use in the now frequent direct appeals to the *people* of other states. Allied with this is the fallacy that power is measurable and quantifiable just because you can add up and compare such things as the numbers of soldiers under arms, the tonnage of battleships, the potential of the steel industry serving war needs, etc.

In order to explain power in international relations in its broadest meaning it is convenient to distinguish between relations that include an element of coercion and those that do not. In fact it may be advisable to accept, as Harold Sprout does,[3] the military connotations of the term power and to limit it to actions and situations having within them an element of coercion. The other, non-coercive aspects of power can then be called 'influence'. It is unfortunate but symptomatic of our preoccupation with coercion that our language lacks a more precise term for these aspects. Perhaps we cannot find it because the coercive and non-coercive elements cannot be clearly separated. Gentle, persuasive diplomacy works much more efficiently if backed by guns and missiles, although these need never be mentioned; coercive elements, if used starkly, are very useful since they can lead to desperate opposition. The use of force, actual physical coercion, is not a logical exercise of power. On the contrary, it is a manifestation that power is deficient.

State power involves several important elements usually referred to as capabilities, which will be discussed in turn, but these elements do not add up to a full explanation; indeed, the fact that some of them can be quantitatively expressed should not mislead us into thinking of power as a quantifiable entity. The power of states is better understood through an analysis of their actions rather than of static elements; as the etymological origin of the word in several languages (*dynamis, potentia*) indicates, it has a potential character. Harold Sprout goes so far as to call the combination of the coercive and non-coercive elements 'potential'; Klaus Knorr calls them 'putative' as against actualized power.

It is possible to conceptualize and compare the power of individual states in various ways. Three dimensions seem to be particularly important: *weight* describes the degrees to which the policy of the target state is affected; *scope* refers to the functional aspects, the range of issue areas in which power is effective—it may, for example, be limited to economic or military issues, or it may be comprehensive; *domain* refers to geographical aspects, the regional, subregional, or global scope of power and the number of states and other targets affected.

The point must be made that, although power plays a role in most international transactions and is central in many, it is not an ingredient in all. We speak then of 'non-political' or 'technical' matters. It is often impossible to agree whether an issue is political or non-political, but the distinction is nevertheless very important. It is, for instance, at the centre of the recurrent controversies between the United States and its allies regarding trade with Communist states. Trade, if regarded as predominantly technical, non-political, is governed by quite different considerations from trade considered as political, as a factor which can strengthen a hostile state.

It is the will of states alone that determines the political character of issues, anything which can even remotely affect the vital interests of the state is political. When it becomes the subject of an international dispute, the state refuses to regard the dispute as legal, that is, suitable for being decided by an impartial arbiter; it reserves the right to secure terms of settlement which are acceptable to itself, in the last resort even by the use of force. The character of activities does not fully determine their non-political nature even when they are so obviously humanitarian as the abolition of slavery or of forced labour, or protection of human rights in general; they become pronouncedly political when directed against a specific state, as happens with the debate over the implementation in the Soviet Union of the obligations regarding human rights under the Final Acts of the Helsinki Conference in 1975. The identity of the states involved is just as important as the character of the activity. Obviously Switzerland is much less likely than the United States or the Soviet Union to regard her trade issues as political; furthermore, Swiss trade with a small neutral country like Eire is less likely to give rise to political issues than her trade with one of the superpowers.

All the analytical categories employed in the discussion of the power of states are fully applicable to that of other international actors. When analysing their international behaviour, we are concerned with the effects of their activities upon the behaviour of other actors, as we are with states. The reasons why traditionally analysis is limited either to states or to non-state actors lie in the difficulties not so much of conceptualization as of comparison of the actual behaviour of actors which are not fully comparable: their legal positions are different, as only states are sovereign and in control of a territory, and their capabilities lie in different areas. It is, for example, very difficult to assess in general terms to what extent the economic power of a multinational corporation can prevail against the political will of a state. The latter may be dependent upon the multinational to sell its minerals, which constitute the main source of its income, but may count on the strong support of other radical Third World states. All these factors cannot be readily compared.

Capabilities

Although an analysis of capabilities seems indispensable for the study of international relations, the warning must be repeated that the mechanical sum total of these elements does not take us very far in explaining the actual power potential available to a state. Despite the great progress made in statistical analysis in the twentieth century, the assessment by Francis Bacon is still applicable:

The greatness of an estate, in bulk and territory, does fall under measure; and the greatness of finances and revenue does fall under computation. The population may appear by musters, and the number or greatness of cities by cards and maps; but yet there is not anything, amongst civil affairs, more subject to error than the right valuation and true judgement concerning the power and forces of an estate.

Power can be realistically estimated only in action, and discussion of capabilities can take us no further than an understanding of the state's potential—or its theoretical capacity for such action.

Some general points should be borne in mind whenever one analyses any particular element of power of any specific state. First, all power elements are relative to those possessed by other states, especially neighbours and possible rivals and opponents. The statement that Britain has a population of over 55 million is meaningless in terms of power relations unless we compare it with the populations of her larger European neighbours (to which it is roughly equal) and those of the superpowers (which are much more numerous). Second, mere quantities are fairly meaningless. Population figures must be broken up according to age, sex, skills, education, etc.; numbers of aeroplanes according to range, speed, weapon-carrying capacity, etc.

Third, single capabilities play their part in the complex totality of the state's power and can be evaluated only against this background. No one element will suffice if the state is deficient in others; for instance, military power alone is inadequate unless it is backed by sufficient population and industrial resources to keep pace with technological advance and to replace possible losses. Thus, with a population of barely seven million people possessing few mechanical skills, Saudi Arabia could not readily become a major military power, despite her lavish expenditure on armaments in the seventies and eighties, backed by a commanding position among oil exporters and enormous financial resources. Whenever a state has a surplus of an element of power, over and above actual and likely future needs, this surplus is only marginally relevant as remote strategic reserve. Thus the United States is not rendered much stronger by the capacity of its steel industry, well above its military and civilian needs. The large numbers of China's or India's populations are in one way an element of strength but in another of weakness, since they create problems of control and sustenance. In fact, what is usually an element of power can become a liability—for instance, if a state deficient in other elements possesses large deposits of rare minerals, such as fissionable materials, which make it a coveted prize for the great powers.

Fourth, capabilities may be utilized either more or less efficiently. It is conceivable, though not quite certain, that, although Soviet steel production both in absolute quantities, and *per capita* is lower than that of the United States, it may be equally adequate for the purposes of maintaining the Soviet power position because the Soviet consumer industry needs are considerably lower. The power value of a detachment of troops or weapons varies according to the strategic doctrine they are serving; thus during the Nazi attack on France in May 1940, a tank in the hands of the German command was strategically much more valuable than a mechanically equivalent tank in the hands of the French.

Fifth, since we live in an area of uniquely rapid technological advance, the relative importance of the various capabilities is constantly changing. Oil has replaced coal as the main source of energy and may itself be replaced in the future by uranium; uranium will lose its value if nuclear processes are mastered to the point of releasing energy through fusion, for which only very limited fissionable material is necessary. Weapons are constantly going out of date—submarines have rendered useless capital ships and ballistic missiles have gone a long way towards supplanting manned aeroplanes. And it is not only technology that changes. A profound disturbance in power relations can arise not only from the evolution of new raw materials or new weapons but also from less tangible though equally important changes in the efficiency of government or in the morale of the people.

Finally, the aspect of readiness must not be neglected. Even in the past all strategists readily distinguished between soldiers actually under arms (forces in being) and soldiers who had to be mobilized, between operational ships and those laid up, between aeroplanes which require hours to be ready for flying and those on the alert. By the mid-eighties the time-scale had become further compressed: only minutes were available for warning against ballistic missiles and the Americans were engaged in developing the technology for their Strategic Defense Initiative (SDI), the aim of which was to destroy missiles immediately after they had been fired, before they had emerged out of the atmosphere.

Consequently analysis should be limited to the data available on the present or the recent past but must perforce include an estimate of trends both in the elements of power currently considered important and in those likely to become so in the future. Here the main problem is how to make the necessary distinctions between reliable statistics and estimates, and between their timing. If, for example, we compute the Soviet capacity to produce nuclear missiles, we still do not know how many missiles it has actually produced, since they may not be able or willing to use their capacity to the full. While most strategic analyses centre around intercontinental ballistic missiles, the destructive power of biological and chemical weapons is not compared; simultaneously the 'obsolete' manned bombers still play a significant strategic role. A comparison of the American and the Soviet nuclear striking abilities at different dates produces vastly different results; any comparison must therefore employ statistics and estimates strictly comparable in time.

Population

Undoubtedly the power of a state is related to the size of its population. Although the correlation is not absolute, it is valid to the extent that no state with a small population can become a great power. The two superpowers have very large populations: in the mid-eighties the Soviet Union had over 270 million and the United States about 240 million; the most populous states, China with a population of over a billion and India with over 650 million, are serious aspirants to great power status, although they do not in any way approximate the power position of the two less populous superpowers. The sudden growth of the population of Western Europe, especially Britain, in the last three centuries, had led to the establishment of colonial empires but, in the different conditions of our century, a similar expansion of the populations of Latin America, Asia, and Africa cannot possibly lead to comparable results. An estimate of the trends in population development is indispensable for making long-range power calculations. The highly industrialized Western states, which have reached a fairly stable equilibrium between birth-rates and death-rates, are likely to decrease or increase at a very much slower rate than other societies in which the death-rates are being suddenly reduced, while the birth-rates continue high.

Bare numbers do not tell us nearly enough, however. We must ascertain the proportion of the population in the crucial age-group of 20–50 years, which is both the most productive and the best capable of bearing arms. Comparison of this age-group in different countries requires further refinements according to the utilization of women for both tasks. Whereas during the Second World War the Soviet Union employed women in industrial production and to some extent also for military service, the Germans did not; hence the correct comparison is that of German manpower and Soviet man- plus 'woman-power'. Furthermore, the extent of literacy, education, and industrial skills can prove decisive. In 1942 the Germans could challenge the Russians because the population of the Soviet Union, although three times more numerous, was inferior to them in most of these respects. Today, this being much less so, the sheer weight of Russian numbers makes such a challenge less thinkable.

Geography

Geography is so prominent in the make-up of the territorial state that some thinkers belonging to the school of 'geopolitics' have sought the full explanation of foreign policy in geographical influences. Needless to say, like any other explanation which attempts to reduce a complex reality to the effects of one single factor, 'geopolitics' cannot be accepted as an adequate theory even though the geographical element of power does count for much.

Undoubtedly a certain correlation between power and the size of a state's territory does exist, although it is considerably less pronounced than the correlation with the size of the population. The largest state, the Soviet Union, which measures over 22 million square kilometres, is very powerful but not more so than the United States which covers just under 8 million. Despite her small area (just 250,000 square kilometres when including the whole of Ireland), Britain managed to play a leading role in world politics for a considerable time and to build up the greatest colonial empire. In fact, where vast waste tracts of land divide the centres of population, size can be a handicap until adequate communications have been developed; Australia, for example, is weakened rather than strengthened by the extensive but barren waste of her interior.

Shape, location, and topography are all important. For strategic and administrative purposes a state should be compact with a capital more or less in the centre, like France, whereas an elongated state like Czechoslovakia is difficult both to defend and to govern. The 'geopoliticians' have attributed to location a decisive influence—indeed much of the turbulent history of Germany or Poland is due to their respective positions in the midst of the Central European plain, whereas Britain, in her insular isolation, was able to develop the foundations of a world empire, while Spain and Portugal, the Scandinavian countries, and Japan, being located on peripheries, have sometimes effectively withdrawn from the mainstream of power politics. Modern technology has reduced the significance of topography and of such 'natural frontiers' as mountain ranges or rivers, but location remains important.

Finally, climate greatly influences the produce of the land and the character of its people. The great centres of power have so far arisen only in the moderate zone, between twenty and sixty degrees north.

Economics

The economic basis of modern states is paramount both in peace and in war. It determines the living conditions and the well-being of their peoples and provides them with the wherewithal for a successful foreign policy; it also serves as the foundation for an armaments industry and can be regarded as ultimately decisive in war.

The GNP is useful as a general index of economic strength, particularly when supplemented by a breakdown on a *per capita* basis and by an estimate of the growth rate. Unfortunately national figures are computed in different ways and are therefore not strictly comparable; many are also unreliable. Usually two components are distinguished in the economic element: natural resources and industrial production. Again comparisons are inaccurate but nevertheless quite telling as general indicators of strength.

When evaluating the economic elements of power one must always bear in mind the distinction between capacity and actual production. Soviet steel production capacity, for instance, though smaller than that of the United States, is generally more fully utilized while American capacity is generally worked only partly; hence the discrepancy between the quantities of steel actually produced by the two countries is considerably less than that between their capacities. Moreover, while much of American steel is put to a marginally social use, for instance to make the cars even bigger, it is, for power purposes, much less effectively used than Soviet steel which is made into weapons and essential consumer goods. Against that, the quality of the product must be borne in mind; defective end-products which are useless or only partially useful are likely to be produced much less frequently in the competitive American system than in a Communist society where dire penalties threaten factories which fail to produce their allotted quotas, regardless of quality.

If a state is deficient in a raw material or productive capacity, one must investigate how it can overcome the shortage through stockpiling or imports, and under what economic and strategic conditions, or how a substitute could be discovered through technological advance. For instance, one of the strategically important materials which the United States lacks is rubber. For a long time the Americans were dependent on imports from South-east Asia, which put them into a strategically dangerous position owing to the distances involved; to meet a sudden emergency they stockpiled considerable quantities of rubber and finally they evolved methods of producing artificial rubber which, for some purposes, is superior to the natural product. The process is, however, slow. For instance, in the seventies the world was faced with an 'energy crisis', owing to the rapidly growing energy needs and even more rapidly growing dependence upon oil imports to satisfy them. Nevertheless it was by no means clear what this meant in computing the power of states. On the one hand, the dominant position of Saudi Arabia as not only the leading oil exporter but also the only exporter capable of a rapid massive increase in its supplies, was not translated into a position of clear diplomatic influence; on the other, the growing dependence of the United States on oil imports and particularly on Saudi Arabia was not directly translated into a loss of diplomatic influence—the resulting substantial imbalance in payments and the weakness of the dollar were very much more significant. In the mutual relations of Saudi Arabia and the United States the former did not manage to use her advantage to really good effect to prevent the latter from continuing to extend protection to the state of Israel. In the longer run, however, a greater degree of such influence could be anticipated.

Only the two superpowers have approached self-sufficiency, but only for a while, and even then they were dependent on imports of some raw materials. In 1960 the United States imported some seventy key materials totalling about 15 per cent of its entire raw material consumption, and these imports have been rising further. The Soviet Union imports considerably less and is more likely to find at home additional raw materials to meet the needs of increased industrial production in the future. In the late seventies, the United States became a large-scale oil importer, and the Soviet Union, too, was facing the prospect of becoming one.

Strategically important raw materials fall into three groups with a certain overlap: fuels (coal, oil, natural gas, and fissile materials); metals (especially iron, to which coal must be added for steel production; copper; metals used to harden steel such as chromium, manganese, and nickel; bauxite, lead, zinc, tin, titanium, gold, silver, and platinum, etc.); and agricultural produce, subdivided into food and industrial crops. In industrial production, steel output, which is the basis of all heavy industry and particularly of the production of weapons, usually receives much prominence; the chemical and the electronics industries are also important in all advanced economies; from the seventies computers and information technology came to the fore.

Despite a growing challenge from Japan and also from the European Community, the United States clearly leads in advanced technology; with the signal exception of military technology, the Soviet Union trails far behind. A number of other states, often referred to as Newly Industrialized Countries, are also seriously set upon the path of industrialization: some of them are small, like South Korea or Taiwan, but some are big, like Brazil or India. Moreover, economic growth has now become the major goal of all states, which are appropriately referred to in this context as 'underdeveloped', 'less developed', or 'developing'. From the point of view of power relations, states already industrialized are in a much better position than others. Not only can they supply more weapons for their armies and more goods for their people, but they have a much better chance of crossing the threshold beyond which economic growth becomes a self-perpetuating process, as it is in the West and in the Soviet Union. In the longer run, however, as more and more producers compete for raw materials—and despite the fact that greater deposits of these are constantly being found and more efficiently exploited and that substitutes are often found—it is conceivable that states controlling rare crucial raw materials could come to occupy a powerful position, able to command in exchange all that they require. For a while this actually happened with oil.

Government and military organization

The potential elements of power are utilized according to how efficiently they are organized; hence the importance of government. Sudden changes in the power position of a state can be entirely due to a change of government, as happened in Germany when the Nazis replaced the Weimar Republic, or in China, when a Communist government replaced a demoralized Nationalist one.

The contemporary types of authoritarian and democratic governments differ in their respective advantages and disadvantages. An authoritarian government can override the wishes of its people; hence it can act with speed, and, at least in the short run, with efficiency. A democratic government must persuade its people first. This is often a slow and difficult process, sometimes to no avail, but it has the off-setting advantage that the more active consent of the people ensures the stability of the government and enables it to withstand stress. If we compare the systems in contemporary China and India, we find that the Chinese Government was the more able to mobilize the whole population and to divert scarce resources to economic development but it became involved in a devastating 'Cultural Revolution'. The much less efficient and less ruthless Indian Government may have been equally successful although it continues to face severe economic and minority challenges. In the eighties, however, China introduced drastic measures for population control whereas India could not achieve this despite strenuous efforts.

How significant is the quality of the civil service, is demonstrated by the comparison of newly emancipated colonial territories. After emancipation, countries which inherited a reasonable civil service, such as Ghana or Nigeria, fared at first much better than countries in which it had broken down, such as Indonesia or the Belgian Congo. In India the advantage has proved to be more lasting. For international relations, the quality of diplomacy is particularly relevant.

Although, as has been mentioned, its role is often exaggerated, military power is an essential condition for the survival of the state not only in war but also in peacetime, to enable it to pursue policies of effective deterrence and to endow the state with the capabilities necessary for the making of effective allies. Comparisons of military organization are confusing since we must bear in mind at least three separate military elements: the strategic deterrent; the so-called conventional weapons, traditionally divided into air, naval, and army branches; and the strategic doctrine. Moreover, the respective importance of the three is constantly changing. During the immediate post-war years the Americans greatly overrated nuclear weapons to the detriment of conventional ones. Even now possession of nuclear weapons remains a major condition for great power status, and nuclear equilibrium is the major objective of the two superpowers. The role of nuclear weapons in securing great power status for Britain, France, and China is uncertain but probably quite substantial. Moreover quite a few additional states possess the technological ability to produce nuclear weapons and some of them may have actually done so. As despite prolonged international negotiations the prospects of effectively preventing nuclear proliferation are not very promising, the effect on global and regional power balances is bound to be fundamental. This is already true of the Middle East and South Asia as both Israel and India possess the full capacity to produce nuclear weapons.

The value of strategic doctrine lies in choosing military power of the right kind. Thus French military doctrine in the inter-war period can be blamed for the defeat in 1940, since the French were prepared for static trench warfare of the First World War type and not for the mobile warfare of the Second World War, imposed upon them by the attacking Germans. Today the major problem lies in determining the proportion of resources to be devoted to nuclear weapons necessary for deterrence and for a nuclear war, and to conventional weapons useful in other conflicts. The differences between the strategy of deterrence and that to be employed in the minor clashes of the cold war, such as subversion or infiltration, also require definition.

The proportion of the GNP devoted to military ends indicates the intensity of the military effort and offers a clue to the prospects of its durability. In the mid-eighties the Russians devoted some 12–17 per cent of their GNP to military ends, the Americans only some 7 per cent. The latter, additionally, not only enjoy a much higher national product, but also do not fully utilize their industrial capacity. Hence armament programmes are generally not too onerous for them; on the contrary, they stimulate technological advance and employment. Real strains arose only during the Vietnam War and the massive Reagan rearmament in the eighties, when huge deficits were financed by borrowing. The strains on the Soviet economy have been growing steadily, particularly when it began to slow down in the eighties. Although traditionally giving preference to guns over butter, the Soviet rulers have an ever-increasing interest in limiting the cost of armaments.

Comparison of actual military strength is highly technical and need not be pursued here beyond the conclusion that both the Americans and the Russians have more than sufficient 'second-strike capability', that is, enough nuclear weapons to inflict 'unacceptable' damage on the opponent even after having been subject to a devastating nuclear attack; the power-value of the British and French deterrents is controversial. Likewise inconclusive is the comparison of conventional military resources. While we can count the troops and weapons classified according to their striking power, the intangible element of the political attitudes of both the soldiers and the civilians must not be neglected. Support, although often enforced, of the native people for Communist guerrillas in South-east Asia multiplied the power-value of the numerically small active Communists; nationalist, anti-Russian sentiments may greatly reduce the reliability and hence the power-value of the Warsaw Pact troops; certainly Polish troops could scarcely be expected to fight whole-heartedly.

Psychological-social elements

This category embraces all the less tangible elements of power which cannot be easily bracketed within any of the preceding categories.

It is necessary to distinguish the social system from the governmental one. A people united and homogeneous are obviously much stronger than one disunited and heterogeneous. Any major rifts, whether racial, national, religious, or of any other kind, detract, at least potentially, from the power of the state because it may not be able to muster the whole strength of its population whenever factional interests clash. This somewhat intangible element used to augment the power of the United Kingdom while its social system remained stable. It casts some doubts on the ultimate strength of the Soviet Union where important national, religious, and ideological differences clearly exist. While they lasted, the racial disturbances in the United States seriously detracted from its power potential.

Then there is the factor often referred to as morale. Morale describes the extent to which the people support their leaders, believe in the future of their state and in the rightness of their cause. It depends upon a combination of circumstances and the quality of leadership and can be subject to frequent and sometimes sudden fluctuations. Thus French morale was much higher than the British throughout the sixties but was severely shaken by the student riots and general strike in 1968. For over a decade American morale was shattered by the Vietnam War, while economic decline sapped the morale of the British from the late seventies.

A more permanent intangible element is national character. Although the stereotypes of national character can be grossly misleading, there is some foundation for the observation that different nations tend to develop their own peculiar ways of thinking and acting, some of which are more useful than others for the power of the state; there can be little doubt about the advantages of German industriousness or the disadvantages of Polish unruliness in the past. Analysis of national character does not, however, take us very far. First of all, national character, although much more stable than morale, does change. In the seventeenth century the English were reputed to be the most turbulent nation in Europe and in the eighteenth the Germans the most romantic and peaceful, but quite justifiably neither reputation holds today. Second, it is notoriously difficult to agree on what national character actually is or how useful are some of its features. It is fairly easy to catalogue the differences between the Americans and the Russians and to arrive at the conclusion that their national characters are quite different. It is not much more difficult to list the similarities due to the common factors of size and concentration on material achievements, and to arrive at the opposite conclusion.

Prestige is derived from some features of society that involve power and from others that do not, but is an element of power in itself because it helps the state to obtain the desired social response from others. Prestige is built upon the image formed by others of the state's qualities, an image often having little in common with reality—especially when the supposed qualities are merely a matter of the past. The qualities that count for the purpose of prestige vary from period to period, and states tend to evolve their own individual methods for enhancing their reputations.

Military, today particularly nuclear, power is a sound foundation for international prestige. So is economic strength, though here prestige ambiguously embraces several elements: there is the element of economic strength as a basis for and supplement to military power, as the ability to provide largesse abroad, and as a testimony to the soundness of the ideological foundations of a society. In the latter respect, the Russians used to be able to score because their centrally planned economy could boast of one of the highest rates of economic growth sustained over many years. One should not, however, forget the frequently unacknowledged prestige accruing to the United States for its indisputably high standard of living and for all the glossy gadgets its citizens enjoy. Despite all the incidental harm Hollywood films may have been doing to American prestige, they ensure that the whole world is familiar with an admittedly exaggerated image of American standards of living.

In our age which is so acutely aware of human rights, social justice has become important for the reputation of states. Especially since 1975, when the protection of human rights became a legally recognized international concern under the Final Acts of the Helsinki Conference, infringements of such rights when dealing with ideological dissidents have become seriously damaging to the Soviet Union. Particularly obnoxious is racial discrimination, which accounts for the extreme diplomatic isolation of South Africa, a country pursuing apartheid, her policy of separate development of races, despite growing international opprobrium.

International strategic position

State power is determined not only by the combination of all the above-mentioned domestic elements of power but also by the position of the state in the world. No state, not even the superpowers, is fully self-supporting, all depend on military allies, on friends in diplomacy, on suppliers and markets in trade. All the elements of power in their possession can be considerably augmented by outside support. Such support is highly desirable, sometimes indispensable, but its value and cost require careful computation. Although numerical precision cannot be achieved, it seems to be useful to think about international support as a kind of multiplier—positive or negative—to domestic capabilities. On issues of anti-colonialism or racism, any new, developing state can count on sustained support from the Group of 77 and usually also from Communist states so that its capabilities, however slender, are accordingly augmented. By contrast, a state faced with international opprobrium must discount its national capabilities accordingly; for quite different individual reasons, this is the case with South Africa, Israel, and Taiwan. Hence these are sometimes bracketed as 'pariah states', however heterogeneous this category is in all other significant respects.

Foreign support is not very reliable. The ultimate command of the resources which can be called upon from abroad remains in foreign hands: the promised troops may be refused at the last minute, the expected economic aid may be stopped, the raw materials may not be delivered. Excessive reliance on uncertain support is obviously dangerous. Moreover, there are the drawbacks of cost and risk. The concessions necessary to ensure the reliability of an ally may be so great as to reduce the power of the state in relation to this ally, although the alliance strengthens its power in relation to other states. To take the example of American alliances since the Second World War—they have certainly proved costly and, with the exception of NATO, usually both ineffective and precarious. While they have been concluded and maintained in the belief that they increase American power, the contrary could be argued about alignments such as that with South Vietnam, which led directly to American involvement in the Vietnam War.

The value of political support short of an alliance, or even of benevolent neutrality, is obvious in the deliberations of the General Assembly. The United States and the Soviet Union vie in their efforts to secure the goodwill of the numerically preponderant Afro-Asian bloc; much of Soviet diplomatic power in the United Nations comes from the anti-colonial and therefore anti-Western attitudes of this bloc. A state concerned in a matter coming up on the agenda of the General Assembly is compelled to make the rounds of other members, and the isolation of such states as South Africa and Israel greatly reduces their power.

7

Instruments and techniques of state interaction

Some general distinctions

Two important but necessary limitations of the subsequent discussion must be noted in advance. First, it is limited to direct state interaction. A legitimate objection to such a limitation could be raised on the grounds that often what is in form a purely domestic policy can profoundly affect other states—the economic or armaments programme of the United States, for example. It is, however, not unrealistic to assume that any domestic matter with a sufficiently strong international component is bound to be taken up internationally. Second, the international system within which this interaction takes place can be only sketchily referred to here; it will be more fully discussed in subsequent chapters.

In the first instance it is necessary to discuss the degree of choice of instruments and techniques open to individual states. Clearly such choice is limited by the availability of the appropriate capabilities: a militarily weak state is naturally inclined to develop its foreign relations with the aid of non-military instruments and techniques; an economically weak state is limited in its choice of economic instruments and techniques. The choice, however, cannot be made at the will of the state, according to a rational appraisal of its attitudes to the other party and of its power-position. Some inescapable influences arise within the international environment—challenges and opportunities in every field change with the passage of time; international fashions and the 'rules of the game' governing international intercourse are not static. Thus post-war American foreign policy has been justly criticized for its excessive reliance upon nuclear weapons in which the United States is strong, despite the fact that these weapons are useless in most situations and that the major

Communist challenges have gradually shifted to the ideological and economic fields. France and Britain learnt only through the failure of their Suez expedition in 1956 that in the mid-twentieth century armed intervention could be undertaken only with the support of at least one of the superpowers or of the United Nations. For some years the Western powers were rather pathetically complaining that they could not cope with Communist-inspired subversion.

Arms control or disarmament, an agreed reduction of the military instruments, would clearly be in the general interest. Not only would all states save colossal sums of money on an increasingly costly item of expenditure but also the instruments of violence would be limited and hence external threats somewhat reduced. This was the origin of disarmament proposals which started with the initiative of the Russian Tsar at the end of the last century, were abortively resumed in the inter-war period, and have formed a feature of international relations since 1945. Negotiations are conducted nearly continuously in several forums; some include many states and others only the two superpowers. Complete nuclear disarmament, which is the frequently voiced aspiration, would of course be of colossal benefit to mankind and is pressed for by non-nuclear states; the attitudes of the two superpowers and of the three other nuclear powers—Britain, France, and China—are, however, determined by the fears and uncertainties of any feasible scheme. Negotiations aim more at scoring military and propaganda advantages over others than at achieving genuine reductions. Although results have been limited, they do go beyond platitudinous declarations. Most successful were the two SALT agreements between the Americans and the Russians, which limited the escalation of the nuclear arms race for some years. It seems possible that, despite a futile summit meeting at Reykjavik in 1986, the two superpowers are moving towards an agreement to eliminate middle- and short-range nuclear missiles and, in the longer run, to make deep cuts in their strategic arsenals.

Disarmament attempts have been supplemented by attempts to outlaw war, which culminated in a far-reaching prohibition on the use of threat or force in the conduct of international relations.

This is embodied in the United Nations Charter; although frequently ignored it does exercise some constraint: in general, other things not being too unequal, states will tend to choose instruments and techniques compatible with the Charter and likely to find approval with international public opinion as expressed in the General Assembly. Of course the degree of deference varies with the individual states and according to the significance of the issues involved.

The choice of instruments and techniques by an individual state cannot be fully divorced from the determination of foreign policy as a whole. Some variables can, however, be singled out as being particularly relevant to such a choice. To start with, there is the very fundamental issue of the intensity of international relations, which varies greatly in different areas and periods.

While Mesopotamia became the stage of ramified international relations some millennia before our era, the remote Himalayan realms of Tibet and Nepal remained isolated until this century. One cannot appreciate the foreign policy of any state without some idea of how involved it is in its relations with other states—today the United States and the Soviet Union are obviously the most active countries, while many neutrals are trying with varying degrees of success to stay out of the mainstream of power politics. Major issues of foreign policy centre around involvement—for instance to what extent should Britain or France pursue their policies as nuclear powers, as active members of NATO, and as senior partners in networks of relationships with their ex-colonies?

Traditionally, states have tried to escape what they consider excessive involvement through isolationism and neutrality. Isolationism, meaning a deliberate withdrawal from international relations, is no longer possible on the basis of geographical isolation, as pursued by China and Japan until the relatively recent incursion of European influence. Britain's 'splendid isolation' in the nineteenth century did not really amount to non-involvement; on the contrary, Britain actively participated in all major European conflicts except the Franco-Prussian War. The term merely described the operation of the balance of power system, which did not demand from Britain continuous participation but only sporadic interventions. Likewise the 'splendid isolation' of the United States was to a large extent mythical. The Americans were extremely active in the Western hemisphere and watched European politics closely but, owing to the protection of the friendly British Navy, they could refrain from taking part directly.

Fifty years ago neutrality was primarily a strictly legal concept describing non-participation in war, which conferred certain rights and imposed certain duties on the neutral states. The United States in the First World War until its entry or Eire in the Second World War are recent examples. Although more rarely, the concept applied also to more broadly political orientations in peacetime such as the neutralization of Belgium in 1939 or the traditional policies of the classical European neutrals, Switzerland and Sweden. In response to nuclear weapons and the cold war, however, under the new name of 'non-alignment', a policy of neutrality has spread very widely since 1945, especially among the new states. Its basic meaning consists of not being committed to either major bloc and of refusing to participate in their systems of alliances. The term applies to a state's attitude to the cold war alone. The non-aligned states endeavour to avoid commitment to either the Russians or the Americans but they are, in varying degrees, involved in quite intensive international relations outside this context. Moreover, some individual non-aligned states come under the strong influence of one of the superpowers so that their neutrality is by no means even-handed. Ever since its foundation at the Bandung Conference in 1954 the non-aligned bloc has been a major feature of the international system, but its continuation requires consummate diplomatic skills and manoeuvres on the part of its leaders. In 1978 it came under a particularly severe strain owing to the dispute over the large-scale Cuban military interventions in Africa.

Another important variable is *crisis* perception. Definitions of a 'crisis' vary but, according to most writers, it is a situation characterized by high levels of threat to some vital interest; including, according to some, a high probability of military activities; by time-pressure resulting in decision-making generally being conducted higher up the hierarchy and in an accelerated—which inevitably means also simplified—manner; and often also by surprise. Thus, by definition, crisis situations result in a strong bias towards the use of the military instrument and of force. Hence, both from the systemic and from the individual state's point of view, it is important to conceive of methods of crisis prevention and management which would be as effective as possible.

General attitudes to the stability of the international order constitute another important variable. Some states like to preserve stability which, they feel, serves their national interest; they are the defenders of the status quo (*status quo ante bellum* is a legal term used in peace treaties to describe the state of affairs which existed before the beginning of hostilities); others, feeling that the order is against their national interest and that they would gain by changing it, are usually described as *revisionist* powers. These positive or negative attitudes to the existing international order vary in intensity and determination. Not all supporters of the status quo are equally ready to defend it, and, likewise, not all revisionist states are equally determined to strive for the downfall of the existing order. Moreover, states vary greatly in their attitudes to friends, potential enemies, and neutrals. Inevitably they are influenced by these in their choice of instruments and techniques.

In the interaction between states there are no clear-cut divisions between friends and foes, between persuasion and coercion. In most cases relations include varying, even conflicting, elements—a threat of coercion occasionally creeps into the most amicable relationship and even ardent ideological opponents may find it possible to compromise in matters of common interest, such as trade. Peace does not preclude the existence of conflict, even of quite an acute nature, nor does war mean complete severance of non-coercive relations. All the instruments and techniques of international intercourse have some application both in friendly and in hostile relations, in peace and in war, even though some are pronouncedly more persuasive while others are pronouncedly more coercive.

Until the First World War international relations were conducted with other governments alone, but since then relations with the people of other states or other subgroups have been growing in importance. Consequently instruments and techniques suitable for intergovernmental relations have been supplemented and to a certain extent displaced by those suitable for approaching these people. Often dilemmas arise. When determining their relations with unfriendly Communist governments in Eastern Europe immediately after 1945, for instance, the Americans sometimes helped them in their economic difficulties in the hope of securing their goodwill and weakening their allegiance to the Soviet bloc (this was called detachment). The alternative was to appeal to the people of these countries to overthrow their governments and replace them with governments which would be more friendly to the United States and would therefore qualify for assistance (this was called subversion). Obviously these two policies are incompatible.

Foreign policy is not only directed towards other governments but can also use them as instruments. One of the characteristics of the post-war period has been 'aggression by proxy'. The Russians have used their own troops only in neighbouring countries. The many Communist-inspired and supported actions and disturbances which took place elsewhere immediately after the war were conducted by foreign Communists employed as instruments of Soviet foreign policy; only the Yugoslav and the Chinese revolutions were genuinely national. Military intervention by proxy remained in use in the late seventies when it was undertaken on a large scale by Cuban troops in Angola and on the Horn of Africa, with the Russians providing only military supplies and transport.

The various instruments and techniques will be analysed according to the fields within which they operate. A large proportion of state behaviour is verbal and falls within two categories known as diplomacy and propaganda, while economic and military activities, which are of central importance, show specific characteristics.

Diplomacy

The word 'diplomacy' is often employed in a broad meaning which embraces both the making and the execution of foreign policy. In its more technical meaning here employed it has been aptly described as the business of communicating between governments. It is the inevitable outcome of the coexistence of separate political units with any degree of contact; indeed, its origins can be traced to remote antiquity. Greece, Byzantium, and Renaissance Italy made the most notable contributions to the evolution of contemporary diplomacy. At all times rulers have considered diplomacy an important instrument of state policies, but gradually it transcended a purely national role. Although the diplomats were governed exclusively by the dictates of national policy and ruthlessly employed cunning, deceit, and duplicity, as realistically described by Machiavelli in *The Prince*, they slowly evolved a certain orderliness of procedure. In the eighteenth century the common interest in the maintenance of an international equilibrium led to a fundamental reorganization. The balance of power system, which will be discussed in the following chapter, fundamentally affected the conduct of diplomacy. It demanded constant vigilance from its participants; hence diplomatic missions became permanent instead of sporadic. This, in turn, led to the consolidation of diplomatic procedures and practices, which was facilitated by the common aristocratic origin of the practitioners and by the common interest in the existing international order; in 1815, after the end of the Napoleonic Wars, the process was formalized by the regulations of Aix-la-Chapelle.

The interest in international order shared by all states thus transformed the nature of diplomacy. Since the national interests of the several states could not be successfully secured except through the maintenance of the balance of power, diplomacy had to serve the requirements of the system as a whole. Instead of the intrigues and deceit prevalent earlier in history, the qualities of integrity, good faith, and honest negotiation became increasingly stressed. While remaining a major instrument of state policy, diplomacy became also a major agency operating on behalf of international society.

The golden age of diplomacy passed together with the balance of power system; following the fundamental changes in international society since 1918, we then entered an era of what is often called popular or new diplomacy. One fundamental reason for this was the transformation of technology and communications. Already in 1919 the actual heads of the governments of the Allied and Associated Powers spent long periods together, deliberating over the peace treaty with Germany. Since then, the evolution of aeroplanes and telecommunications has greatly increased the speed of diplomacy and has therefore reduced the importance of the diplomats in the field; to a large extent diplomacy now overlaps with policy-making. Moreover, new means of mass communication have opened the way to a direct approach to the people of other countries through propaganda. This not only detracts from the importance of diplomacy but sometimes conflicts with its basic purpose as well as with its day-to-day operation.

In the West, moreover, public opinion has forcibly intruded into the conduct of foreign policy and has weakened the esteem in which diplomacy had formerly been held. The people were suspicious of power politics and of the balance of power system which had led to the First World War; hence they suspected diplomacy as the major instrument of foreign policy and attacked its traditional secrecy. President Wilson, the most influential spokesman of the new view, formulated the ideal in the very first of his famous Fourteen Points:

Open covenants of peace, openly arrived at, after which there shall be no private international understandings of any kind, but diplomacy shall proceed always frankly and in the public view.

Open diplomacy means two things—first, that there should be no secret agreements; second, that negotiations should be in the open. While the former condition is reasonable and is firmly rooted in democratic theory, the latter has proved embarrassing. Once the diplomats have stated their national demands in public, they generally cannot agree to a compromise without loss of face; in other words, they cannot effectively negotiate.

The composition of international society has now completely changed. Europe is no longer the exclusive centre of international affairs and, since the Second World War, power has become concentrated in the hands of two non-European states, the United States and the Soviet Union. The members of international society have swollen in numbers with the emancipation of colonial territories in Asia and in Africa; the new states are much more remote from European diplomatic traditions than even the two superpowers.

Moreover, the United Nations has become an important supplementary and, to some extent, competitive channel for international intercourse, some of which is conducted in the traditional manner by the diplomatic representatives to the United Nations, whose private negotiations are particularly useful to states which do not maintain direct diplomatic relations. However, the United Nations also represents a new dimension in diplomacy, sometimes called diplomacy by conference, or forensic diplomacy. In addition to traditional confidential contacts, this diplomacy is conducted openly in conferences or assemblies, and, instead of the art of compromise, it requires the art of persuasion to secure the votes of as many members as possible. Since the egalitarian nature of international organization ensures one vote for each state, the wooing of many becomes essential.

Finally, instead of operating within a fairly stable international society based upon the operation of a balance of power in which all the members were interested, diplomacy today operates in a world in which the rival blocs are rent by ideological rifts and have only limited common interests. While the new states are interested mainly in economic growth and in preserving their newly won independence from entanglements, the Communist and the Western blocs continue to suspect each other's intentions. Although it is logical to assume that both share a vital interest in the continuation of the present balance and in the prevention of the spread of nuclear weapons which could upset this balance, the implications of this common interest have not as yet been fully absorbed by diplomacy.

The organization of the diplomatic machinery has remained unaltered since the beginning of the nineteenth century but, owing to the multiplication of state units, only superpowers can maintain separate diplomatic relations with nearly all of them. Provided no difficulties of recognition arise, most states exchange diplomatic missions only with the superpowers, with neighbours, and with other states with which they have much business. These missions are either embassies headed by ambassadors or, less frequently and on a lower ceremonial level, legations headed by ministers. Whereas in the nineteenth century ambassadorial status was granted less frequently—only to important powers—nowadays it has become more a mark of good relations and an expression of goodwill. The chief functions of diplomacy remain the protection of the interests of the country and of its citizens abroad, representation (legal, symbolic, and social), observation, reporting, and, most importantly, negotiation.

Negotiations cover an extremely wide range of international transactions and can be conducted in various ways—by the ambassador of a country in the capital of another, or by its foreign ministry in its own capital; heads of government or foreign ministers engage in 'summit diplomacy' or use their personal agents; diplomatic representatives accredited to the United Nations or to a third country may be in charge, especially if the two countries have no direct diplomatic relations; special international conferences may be convened. Negotiations may be formal, conducted through an exchange of notes, or informal, through personal, sometimes unofficial contacts. The basic objective of all negotiations is to obtain from other states consent to what is considered to be in the national interest—it may be an agreement on limitation of armaments, or support in the General Assembly of the United Nations, or the conclusion of a trade agreement, or protection of the interests of nationals living in the other state, or anything else which may be quite vital or merely trivial. Negotiations necessarily begin with an exchange of statements of the views of both parties and consist essentially of bargaining, of seeking a compromise between these views. Areas of mutual agreement are defined and as far as possible enlarged, areas of disagreement are defined and as far as possible reduced through mutual compromise until accord is reached. This may be entirely informal or it may be embodied in a formal international treaty.

When the parties are basically antagonistic, negotiations are often conducted not with the usual purpose of securing agreement but to damage the position of an opponent and to express hostility. It happened in the past, for instance, when the Chinese were negotiating with Lord Napier at Canton in 1830 or when the Russian Bolsheviks met the Germans at Brest Litovsk in 1919; it has happened frequently since 1945 under the impact of the cold war. In spite of their avowed desire to negotiate, both the Communists and the Americans frequently appear to be intractable; it is possible that during the prolonged negotiations on disarmament neither side have ever seriously contemplated or desired a compromise. While 'negotiating from strength' remains the rule, desire to secure the approval of the United Nations partly instigates the clashes.

Public announcements and behind-the-scenes negotiations do not always coincide. When the Russians and then the Americans resumed nuclear testing in 1962, they accused each other in public of committing crimes against humanity. But, because they wished to prevent other powers from developing nuclear weapons, these public condemnations did not prevent them from privately seeking an agreement to ban tests, though not before they themselves had completed a further series. Such divergence between public announcements and private behaviour may appear cynical, but in fact the two powers quite reasonably combined vital national interests with propaganda warfare.

In all negotiating it is imperative to save face. In the Cuban crisis in 1962, for instance, President Kennedy forced Khrushchev to withdraw his missiles from Cuba but enabled him to cover up his retreat by undertaking not to invade Cuba. Failing such a face-saving formula Khrushchev might have found a withdrawal impossible.

Disarmament talks under UN auspices have continued throughout much of the post-war period, not in the hope of reaching any substantial agreement but largely because the major parties justifiably wished to avoid the opprobrium of breaking them off.

Normally negotiations are the simplest way of reconciling competing national interests; hence they perform a central function not only in the conduct of the foreign policy of every single state but also in the operation of the international system as a whole. They are invaluable in that they offer the simplest method of setting conflicts peacefully; as long as they are continued, the outbreak of violence is less likely. As a rule negotiations deal with concrete issues and details, and parties concentrating on these are diverted from intractable fundamentals with their attendant prejudices and passions.

The basic technique of negotiation is persuasion and compromise. Most issues, however controversial, involve a certain community of interests; when relations between the negotiating parties are fundamentally friendly, persuasion and compromise often suffice. If necessary, inducements have to be offered, either positive, such as military or technical assistance, or negative, such as threats of unpleasant actions, in extreme cases including the threat of force. Different states have developed different national traditions in diplomatic style, and the discrepancies between the Communist and the traditional Western styles continue to impede diplomacy today. Quite a successful theory of international bargaining of general application has nevertheless been developed. It is based on the theory of games, especially on the analysis of threats and promises. The theory is sufficiently flexible to be applicable to bargaining in all situations; it was, for example, useful to the structuring of American–Soviet bargaining both in the conditions of the cold war, when emphasis was laid upon the rational employment of threats and deterrence, and during the subsequent *détente*, when the emphasis shifted to the dangers inherent in these and consequently to promises. Large numbers of participants impede such rational bargaining; as George Kennan once said, the unlikelihood of any negotiation resulting in an agreement grows by the square of the number taking part in it. Characteristically, the most successful arms control agreements have come from negotiations conducted exclusively by the two superpowers.

When mutual attitudes are diffident or hostile and the formulation of an issue or the form of compromise are difficult to reach, sometimes a third party plays a part. It may offer its 'good offices', and bring the two parties together; it may take part in actual negotiations, which is called 'mediation'; it may even participate in the determination of the terms of settlement, which is called 'conciliation'. Even further-reaching is 'arbitration', which means a binding adjudication by impartial arbiters. It was spectacularly successful in the *Alabama* case between Britain and the United States in 1872 and, although it did not rise to the sanguine expectations of its supporters, it is still a potentially significant adjunct to diplomacy. In 1920 a permanent World Court in The Hague was established to further facilitate adjudication.

When successful, negotiations often lead to the conclusion of a formal treaty. The significance of treaties varies greatly, depending on their subject-matter and the identity of the parties; most important are agreements which lay the foundation for future co-operation on vital matters, such as alliances, which are a traditional method of pooling together the power of states with a common political purpose and a common potential enemy. The two important features of alliances are that they can be concluded by states as different as the Western powers and the Soviet Union during the last war, and that their duration fully depends on the existence of the common enemy.

More permanent are alignments resulting from membership of the international institutions. Normally the treaties concerned provide some method for the termination of the institution or the withdrawal of individual members, but the contemporary tendency is to omit such provisions. The United Nations Charter does not mention them, although discussions before the signature of the treaty confirmed that withdrawal remains open; the European Community is meant to be permanent.

Propaganda

By propaganda we generally understand any systematic attempt to affect the minds, emotions, and actions of a given group for a specific public purpose. While propaganda, like diplomacy, is on the whole verbal, it differs from diplomacy in two important respects. First, it is addressed to the *people* of other states rather than to their *governments* (the important subject of propaganda conducted by the government at home need not concern us here); the effect on other governments is rarely more than incidental.

Second, propaganda is selfish, governed exclusively by the

national interests of the propagandist and therefore usually unacceptable to other states. There is here no attempt to find a compromise between competing national interests; the aim is exclusively the national advantage of the propagandist. As far as international order is concerned, propaganda, as it is conducted by the various states, serves purely negative purposes. It is never employed for the purposes of this order, as diplomacy occasionally is, and international efforts to curb at least its most vicious forms have as yet been unavailing.

At the same time the dividing lines between diplomacy and propaganda are not fully clear-cut. Thus, negotiations sometimes degenerate into exercises in propaganda directed at the public and not at the governments. Moreover, the Russian and the Chinese Communists are cultivating extensive relations with foreign groups sympathetic to their ideology. The most important of these are the Communist parties, but there are also numerous other groups, often called cover organizations, such as the national units of the World Peace Council, the World Federation of Trade Unions, the World Federation of Democratic Youth, etc. While all these serve the purposes of Communist propaganda, relations with them are conducted on a quasi-diplomatic, although not governmental level.

Propaganda did not play a significant role in international affairs until the First World War. Previously only the Catholic Church had used it; it had institutionalized the propagation of faith through a special Sacred Congregation (*de propaganda fide*), from the title of which the word 'propaganda' is derived. During the First World War the British Government was the first to organize and systematize the use of propaganda at home and abroad. Its efforts abroad were fairly successful in securing the goodwill of the neutrals, especially the Americans, but less so in appealing to the Germans. Other belligerents did not employ propaganda quite as systematically or extensively and the organizations built up during the war disappeared after its end.

The real impetus to the development of propaganda was given by the growth of the totalitarian regimes in the inter-war period. First the Communists and then the Nazis built up tremendous and costly propaganda machines, and the Western democracies were gradually forced to match their efforts. Despite the defeat of Nazism, post-war propaganda has further increased in scope. The Russians try to stir up discontent and to secure the allegiance of the people in the West while the Americans have parallel aims regarding the people of the Communist bloc. Equally important are the competing appeals of both to the peoples and also the governments of the uncommitted countries. The agencies which are in charge of these propaganda activities, the CIA in the United States and the Agitation and Propaganda Section of the Central Committee of the Soviet Communist Party, have assumed considerable importance and operate on large budgets. Here, as in the field of armaments, other states find it difficult to compete. British propaganda, for instance (officially referred to as information services), although relatively cheap and highly successful, suffers from a chronic lack of adequate and assured finance. It remains decentralized and is conducted by the Central Office of Information, by the Overseas Services of the BBC, and, marginally, by the British Council.

Among the varied instruments of propaganda, short-wave radio is by far the most important since broadcasts can reach audiences anywhere in the world and cannot be effectively blocked. Hence much of the money spent on propaganda goes into radio transmitters and programmes and, in Communist states, also into transmitters which jam foreign broadcasts. While this interference is not fully successful, governments can much more easily prevent the distribution of propaganda materials in printed form and have full control over personal travel.

In all propaganda activities the first problem is how to reach physically the people at whom it is directed; it is largely technological and its successful solution depends on sufficient resources and skill. When the target can be reached, there arise difficult psychological problems which are similar to those in commercial advertising: how to capture the attention of the people and how to achieve the desired response. These determine the method of presentation.

A simple way to conduct propaganda is to present news and information as objectively and factually as possible and to leave the listener or reader to reach his own conclusions. A straightforward information service can be politically effective, especially when it reaches totalitarian societies which try to limit their citizens to sources of information suitably vetted by the government. It has the great advantage of attracting attention since the listeners or readers will be generally interested in correcting the distorted and suspect picture presented at home. Complete objectivity is, of course, scarcely realizable and, even in the most factual and dispassionate services, a selection from the various items competing for attention is generally made to emphasize favourable rather than disparaging news. The BBC has earned a justified reputation for concern with truth during the Second World War and since and, in order to retain the interest and the trust of its listeners, it must constantly guard against deviating too far from its high standards of objectivity. Nevertheless, in presenting news to overseas listeners, the BBC could scarcely be expected to stress the backwardness of some British industries as much as the up-to-date character of electronics or aviation, or the relative inadequacy of old-age pensions rather than the more advanced nature of the National Health Service.

The opposite technique is that of the 'Big Lie'. It was effectively used by Hitler, who acted according to his argument developed in *Mein Kampf*, that a lie, provided it is sufficiently big and is frequently repeated, will be at least partly believed by the masses; most people lack the imagination to conceive that, although repeated, statements are not all true. The censorship of alternative sources of information is essential for this technique to be effective. Falsehood on a minor scale is much less useful and can undermine trust in the sources of information. Hence the United States calls its information activities since the Second World War a 'strategy of truth' and, without quite achieving it, tries to earn the reputation of objectivity enjoyed by the BBC.

The form of the news must be reasonably attractive in order to gain attention. The public are not interested in ponderous analyses of the rights and wrongs of any issue but readily respond to simple slogans, however loosely related to it, provided they contain such emotionally valuable words as 'peace', 'aggression', 'human rights', 'self-determination', etc. Visual impressions and physical demonstrations add greatly to the influence of propaganda. Nuclear explosions and launchings of satellites now supplement the age-long tradition of military parades and naval demonstrations. Visits by prominent politicians, leaders, and artists, even travel by the man in the street, all play a part in drawing attention to the propagandist state.

Not only attention but also positive response is required, and the propagandist must establish a degree of rapport between himself and the people who are his target by appealing to their own local interests, experiences, and outlook. Hence propagandists tend to stress common characteristics and interests—the Japanese spoke of the 'co-prosperity sphere', the Nazis of the Aryan race, the Russians of the solidarity of the oppressed and underdeveloped countries, the Chinese of the Asians and the 'true' revolutionaries. Where such solidarity is not effectively established, propaganda fails, as is shown by the futility of American appeals to anti-Communist sentiments which are not fully shared by others. The influence of propaganda increases greatly through its frequency and consistency over a long period of time and also through the elimination or obstruction of competing sources of information.

Economic instruments

Economic instruments differ from diplomacy and propaganda in that they are not necessarily directly operated by governments. Indeed, in the nineteenth century, international trade, which was dominated by the City of London, gave the appearance of being divorced from politics and completely autonomous—although, as E. H. Carr has forcibly pointed out in *The Twenty Years' Crisis*, this illusion was possible only against the background of Britain's unchallenged naval supremacy. In the twentieth century, the close connection between international politics and economics has been re-established. Private interests are still paramount in the international trade of Western powers, but clearly under a degree of governmental direction. In Communist and also in some new, underdeveloped countries, trade is conducted by governmental or government-controlled agencies.

The other characteristic peculiar to economic instruments is their great advance towards internationalization. As soon as the governments had assumed substantial economic powers, they began to yield some of them to international institutions. Western trade is circumscribed by the provisions of the GATT, and manipulation of exchange rates of national currencies by the membership of the International Monetary Fund; members of the European Community and of its Eastern counterpart, the CMEA, have surrendered some of their economic sovereignty to these organizations. There are two reasons why the economic instruments are being internationalized in advance of others. First, considerable economic advantages are secured. Second, although the close connection between economics and politics is now fully appreciated, the direct and immediate impact of economic internationalization on state sovereignty is considerably less than would be the impact of internationalization of such politically sensitive elements as armaments. For the time being, at least, while the most important economic institutions include only Western states and Japan, with rare though significant exceptions, the problems arising from their existence have not been politically grave.

Economic instruments are widely employed both in peace and in war: in peacetime international trade and aid are most important, whereas in wartime and during the cold war various measures of economic warfare are employed.

To some extent all countries must engage in international trade in order to obtain some goods which they cannot produce economically at home, and to sell others with the proceeds of which they can pay for their imports. Beyond this indispensable minimum, international trade provides the benefits of an international division of labour under which the various goods can be obtained from the most efficient and therefore cheapest producer. Free trade, which was actively pursued by Britain between 1846 and 1932, meant to the British an economically most advantageous world-wide arrangement. To the majority of other countries it meant a perpetuation of a situation in which they had little chance of developing their own industries in open competition with the established, more efficient British exporters. Protective tariffs, the most important instrument for controlling international trade, thus arose mainly for economic reasons—to shelter budding domestic industries from foreign competition. These industries, however, were desired not only for economic welfare but also for general political purposes, as an element of state power. The Great Depression, which began in 1929, brought in its train an enormous increase in protective tariffs and also in other devices to keep out imports, such as quantitative controls (quotas) and currency restrictions.

Apart from this protective role, tariffs serve to secure better terms of trade through reciprocal arrangements but they can be used also for more clearly political purposes, as bargaining weapons in negotiations and as instruments of retaliation. Here the elements of size and of relative importance in the foreign trade of the country concerned are decisive. The main buyers of a country's produce or the main suppliers of its vital imports are obviously influential. The Southern States used their position as the major suppliers of cotton for the Lancashire textiles industry in their endeavour to secure British support during the American Civil War; the Austrians were able to bring Serbia to heel by declining to buy her pigs during the so-called 'Pig War' in 1905; Britain exercised a similar pressure on Ireland through the 'tariff war' of 1932–6; Hitler dominated Eastern Europe in the late thirties by offering the only available large-scale market for its agricultural exports—he enjoyed a position which approached monopoly.

Through a deliberate policy, international trade can be directed towards a group of states not only to enhance its economy but also to reinforce its political coherence, for instance in the various colonial systems, or in the Communist bloc, and in the European Community today.

The post-war trend towards the liberalization of international trade and the establishment of international economic institutions greatly reduced the freedom of states to control their trade individually. Within the blocs, individual control was being partly superseded by an institutionalized co-operation while the inter-bloc trade was, to some extent, restricted. The situation changed dramatically in the seventies when a long period of rapid growth of international trade was superseded by a prolonged recession started by the energy crisis in 1973. On the one hand, a strong trend towards protectionism arose in large numbers of market economy countries; on the other, inter-bloc trade significantly grew to meet the complementary needs both of the Western exporters needing markets and of the Communist importers needing access to Western technology—and also of the new states requiring both consumption and capital goods. As will be discussed from the systemic angle in the next chapter, international trade has become 'high policy'. Naturally this has confusingly altered its use as an instrument of foreign policy and so far the implications are unclear.

In the early seventies, moreover, the growing scarcity of oil, and the use of the 'oil weapon' in 1973 by the Arab exporters against the United States and the Netherlands for what they regarded as excessively pro-Israeli policies, raised the possibility of trade in other crucial raw materials becoming politicized also. The experience with oil was, however, inconclusive. As Iran did not support the policies of the Arabs, the oil weapon had only marginal effects; moreover, despite her leading position not only as the largest exporter of oil but also as the only potential source for large additional quantities of oil in the near future, Saudi Arabia was signally unsuccessful in directing United States' policies against Israel. This could be attributed to Saudi mutual dependence on the West as a market, a venue for the investment of the wealth amassed from oil, and a major supporter against Communist subversion, and also to lack of diplomatic experience. It is impossible to predict with any confidence when more propitious conditions will arise for the development of this new instrument of economic policy—in fact whether they will ever arise at all.

Investment in foreign countries has always been basically private and for economic purposes. It has continued to be so from the time of the great banking houses of the Fuggers in the sixteenth century, or the Rothschilds after the Napoleonic Wars, to the industrial empires and the great oil companies of our own generation. Investments by such concerns have not been divorced from politics—the national governments encourage or discourage them to suit their political aims—but the usual form of direct governmental intervention is assistance and not investment. In all periods economically weak allies have had to be buttressed by military supplies and political loans or grants but, since the Second World War, grants have surpassed all precedents. By the colossal expenditure of over $20,000 million, especially through the Marshall Plan, the Americans helped to restore the economies and modernize the armed forces of Western Europe. They were dispensing money for military support and economic aid outside Europe also and were conspicuously successful in restoring the economy of Japan; the funds are continuing to flow out at a diminishing but still substantial rate. In the mid-fifties the Russians began to offer economic assistance, and their competition with the Americans became an important feature of the cold war. Sometimes the superpowers courted the same governments, for instance those in India, in Afghanistan, or in Egypt. More often each supported friendly governments; thus the Americans were helping the Philippines, South Korea, South Vietnam, and Taiwan, while the Russians were supporting Cuba and Vietnam. All the colonial powers, especially France and Britain, have given considerable assistance to their colonies and ex-colonies.

Oil revenues have been the source of extensive aid dispensed by the larger oil exporters, originally for political purposes, especially by Libya, but later, after the raising of oil prices in 1973, largely for helping the poor importers of oil to pay for their imports. Much of the revenue was, however, deposited in Western banks which, in turn, 'recycled' it, financing generally uneconomic projects in developing and socialist countries. When international trade and the flow of new capital slowed down in the late seventies, many of the debtor countries found it impossible to service the debts, which led to an acute and continuous international finance crisis.

Even in peacetime the unfriendly purpose of economic policies can justify their classification as economic warfare. Such is the boycott of trade which is usually conducted by the people rather than the government, but which may have governmental support—one example is the Chinese boycott of British and Japanese goods in the inter-war period. Or it may be an action against the currency of another state, as in London in 1923 when the French occupied the Ruhr against the wishes of the British.

A state may resort to 'dumping' in order to dislocate production and the world markets—thus in 1958 the Soviet Union resold, with disruptive results, quantities of Chinese tin at a price less than what they themselves had paid to the Chinese. Economic warfare can also take the form of the closing and opening of markets. In 1960, when the Americans became convinced of the hostility of the Castro Government in Cuba, they gradually brought to a halt the imports of Cuban sugar which had enjoyed a privileged market in their country; as a counter-move in economic warfare, in order to stabilize a regime hostile to the United States, the Communist bloc stepped in and offered new markets for this sugar.

In wartime a belligerent may resort to 'pre-emption' of vital strategic materials from neutrals in order to deny them to the adversary, as the British tried to do in the Second World War with Spanish copper and Turkish chrome.

The best-established war measure is naval blockade. Britain has been employing it since the times of Elizabeth I; it played an important part in the Napoleonic and the two World Wars, and it is still by no means obsolete. The effectiveness of economic measures gave rise to the idea of 'economic sanctions', which were embodied in the League of Nations Covenant as a promising expedient for curbing aggression without military intervention. The League applied such sanctions only once, against Italy in 1935 for her aggression against Ethiopia. The sanctions failed but probably only because the members were half-hearted in their support. In 1951 the United Nations decided in favour of economic sanctions against Communist China, in 1962 it was moving towards such sanctions against Katanga, and, in 1963, against South Africa. It employed them, again rather ineffectively, against Southern Rhodesia and, in the eighties, against South Africa.

The cold war led to many measures which can be called economic warfare. Each bloc tried to deprive its opponent of supplies of strategically important materials and products. Communist international trade is rigidly controlled, and the

Americans made strenuous but not fully successful attempts to curb Western exports of 'strategic' materials to the Communist bloc. As has been noted, the situation changed in the late seventies when the complementary needs of both sides resulted in a relaxation of restrictions and an increase in the flow of trade. Consequently, to some extent, inter-bloc trade has stopped being used as an instrument of policy and has become governed largely by economic considerations.

Military power and war

In contrast to economics, the military field has been fully monopolized by governments. A few individuals and groups have always possessed weapons independently of governmental control, but these used to be quite insignificant in international relations unless they managed to stage a successful rebellion. Only in the sixties and seventies did resistance groups rise to the position of significant military factors, as epitomized by the PLO discussed in Chapter 4. The states are nevertheless strongly circumscribed by international considerations. A unilateral military strategy would be possible only for a state sufficiently powerful to be able to cope with its rivals by itself, or under a policy of isolationism which, as has been explained, is not feasible in the world today. Whether employing the expedient of alliances and coalitions, or participating in any scheme of collective security in the future, states are no longer in full control of the military instrument.

This instrument looms large in all considerations of foreign policy and is extremely costly; in all states, including the superpowers, it swallows up a large slice of the national product. Moreover, technological change and the resulting changes in the structure and operation of international society raise a host of questions about the usefulness of the instrument, questions which are of such a fundamental nature that some of them cannot yet be adequately formulated, let alone answered.

The problem can be easily grasped both from the global expenditure on armaments which, according to UN estimates, rose to some $1 trillion ($1,000 billion) in the late eighties, and from a glance at the issues of a national defence policy. Thus in Britain, for example, the frequent criticisms of defence policy have arisen from the two connected views that this policy has been excessively costly, to the detriment of pressing social needs, and that it has been ineffective, incapable of securing vital national interests. The second criticism is more fundamental, and opinions about cost obviously depend on the answer it receives. Particularly violent has been the argument about the usefulness of nuclear weapons. While the unilateral nuclear disarmers regard the whole expenditure on the nuclear deterrent as immoral and wasteful, more moderate critics stress the illusory character of the 'independent deterrent' and the inadequacy of conventional armaments due partly to the diversion of funds to nuclear weapons, and partly to the inefficiencies resulting from the conservatism of military thinking and from the competition between the three traditional services, the Navy, the Army, and the Air Force.

In the United States, concentration upon nuclear weapons in the late forties has given way to a parallel effort in conventional armaments. Although the American economy can sustain both, and massive aid to allies too, the questions of the future size of the defence effort and of its adequacy for ensuring the defence of the country are periodically debated. Japan maintains only a slight 'self-defence' force and, until 1986, limited defence expenditure to under 1 per cent of GNP. By contrast France has maintained a basic consensus on extensive defence forces, including a nuclear deterrent and compulsory military service. Both the Soviet Union and China have been giving absolute preference to guns over butter, despite their poor standards of living; attempts at democratization in the late eighties could affect their freedom in this respect.

In order to tackle rationally the involved problem of the military instrument, we must clarify its actual role in international relations. Many of the criticisms of military expenditure somewhat naïvely assume that such expenditure, if more efficiently managed, could ensure national security and major national interests. This assumption is untenable. We should not exaggerate the value of the military instrument; complete security is unthinkable in the nuclear era and other, non-military instruments are growing in importance, especially in dealings with the uncommitted countries.

Another source of confusion arises from the fear of another total war and from the resulting attempts to eliminate violence from international relations altogether. Weapons can be used in two capacities—in attack, in order to secure a change, or defensively, to deter a possible attacker and repel him if an attack actually takes place. The policy of nuclear deterrence is not a complete innovation, but merely a modern adaptation of the old Latin adage *si vis pacem para bellum*. The Second World War was a catastrophic disappointment to the naïve disarmers and supporters of disarmament and international organization who had believed that violence could be eliminated from the world without an adequate supervisory military force. Nevertheless, although the central role played by the military instrument is now more generally appreciated, the situation is still often obscured by unrealistically sharp distinctions between the states of war and peace and between nuclear and conventional weapons.

As has been repeatedly stressed, state interaction combines both antagonism and community of interests. This means that conflict is never fully separated from co-operation nor co-operation from conflict. Indeed, different periods of history combine the two in varying measures, and the difference between the states of peace and war lies merely in the degree to which one of these elements predominates. If negotiations are the general way in which international issues are tackled and if force is employed only marginally, we speak of peace; if violence is openly employed as the main method of settling such issues, we speak of war. This state of affairs was not altered when the Peace Treaty of Westphalia established peace as the normal mode of international relations in Europe or when international lawyers developed two separate bodies of rules of international law known as the law of peace and the law of war. The cold war, the name commonly given to the immediate post-war period, makes clear how unreal the distinction is. The cold war was neither peace nor war; hostile relatings predominated, but not to the exclusion of negotiations, and the use of violence remained circumscribed. We cannot fully explain the place of the military instrument in the cold war either in terms of peace or of war.

Despite our natural preoccupation with the prevention of war, we must not lose sight of the fact that war has traditionally filled an important social role in international society. Whenever a state wishes to enforce a rule of law which is in its favour but is disobeyed by another state, or to alter an adverse rule, in the absence of any superior authority to deal with these matters, it must unfortunately be ready to resort to violence. It is difficult, if at all possible, to deprive the states of their ultimate right to wage war unless some other effective method of enforcement of law and of peaceful change is devised. Otherwise the world would be frozen without the possibility of change to conform with the demands of justice and with changing social conditions, and even existing rights could be violated with impunity. It is arguable that the General Assembly already acts as an agent of peaceful change, but only in a limited fashion. It was instrumental in hastening colonial emancipation but is still helpless even against not particularly powerful members like South Africa or Israel who, defending what they regard as their vital interests, consistently refuse to comply.

The other unrealistically sharp distinction· is that made between conventional and nuclear or, more broadly speaking, mass destruction weapons. The former are less destructive and better understood, their use could be left unlimited or slightly circumscribed by international law without endangering the continuation of the national states or of international order as these exist today. The latter have enormous destructive potential, the political implications of which cannot as yet be clearly perceived; hence their control or, if possible, elimination is the only solution. In practice the distinction is much less clear. The devastating Second World War was fought in Europe with conventional weapons alone; some of the 'non-conventional' weapons, such as low-yield tactical nuclear devices or mild forms of nerve gas which only temporarily disable human beings exposed to them, are less destructive than the most powerful conventional weapons. The dangers of 'escalation'—a milder form of warfare gradually leading to more severe forms—are in any case such that a rigid dividing line is untenable.

The military instrument provides the background of assuredness and stability for diplomacy. 'Negotiation from strength' is a sound precept; without the backing of military power, no state can avoid concessions detrimental to its vital interests if irresistible pressures and threats are brought to bear upon it. The Western powers withstood Soviet pressures on their exposed position in Berlin, both during the Berlin Blockade in 1948 and 1949, and again, after November 1958, only because they were militarily strong.

Strength alone is insufficient unless the prospective opponent is aware of it and takes it into account. Hence international relations in most ages, particularly during the cold war, abound in references to and demonstrations of strength. Armaments and troop formations are displayed during national day parades; naval demonstrations are staged; troops are mobilized or massed along frontiers or shifted to bases in sensitive places. A show of force is a much easier and cheaper expedient than its actual use and it may sometimes be quite effective. It is possible that the Chinese Communists were eventually forced to conclude the dragging armistice negotiations on Korea only by the dispatch of American nuclear weapons to Okinawa, a show of strength implying that they might be used.

Finally, the military instrument may be actually employed. It is here that the notion of the dichotomy between war and peace constitutes a serious obstacle to understanding, because the use of violence is by no means limited to war. Even the classical international law of peace permits the employment of violence which falls short of war under such names as reprisals, measures tinged with a hostile character, pre-belligerent measures, or measures short of war.

An actual example may explain the distinction made here, and it is best chosen from relations between unfriendly countries in which the military instrument is much more prominent than in relations between countries which are friendly. Since the Arab countries are hostile, to a very large extent Israel relies on the military instrument. She came into existence through the use of violence, as a result of the victory of the Jewish military forces in the war against the Arabs in 1948. She still relies upon this instrument for her survival, being faced, as she is, with the desire of some Arabs to terminate her independent existence. In order to remind their neighbours of their military strength, the Israelis often parade it and occasionally use it in frontier raids (which serve also the narrower objective of warning against Arab infringements of the border). In 1956, when faced with growing danger from the Egyptians who were receiving military supplies from the Communist bloc, the Israelis used their forces for a large-scale military operation in the Sinai peninsula. They scored a victory over the Egyptian forces and greatly damaged Egyptian morale but were forced to withdraw under pressure from the United Nations. Then the Israeli military instrument reverted to its previous deterrent role and was actively used only in minor frontier skirmishes, but in situations similar to 1956 it has again been used fully: in the lightning 'Six Days War' of 1967; in the Yom Kippur War of 1972; in 1978 and, on a much larger scale, in 1983 for intervention in Lebanon to contain Palestinian guerrillas.

It is important to note the fact that only conventional weapons have actually been used since 1945, and invariably in a somewhat restricted form. The Americans and the Russians have refrained from a direct clash and, in all conflicts, at least on one side, fighting has been done by proxy. The situation shows gradations from guerrilla warfare, sometimes conducted by extremely small groups, as in Laos in 1961 and 1962, to such approximations to a major war as the conflict fought out in Korea in 1950–1 and in Vietnam in the late sixties. Armed forces have also been used extensively outside the context of the cold war, particularly in numerous colonial struggles.

In the policy of deterrence nuclear weapons have served only as a general background for diplomacy and have not been actually employed. The basic principle of this complex policy is simple, the weapons are produced and deployed not in order to strike but in order to inspire the opponent with the conviction that they would be automatically employed following any serious attack by him. As long as this policy is successful, nuclear weapons will not actually be used. Since deterrence is rightly considered as fundamentally important, both sides resort to frequent reminders and demonstrations of their nuclear power; the launchings of satellites and nuclear tests serve these, as well as purely technological ends. Moreover, the Americans, at least, have been devoting much thought to making their deterrent credible, to ensuring that the Russians would be in no doubt as to whether the weapons would be used, if necessary.

It may be added that there is little justification for equating the existence of nuclear weapons with the danger of an all-out nuclear war. Admittedly, the ingenious American doctrine of 'graduated deterrence', based upon the possibility of nuclear conflicts limited in scope, does not sound very convincing. The argument runs that, even if nuclear weapons were employed in any future conflict, neither side would be likely to resort to an all-out attack on the opponent's cities, which would provoke immediate retaliation; hence a war would be fought by small-scale, tactical nuclear weapons alone, or be limited to an attack on the opponent's 'counterforce'. Such limitations are not very credible, however, owing to the dangers of escalation; the side suffering a disadvantage at any level would be sorely tempted to escalate the conflict in order to recoup its fortunes, until an all-out war was eventually reached.

Deterrence, or the nuclear balance of power, provides a basis for a certain degree of stability of the present international order, and we have not as yet found any possible substitute. The basis of stability is, however, brittle. It may be destroyed by the proliferation of nuclear weapons or by a technological breakthrough, for example the American SDI, started in the eighties. The strategy has become increasingly challenged by peace movements in the West, representing the growing concern with the elusiveness of meaningful disarmament agreements; the publicized possibility of the complete obliteration of the human race through a 'nuclear winter' following a major nuclear exchange has further lowered the credibility of deterrence in popular eyes. Even some leading strategists and military leaders have begun to favour a shift towards conventional strategies, especially based upon emergent technologies. Moreover, deterrence serves mainly conservative aims, to preserve the status quo. It does restrict practical revisionist policies by eliminating the likelihood of an immediate all-out nuclear war whch would be pernicious to all, but if the limited struggles do not succeed escalation may eventually lead to it.

So far, war and the use of force have been discussed only as techniques of foreign policy. Their place in international relations can be more fully explained only within the context of international order.

8

The international system

The nature of the international system

The argument now shifts from the micro-level, the activities of the states and non-state actors, to the macro-level, that of the international system. At the outset this term must be defined.

In the broadest sense, a political system denotes a collection of independent political entities which interact with considerable frequency and according to regularized processes. The term is now increasingly used instead of the partly overlapping traditional terms of 'family of nations', 'international society' or 'community', and several others. It has the advantage of taking us away from the political rhetoric with which the older terms are laden and enabling us to think systematically, by employing the concept of analytically distinguishable variables evolved in the general systems theory and applied to many other social affairs— social or economic 'systems', for example.

Some writers therefore approach the analysis of international systems using a 'structural paradigm' evolved in systems analysis. Others focus on a Marxist conception of class conflict, and others again on liberal traditions centring upon the rights of the individual. Each approach has a contribution to make, but they cannot be blended with the conventional power-political approach, employed here. The latter has been preferred for the simple but persuasive reason that it focuses on the central power-political features of the international system which would otherwise get insufficient attention. The international economic system, though growing in importance, has not become integrated in the politico-strategic system; hence it is separately treated at the end of the chapter.

International systems lack the two prerequisites of domestic political systems—the social basis of a community and the political structure of a government. Instead of unconditional agreement on co-operation, on the precedence of some basic common good over subgroup or individual interests, international systems can build only upon a limited and conditional co-operation which sometimes degenerates into anarchy. They lack a hierarchically arranged government which determines the jurisdiction of all the social subgroups and has the means to enforce its norms of law. The meaning of sovereignty is quite different in both contexts. While internal sovereignty means that the government is supreme within the political system of the state, that the whole takes precedence over the parts, external sovereignty means that the governments are supreme within the international system, that the parts take precedence over the whole. In other words, while political systems are strongly centralized within the states, international systems are strongly decentralized—they are 'subsystem dominated'.

Nevertheless, as the very terminology employed indicates, international systems do not entirely lack structure and sets of norms which regulate the behaviour of their members, although these structures are invariably much looser and the sets of norms much weaker than those distinguishable within states. These are discussed in the next chapter. The interplay among the units and the international order as a whole, is affected by the nature of each historical system. Clearly understanding the 'logic of the system' is as essential for effective foreign policy as is the understanding of the market for anybody operating within it—it is necessary both for operating within the existing structures and for seeking ways in which these structures could be improved.

Hence an analysis of the nature of the system operating at a given time and place is essential for the understanding of international relations taking place within it. The study of the behaviour of single states, or of states in mutual interaction, is insufficient in itself. From the point of view of the states and other international actors, the international system is no more than the external environment within which they act, offering both challenges to which they have to react and opportunities which they like to exploit. From the systemic point of view, however, the system can often be greater than the sum of its parts. It not only embraces the uncoordinated though interrelated activities of the actors but, in the process, it develops characteristics and a momentum of its own which can lead to unplanned and often very undesirable international events—arms races and wars are the most prominent of these.

Owing mainly to two connected phenomena—the rapidly growing interdependence of states and the crisis of the territorial state—the internal dynamics of the international system have now greatly increased, extending to a host of economic and ecological problems which cannot be effectively tackled at the state level. Hence the issues of international politics and of the international system in general have been attracting increasingly more attention, both from statesmen and from scholars. Many, perhaps most, of the latter think in terms of some form of 'systems analysis' and limit themselves to the present and the very recent past. Their thinking should not, however, be divorced from its historical matrix as often they either unknowingly use the frequently inapplicable and misleading insights of their predecessors or they ignore them, at the cost of a great intellectual loss. The modern European tradition of thought about the international system can be broadly divided into three major streams—first, the realist or Machiavellian school, concerned with conflict and power; second, the rationalist or Grotian school, stressing rationality and co-operation; third, the revolutionary or Kantian school, stressing the solidarity of mankind and tending to look at the international system as 'the commonwealth of man'. In the twentieth century intellectual interest in the international system has quickened. One can distinguish four broad phases: major contributions came first from international lawyers and then from historians, behaviourists, and, finally, systems analysts.

Conceiving international society as a system and its major components, both the states and non-state actors, as subsystems, conceptualizes reality in a sensible manner. If one begins at the traditional starting point, that the international system consists primarily of power relationships between nation-states, one extends the analysis both horizontally and vertically: horizontally, by replacing the notion of states as units by that of 'national groups' and recognizing the existence within them of sub-national systems; vertically, by extending the network of international relationships beyond power to other issue-areas, notably economic, ecological, and psychological. Thus we end by differentiating a multitude of concrete systems—national, international, extranational, subnational, transnational. Some thinkers, endeavouring to balance the excessive concentration upon states in the past, tend to shift the emphasis to the transnational activities of non-state actors and to arrive at a simplified model of the modern international system as one of a web of world politics in which state activities are becoming increasingly less important and state boundaries mere discontinuities in many fields of human endeavour. This is largely normative, wishful thinking. The multidimensional model proposed here is a much more realistic representation of international reality at the time of writing and the web of world politics model is unlikely to become more useful in this century, if ever.

If, as the systems analysts do, we assume that, along with their historical differences, all international systems show also a certain degree of similarity—they sometimes call it 'cross-systemic isomorphism'—we can fruitfully discuss 'ideal types' of international systems. Thus, for instance, allowing for the fact that most systems fall somewhere in between, we can distinguish two extreme types: one which is completely dominated by the units and the other by the central institutions of the system. It is also possible to concentrate on historical international systems, particularly modern ones. We shall try to combine both approaches. While it is obviously important to study the balance of power system which operated from 1648 to 1914, since it has been the basis of contemporary international society and the source of much of our terminology, it would be difficult, if at all possible, to specify the causes for its disintegration and to estimate the significance of subsequent changes without some theoretical appraisal. Of necessity we must break up the chronological flow of events into tidy units, periodize and systematize, and it is preferable that we undertake this operation consciously, explicitly stating the underlying theory.

Analytical categories

Clearly, thinking about the contemporary international system as a whole, in all its complexity, is bound to confront us with great difficulties, especially as the categories employed have been developed largely in the context of its much simpler predecessors. In the first instance, we must take account of the *extensity* of the system, which can be analytically broken down into two clear-cut components—(geographical) *scope*, and (functional) *domain*—and the *intensity* of interaction which can be measured by the intensity of the use of force as well as by various indices of social communication of which international trade is one of the most important. In all these dimensions the contemporary system shows considerable advances on its predecessors; its analysis should therefore take as full an account as possible of the degree and nature of these advances and of their implications.

Second, it is useful to distinguish in the international system the elements of 'structure' and 'process'. By *structure* we mean the characteristic relationships between the actors across time, such as the main types of association and basic types of inter-action, whereas *process* refers to forms and modes of interaction, distinguished from structure both by their short time-scale and by their analytic properties.

Third, two categories recurrent in all analyses are those of *stability* and *change*. From the systemic viewpoint, 'stability' may be defined as a probability that the system will retain its principal features; that most if not all of its members will survive; that no one state will attain dominance; that adaptation to change will take place without a major war. Of course all social systems change constantly, adapting to changing circumstances. All attempts to make them adapt according to a fixed plan—an ideology—seem to lead to coercion and ossification; this has been clearly demonstrated by the recurrent issue of bureaucratization which has been dominating all Communist systems, despite the great differences in their national variants. Hence blueprints to ensure the stability of the international system cannot be ex-pected to show much promise.

The stability of the international system is often associated with a further dimension, the *concentration of power*. There is fairly general agreement that dominance by one state is undesirable but strong disagreement about what type of system is more conducive to stability: bipolar or multipolar. During the cold war, scholars showed a general tendency to believe that a bipolar system was the less stable as it is less flexible and results in the two antagonists giving each other 'critical attention'. However, despite the largely bipolar structure of the international system, the cold war gradually changed into a *détente*. The opposite conclusion then seemed to carry more weight: that the concentration upon one another of the protagonists has the positive results of each giving full attention to the other one, and that many of the complexities of a multipolar system are thus reduced—notably the issues of responsibility are clearer and peripheral conflicts do not as readily spread and escalate. Recent historical evidence thus seems to indicate that, despite its prominent place as a structural characteristic, the issue of bipolarity/ multipolarity is not a decisive determinant of stability. Perhaps the most promising explanatory variable is found in the *propensity to risk-taking*. On this basis it is plausible to hypothesize that the contemporary international system is stabler than its predecessors because this propensity among the superpowers is very much reduced owing to the fears of a nuclear war.

Although this is rooted in the traditional state-centric approach which is no longer fully applicable, seeking categories relevant to the issue of avoiding a major war therefore seems to retain a degree of validity, and we may continue to seek the criteria for periodization in a combination of three interrelated elements for which Stanley Hoffmann has suggested the name *stakes of conflict*. First, there is the fundamental question of the identity of the units, a question the importance of which can be seen in the transition from the Roman Empire to the medieval system, or from the nineteenth-century system of multinational and colonial empires to the multiplicity of independent states and other non-state actors in the present. Then, there is the question of technology, a fundamental change in which, like the invention of gunpowder or of nuclear energy, completely alters the scope of possible actions. Finally, there is the question of what the units want to do to one another, whether they are prepared to co-operate within the existing order or whether some of them are attempting to revise it. Attitudes to the existing order are conditioned by the environment, both international and domestic, but influence this order in turn. It is impossible to determine to what extent changes in human ideas, attitudes, and desires are the cause or the effect of changed circumstances. Undoubtedly there is a certain amount of circularity; a fundamental change in any of these elements is likely to lead to a fundamental change in others.

A distinction should be made between stable international systems in which the three elements fluctuate only moderately, and others in which changes are so violent that they become revolutionary. The reasons for and the implications of the relative stability of the international system preceding the First World War offer a promising approach to the understanding of the character of the contemporary system.

Incidentally, here we become involved in the perennial argument between the supporters of stability and order and the supporters of revolution and change. This is primarily a normative issue which will be briefly touched upon in the concluding chapter. It does, however, require a mention in connection with the analytical categories because stability—or revolution/change—is often assumed as given. Although it seems impossible to design a fully value-free attitude which would accommodate both, it seems worthwhile to think in terms of *adaptation* of the system, that is, of change which is acceptable, although not for the same reason, both to the order-orientated politicians because it does not change too much, and to the change-orientated ones because it does not preserve too much.

We can now proceed to a brief outline of the historical international systems, which will be discussed largely in terms of the 'stakes of conflict' and the 'extensity' and 'intensity' of the systems. It is a consciously Euro-centric account, not only because the author's viewpoint is inevitably rooted in Western European traditions but also because the Western political system has been the fount and origin of the present global system. Through a complex process of disintegration, followed by expansion and now by a degree of global integration, the Christian

Commonwealth of medieval Europe has provided the foundation of the contemporary global system. This is the justification for starting the historical account with the formal ending of the medieval order through the Peace Treaty of Westphalia in 1648.

The balance of power system

The expression 'balance of power' is used to describe a tendency towards an equilibrium which some writers discern in international relations as well as in many social and physical domains; it denotes also state politics aiming at such an equilibrium. Here it is used strictly as a name for the international system between 1648 and 1914. This system lasted over the relatively long period of nearly three centuries and showed remarkable stability in surviving the challenge of the French Revolution and the Napoleonic Wars. Some of the most pertinent questions to be asked are about the nature of this challenge and the way in which it was met.

There are good reasons for regarding the balance of power as an important innovation in the history of mankind. For the first time since the destruction of the Roman Empire, Europe achieved a fair degree of stability; moreover, it was a stability not of the objectionable hegemonical type based on conquest and domination by a single power. In conformity with modern ideas and with the forces of nationalism, the new system was plural; it embraced several great powers and it gradually transcended the boundaries of Europe. Also, for the first time in the modern period of history, all the participants accepted that the system was important for them. This did not mean that considerations of international order generally prevailed over the selfishness of states, that a community feeling transcending single states became strong. On the contrary, states remained competitive and suspicious, each continuing as the supreme arbiter of its own behaviour, ultimately free to break the rules of the system. As in all previous systems, this selfishness could and actually did lead to attempts by states with sufficiently promising power to conquer others and upset the system.

Simultaneously, however, the balance of power was a much

more articulated, thought-out system than any of its predecessors. If the member states were not invariably ready to accept the norms it was imposing upon them, they were conscious at least of their common advantage in protecting those norms from being violated by others. When a state made a bid for power, other states tended to join forces in defence; the major challenges of Louis XIV, or Napoleon, or the Kaiser, all eventually ended in defeat at the hands of opposing coalitions.

Stability was based upon the balanced redistribution of territory by the Peace Treaty of Westphalia which established several major states capable of maintaining an equilibrium of power among themselves. Legitimacy was the foundation of the post-Napoleonic settlement and no major changes in units ensued. During the nineteenth century the Ottoman Empire gradually disintegrated, but this empire had never been essential for the system, and the event was less important in itself than as a harbinger of the disintegration of multinational empires during and after the First World War. Order was more seriously disturbed when powerful new units arose through the unification of Italy and Germany.

Although all states, large and small, powerful and weak, were participating, theoretically on the basis of sovereign equality, in fact that balance was maintained only by the few powerful states; it was a balance of power among the great powers and the system depended on their coexistence. Fortunately there were several such powers, as five seems to be a convenient minimum number facilitating a steady equilibrium. Two great powers would tend to end in a headlong clash or try to carve up the world into two competing spheres of influences; four would tend to form two rigid combinations of two states, each of which could be altered only by an extremely dangerous reversal of alliances. Like triumvirate governments, a balance of power based upon three units would be inherently unstable since a state would have little opportunity for realignment and would therefore have a strong incentive for striking first; the only possible regrouping following a war would be an obviously risky and therefore unlikely combination of the weaker of the victorious powers with the defeated power. Thus it was for the benefit of the system that there were so many great powers.

Stability was increased by several favourable circumstances. There were no dramatic technological changes like the recent invention of nuclear weapons; there was ample room for economic development; overseas expansion was a useful safety-valve which enabled states to increase power without seriously endangering rivals and offered wide scope in the game of compensations necessary to maintain balance. Industrialization and colonial expansion were much more promising means of augmenting state power than the subjugation of another European state. Territorial expansion in Europe was impeded not only by other members of the system who were apprehensive that the equilibrium might be destroyed but also by communications, which remained very poor until the end of the nineteenth century, and by the growing influence of nationalism—Bismarck would have found it very difficult to occupy France for any length of time after the Prussian victories in 1870–1.

The system was based on the continuation of the traditional pursuit of security by each state through its own efforts, but it offered opportunities for negotiations instead of fighting and for the conclusion of temporary alliances to counterbalance the power of others. When challenges to the equilibrium could not be staved off in a peaceful way, wars did break out, but they were not fought to eliminate the opponent. Restraint in victory was not due to altruistic reasons but to a realistic concern with the system, to preserve the vanquished state as a potential future ally.

Domestic pressures became less cogent. Religion lost its fanatical appeal, mercantilism and absolutism gradually weakened within the great powers. The rulers and diplomats of all countries were conscious of their 'corporate identity' and agreed upon the legitimacy of the balance. Hence they found no reason to interfere with powerful and growing transnational ties, the intellectual links based on the Enlightenment, and the commercial links of international trade. Tolerance at home and abroad extended to the domestic systems of other states. Since full flexibility of the balance of power demanded that states should be completely independent, the lawyers perfected the theories of state sovereignty, impenetrability of territory, and non-intervention.

Only the more powerful states were necessary for the mainten-ance of the system but the theories of sovereignty were extended to lesser powers too, first in Europe, then in Latin America, and subsequently throughout the world. These smaller states were admitted on the basis of 'sovereign equality', but their role in the system was mainly passive. They were not so much potential allies who could make an impact on the power of the alliance as potential areas of expansion for a great power which could, through conquering them, become dominant. Though in them-selves the smaller states were not essential for the working of the system, their elimination presented problems too difficult to be worthwhile. Within the framework of flexible alliances, the great powers could not agree upon any workable division of Europe and they usually preferred to make use of the much more profit-able and politically less dangerous opportunities for expansion outside Europe. Only one smaller state was divided, and the experience was scarcely encouraging: Russia, Prussia, and Austria carved up Poland rather gingerly in three consecutive partitions towards the end of the eighteenth century, but the Polish question remained one of the most explosive topics of international politics. The incorporation of dissatisfied Poles who occasionally rose in arms scarcely enhanced the power of the occupants. They managed to maintain an equilibrium in Eastern Europe but probably could have done so more efficiently had Poland been left independent.

The system was severely challenged by the French Revolution. In the first place, the Revolution introduced changes at home, with a new regime which assumed full and intolerant govern-mental control over the citizens and prepared the path for Napoleon with his exorbitant ambitions. Internationally, the Revolution destroyed the solidarity of a homogeneous Europe through its ideas, and the balance of power through its military victories; as the result of the Napoleonic Wars all frontiers became unstable and Europe was rent by ideological and national antagonisms of a fundamental nature. The victors decided in favour of legitimacy, of the restoration of the pre-war system in preference to the accommodation of the new forces. The balance was restored and so was France as one of its essential units, under her previous Bourbon rulers and within her pre-revolutionary boundaries.

Between 1815 and 1914 the system evolved the Concert of Europe. Britain rejected the Russian proposal for a much further-reaching Holy Alliance, a loose world government to be worked jointly by the great powers, with the right to intervene in the domestic affairs of other states. The Concert was merely a loose consultative institution which refrained from intervention in the domestic affairs of states. It permitted many small wars, but prevented these from becoming general and thus upsetting the balance of power. Nineteenth-century Europe thus neatly balanced conservation and change and can be credited with many positive achievements. The behaviour of the great powers was, on the whole, moderate, as epitomized in the lenient peace concluded by Bismarck with Austria after her crushing defeat at Sadowa. There was general stability and no states disappeared; such major political changes as the emancipation of the Balkan people from Ottoman rule and the neutralization of Switzerland, Belgium, and Luxembourg were achieved with little violence; international law developed and, towards the end of the century, colonial expansion came under a degree of internationally agreed regulation. It must, however, be borne in mind that these achievements cannot be credited to the balance of power and the Concert of Europe alone since they were made possible by exceptionally favourable conditions for the economic and political expansion of the system.

In the latter part of the century these conditions began to deteriorate, as did also the attitude of Germany, one of the five great powers. The process of colonial expansion ground itself to a halt when there were no further lands available for occupation, and economic expansion degenerated into competition among rival national economies; in contrast to his great lenience to Austria, which had been defeated only four years earlier, Bismarck severed Alsace-Lorraine from France after the 1870–1 war. This led to a continuing French grievance and deprived the international system of a great deal of its flexibility: from 1871 France was permanently aligned against Germany. Instead of working through fluctuating alliances, the system broke up into two opposing camps; slowly but gradually the diplomatic fronts hardened, eventually clashing in August 1914.

This account, concerned with power relationships, has already covered the issue of the expanding geographical scope of the international system. The functional domain equally expanded: the ideas of the French Revolution had a widespread impact; international trade, functional links across national boundaries, and travel all grew apace; the first international institutions were established. None of this was sufficiently recognized by contemporary analyses of international politics. This was partly due to the tendency of the governments, especially those of the dominant power, Great Britain, to divorce them from power politics, and partly owing to the difficulties of conceptualization.[1] These two difficulties were to persist in the subsequent inter-war period. Despite the fact that, in contrast to the nineteenth century, economic problems have today assumed a central importance, especially as a result of the Great Depression, only since 1945 have they become issues of high policy ranking equal with territorial and ideological clashes.

Search for a new order

Being the only known modern form of international order, the 'balance of power' dominated political thought and activities in the first half of the twentieth century. Attitudes to it varied. Some thinkers considered it as the only possible hope for peace, others rejected it as having been ultimately responsible for the First World War. Whether endeavouring to improve the working of the existing system or to replace it by something new, they were all thinking in terms of the nineteenth-century experience and employing the concepts inherited from it.

The system gradually changed from a European to a global one. Around the beginning of the century, two non-European states, the United States and Japan, were admitted to the status of great powers but, as their participation did not become as intimate as that of the European states, the system thus became looser. At the same time, through her naval challenge to Britain, Germany made a bid for the extension of the balance of power system from Europe to the oceans of the world. She confidently but vainly expected that, provided there was a sufficiently powerful German navy to form the nucleus of a naval coalition counterbalancing the British navy, other naval powers would rally against Britain to establish an equilibrium in naval power similar to the balance of power in Europe. The distrust of Germany's power and intentions was such, however, that instead of pursuing the balance of power formula and joining the weaker side, the two great naval outsiders, the United States and Japan, preferred to align themselves with Britain.

With sporadic intervention by the United States, the Concert of Europe managed to settle several acute crises early in the century, but it gradually lost all remnants of its flexibility. In vain did Sir Edward Grey try to galvanize it into another effort in 1914. It finally came to an end with the outbreak of war in August.

The First World War was a traumatic experience for mankind. Having been lulled into a feeling of false security, people found it difficult to adjust themselves to a long war, unparalleled in the scope of the destruction it wrought, and to contemplate the possibility of its recurrence. To many, the war meant the complete bankruptcy of the old system and a challenge requiring a completely new response. They sought this response in a much more tightly organized new type of international order. The states kept their positions in it; indeed, the League of Nations Covenant guaranteed the perpetuation of their territorial integrity and political independence, while the principle of national self-determination gave them a powerful moral and ideological justification. They retained also the ultimate right to resort to war in pursuit of national ends but the League of Nations introduced a collective security system which was to replace the insecurity of fluctuating national alliances.

The inter-war world was profoundly disturbed. All the three elements determining whether a system is stable or revolutionary pointed towards revolution. First of all, the composition of international society changed. Two great powers, defeated Germany and Russia, in the throes of a Communist revolution, were temporarily out of the game, many new states had come into being, and Europe had ceased to be the exclusive centre of world politics. With the advent of the totalitarian ideologies, first Communism, then Fascism, and finally Nazism, international society became extremely heterogeneous and some of its members intolerant and expansionist. Second, the technological changes—the development of the aeroplane, the tank, the radio,—provided new instruments for expansionist policies in peace and in war. Third, the totalitarian regimes determinedly set out to use these instruments and pursue such policies.

The horrors of the First World War failed to persuade the people of all or even the majority of states that their interest in peace demanded a world order which must take precedence over their traditional national interests. The collective security system was ineffective because the great powers, both within and outside the League, were insufficiently determined in their support for it. Indeed, in terms of power politics, it proved pernicious: it destroyed the possibility of flexible arrangements and reduced the likelihood of action against an expanding nation. This was due to the simple fact that the states directly interested and hence ready to act had to persuade and carry all those less directly concerned. The inter-war period witnessed an uneasy and inconclusive struggle between the new idea of collective security and the traditional one of the balance of power. From the very inception France tried to revive the latter, first by seeking a guarantee from the United States and Britain, then through a ring of alliances, the *cordon sanitaire* around the defeated *Reich*, then through the Locarno Agreements with Germany which ambiguously attempted to reconcile balance of power considerations with the collective security system, and finally by seeking an alliance with the Soviet Union.

The geographical scope of the international system had already encompassed all the accessible parts of the globe in the nineteenth century and only the frozen wastes of Antarctica were added in the inter-war period. The domain of the international system increased with the establishment of the League of Nations and the ILO. Nevertheless, when economic issues disturbed the world—like the abandonment of the gold standard in the early twenties and, much more acutely, the Great Depression from 1929 onwards,—despite some ineffective *ad hoc* efforts to seek an international solution, they were dealt with by individual states, at the cost of severe economic setbacks and widespread unemployment. In retrospect, the need for some effective form of international co-ordination of individual national policies became so obvious that it laid the foundation for a wide extension of the domain of the international system in the post-war period. Simultaneously, the rapid advance in the technologies of transport and communications provided the means for a great increase in the intensity of international interaction.

When planning for the post-war order, adherents both of the balance of power and of collective security agreed that a stable order in the inter-war period had been precluded by the lack of co-operation among the great powers, notably the recurrent differences between the French and the British, the isolationism of the United States, the long exclusion from international society of Germany and Russia, and the lack of co-operation between the Western powers and Russia in the late thirties. Franklin Roosevelt at first envisaged a world order founded upon the idea of the great powers policing their spheres of influence, a system of loose world government which de Gaulle called permanent intervention. This did not appeal to the outsiders and anyway became impossible owing to the differences between the Soviet Union and the Western powers. Nevertheless, the idea of a concert among the great powers served as the basis for the United Nations, which attempted to establish a collective security force supplied mainly by these powers and permitted regional security subsystems. The collective security system did not materialize, however, and only the latter survived. Even before the end of the war institutions were established to co-ordinate the important domain of international economics. In 1944 at Bretton Woods there were established the International Monetary Fund (IMF) and the World Bank; talks were started for the establishment of an International Trade Organization which was not, however, destined fully to materialize.

Attempts to establish a new stable international order failed for the fundamental reason that the great powers that really mattered were reduced to the two superpowers—the United States and the Soviet Union. Germany and Japan, the two defeated states, were temporarily eliminated; China was still very weak and France had not yet recovered from defeat; Britain was economically exhausted and it did not take many years to show that she could no longer rank as one of the 'Big Three'. Independently of the fundamental ideological differences, disagreement between the two superpowers was partly the consequence of their number; neither a balance of power of the nineteenth-century type nor collective security could possibly work with only two protagonists.

The bipolar system and its evolution post-war

According to the criteria previously suggested, the post-war system was highly revolutionary. Its composition was rapidly changing—the superpowers were new to their status and responsibilities, the other great powers to their loss of status, the rapidly multiplying Asian and African states to their independence. The nuclear weapons and the ballistic missiles were new and terrifying instruments of destruction. Both superpowers were governed by ideologies which rendered them intolerant in international relations; the expansionist ambitions of Communism were confronted by determined American opposition.

Until 1947 it was not clear that the world was becoming bipolar. It did not seem likely that the United States, unravaged by war and the only possessor of nuclear weapons, could be effectively challenged by the Soviet Union, for some time at least. The antagonism between the Russians and the West soon deepened, but at first it was Britain, and not the United States, which was the main opponent. It seemed likely that the Americans might withdraw into their traditional isolationism, as the Russians undoubtedly hoped they would. The Americans, however, took over the lead when the British were incapable of bearing the financial strain of continuing to play their world role: in rapid succession there came a British request for financial aid, an agreement to merge the British and the American occupation zones in Germany, and a withdrawal of British aid to Turkey and Greece. The watershed was the Truman Doctrine of March 1947, in which the President announced that the United States would not only take over British responsibilities in Greece and Turkey but also that it would assist any country willing to resist Communism. The cold war was joined.

Without attempting to apportion the blame for starting the cold war, it may be regarded as a sparring match between the two giant states, a succession of moves and countermoves. The process of involvement was gradual. The acute conflict between the United States and the Soviet Union was at first confined to Europe but gradually spread to other continents—first Asia, then the Middle East, and finally also Latin America and Africa.

With a speed surprising to the West, the Russians developed nuclear weapons. Eventually, the Soviet Union and the United States were not only threatening each other with nuclear extinction but were confronting each other everywhere; any change, in whatever part of the world, could affect the delicate equilibrium between them. This balance of power was quite different from the nineteenth-century one which had been based on the interplay among five great powers, every one of which had an interest in the survival of the others. Neither the Americans nor the Russians had a real interest in each other's survival since each would have found the world safer without the other. Apart from mutual fear, no powerful external restraints existed to prevent them from destroying each other. Admittedly, during the brief period of its nuclear monopoly, the United States did not act on the advice of the few extremist though logical advocates of a preventive war against the Soviet Union but simply used this monopoly to counterbalance Soviet preponderance in other, conventional weapons. Then the Russians developed their own nuclear weapons and the struggle resolved into the uneasy equilibrium of deterrence. In non-nuclear matters the balance remained precariously delicate since a light swing in favour of either side could sway the scales, perhaps irretrievably.

The United Nations' idea of a concert of the five permanent members of the Security Council was hopelessly out of date. The United Nations continued negotiations on collective security, disarmament, and some other aspects of international order, although with rapidly decreasing prospects of success, but the emerging international order was clearly bipolar. In the cold war, states were inevitably attracted to one of the gravitational poles, either through the pressures of one superpower or through fear of the other. The Soviet Union consolidated a ring of Communist regimes around her Western frontiers, and the United States successfully counteracted this move by giving economic and military support to Western European states and by forming the NATO alliance. Since the NATO formula worked well in Europe, the Americans used it in other regions, supplying aid, establishing bases, concluding alliances. Two supranational blocs seemed to be gradually emerging; the world was being sharply split into a Communist part and what the Americans call the 'free world'.

For a short while the trend seemed more or less inexorable. There was no place for neutrals in the bipolar world and both the Russians and the Americans regarded such states as India with suspicion; both applied the maxim that he who is not with us is against us. The bipolar character of the post-war world was revealed so suddenly that many people were blinded to other aspects of reality and became convinced that eventually the whole world would become rigidly divided into two antagonistic blocs facing each other—that the bipolar system would become increasingly tight. The prospects seemed poor, both for mankind faced with the danger of an atomic holocaust, and for the individual national states which seemed to be increasingly at the mercy of the superpowers. The Soviet Union organized her empire rigidly and maintained sufficient troops in and near her 'satellites' to ensure compliance; the Americans used subtler pressures, but their series of alliances amounted to no less than a counter-empire, less brutally run but nevertheless clearly centring around the United States.

Then the forces of nationalism successfully asserted themselves. Instead of becoming tightly bipolar, the international order began to take a different direction. By the late forties consolidation had not made much progress within either bloc. Attempts to establish a 'Third Force' in Western Europe proved abortive but in 1948 Yugoslavia successfully defied the Soviet Union. The Soviet–Yugoslav dispute was misleadingly clad in an ideological garb but was in fact fundamentally an assertion of national ambitions against Soviet tutelage. Although this was not clear at the time, the dispute indicated that, after all, the Russians would be unable to consolidate their empire fully, and that consequently there was no prospect that such an empire and its American counterpart would swallow up the whole world.

The world outside the two opposing blocs also refused to be moulded into tight bipolarity. Particularly important was the stand adopted by India. With the background of their traditional tolerance and their abhorrence of polarities and of militarism, the Indians chose to stay out of the two rival blocs. They, with the Yugoslavs, offered a pattern of behaviour for other emerging states in Asia and later also in Africa, which preferred to remain non-committed. Gradually it became clear that one-third of mankind had decided against joining the two rival blocs, that a large portion of the globe would remain non-aligned.

In the fifties, also, the two opposing blocs loosened somewhat. Western European powers, with a restored economy and revived spirit, were unwilling to follow American policies slavishly. In 1956 Britain and France engaged in their abortive Suez expedition; de Gaulle's challenge to United States' leadership plunged NATO into a prolonged crisis. The nationalist riots in Hungary and Poland were a clear warning to the Russians that their 'satellites' could not be subdued and exploited indefinitely and led to some loosening and liberalizing of the Eastern bloc. In Poland the process was halted, but in 1966 Romania began to pursue an individual foreign policy, rejecting Soviet direction, and in 1968 the Czechs liberalized their domestic regime, eventually provoking the Russians into a large-scale military intervention. Perhaps most importantly, the Sino–Soviet rift, which had come into the open in 1958, gradually developed into an acute conflict, and eventually, from the early seventies, China gradually began to restore relations with the United States.

Nor did the two superpowers retain their nuclear monopoly. Britain, France, and China have produced operational nuclear weapons and a number of further states have acquired sufficient nuclear technology to be able to produce them. Although the existing and, even more so, the potential weapons could not possibly equal those of the United States and the Soviet Union, and would not be likely to affect the balance of nuclear power between the two, they endow their owners with some scope for a measure of independence in their foreign policies.

Even in the mid-eighties the outlines of the emerging new international system were still dim and fluctuating. It was possible to discern the three blocs established in the fifties and sixties—Western, Communist, and non-aligned, the latter very much looser than the other two—but it may be better to call the system 'polycentric' since the centres of power are many and include not only blocs but also single states and international organizations. Apparently the national states are not going to lose their importance. Not only the two superpowers but other, less powerful states are playing a significant part in international relations. When it comes to purely regional issues, the weak African states working in concert successfully prevail against either superpower. They have adopted the General Assembly as their favourite forum and the United Nations has become a spokesman on their behalf. The future of nuclear weapons is confused. While deterrence continues to keep nuclear danger at bay, it remains uncertain whether further states will acquire nuclear weapons and unclear what the implications would be. The Nuclear Non-Proliferation Treaty, which came into force in 1970, although strongly supported by the superpowers, does not seem to offer much hope.

The historical pattern of the balance of power thus cannot be adapted to modern realities, while the blueprints for collective security seem unrealistic. An additional reason for uncertainty is the dramatic growth in both the extensity and the intensity of the international system, which further complicates the task of dealing with the traditional issues of international peace and security. First of all, the geographical scope has drastically extended through the growth of the technological means for the exploitation of the oceans and for the use of outer space for communications and, at least potentially, for military purposes also. Second, the functional domain of the international system has extended in many areas and the number of international institutions has multiplied. Finally, the intensity of international activities has grown, not only within their new scope and domain but also within the traditional ones. It is impossible even to conceptualize, let alone actually to accommodate, all these changes into a traditional model of an international system. The new post-war international order is still at an early stage of its making and the elements already visible may completely change. All we can do at the moment is to try to identify some of the main problems it is facing. Needless to say even this task can be performed only tentatively. Blinkered as we are by past experiences and present problems, we may fail to identify what is going to be important in the future. The problems of today, pressing as they are and important as they are likely to remain in the near future, may be superseded within a few years by new problems, without necessarily having been fully resolved. In the late eighties the East–West and the North–South conflicts remained unresolved while urgent new economic and financial issues became important.

The international economic system

Much intellectual effort has been devoted to issues of 'interdependence', the concept being suggested as an alternative focus to the traditional model centring on power-political interactions largely followed in this analysis. This is obviously an area of central importance which has become intricately connected with power considerations: not only the security but also the prosperity of the individual states now closely depend upon developments in the international system. Both the theoretical conceptualization and the actual governmental attempts to include international economics in their foreign policies are, however, fraught with difficulties. Owing to their complexity they can be only sketchily outlined here.

To start with there are some fundamental differences between the international economic and political systems. First of all, the former is not fully integrated at the global level: it relates only to what is sometimes called the 'free world', which maintains only tenuous links with the Communist bloc though the Soviet Union is the second largest individual economy in the world. Second, instead of the basic bipolarity of the political system, in the economic system we are faced with a clear plurality of the major actors. The United States and Japan are the leaders but, despite a large gap behind them, the Federal Republic of Germany, and also Britain and France, carry real weight. The leadership of the economic system was gradually institutionalized into the Group of Five; from 1986 it began to include also the two close runners-up, Canada and Italy, to form the Group of Seven. Third, whereas states remain the predominant actors in the political system, their control over the more powerful multinational corporations is somewhat limited and they have found no effective means of controlling the volatile financial markets.

Contrary to conventional wisdom, economics is not a precise science; its liberal use of quantification disguises an utter lack of precision. The first, obvious need is to grasp the logic of the system in order to be able to pursue as rationally as possible one's economic objectives and also to have a chance to improve the system. Unfortunately the development of the post-war international economy has been too sudden to comprehend, let alone to control. The traditional focus of attention has been international trade. Here the system was at first highly successful: the post-war surge in industrial and agricultural production was phenomenal, but under the leadership and with the lavish assistance of the dominant power, the United States, world trade grew at about double the rate of world gross product.

The financial base of the nearly continuous boom was, however, brittle; the countries rapidly reconstructing from the ravages of war were often paying themselves over-generously; as their economies grew, the Americans gradually lost their predominance and, moreover, financed with credit the enormous cost of their Vietnam involvement. In the early seventies OPEC, the cartel of oil producers, suddenly quadrupled the price of oil. The effects were dramatic: economies slowed down and the growth of international trade faltered. Moreover, the stability of international exchanges was disrupted when the Americans were forced to abandon the stable though unrealistically low gold standard of the dollar, the main international currency, thus spelling the end of fixed exchange rates.

The Americans were no longer able or willing to underpin the international economic system, although, as the French constantly pointed out, it had enabled them to enjoy free credit in the form of their dollars held all over the world and to dominate the international economy. Nevertheless, the international economy has proved to be resilient. Despite the disruptions, international trade has continued to grow and to become further liberalized, although much more slowly. Utilizing improved seeds, fertilizers, and pesticides, agricultural production has grown dramatically all over the globe, with the exception of the Soviet Union and some drought-stricken areas in Africa; in world trade terms the spectre of world shortage has been replaced by a glut. Oil markets have undergone a similar transformation: by the mid-eighties new oil finds, lowered consumption, and improved conservation methods had turned the anticipated shortage into a glut with a corresponding drop in price.

The greatest problem has arisen in international finance. As the suddenly enriched Middle Eastern oil producers deposited colossal sums in international banks, the latter, with the approval of Western governments, recycled much of the monies into developing countries and some Communist states, into generally unsound and uneconomic investments. As debts and interest charges mounted, reaching some $1 trillion by 1987, the borrowers could not pay except by incurring further debts. By the end of the seventies the international financial system was in a grave and, so far, chronic crisis; by the late eighties no single government had been declared bankrupt but the illusion of solvency was having to be maintained through increasingly strenuous rescue operations and at the cost of deflation savaging the standards of living of the debtors. Reluctance to pay the interest had grown to the point of jeopardizing the whole international banking system.

Another major imbalance has gradually evolved in international trade: Japan, and to a lesser extent the Federal Republic of Germany, have developed increasing export and balance of payments surpluses, whereas the United States has run into growing budgetary and balance of payments difficulties; from being the major source of capital for the world after the war, by 1986 the United States had become the largest international debtor.

Finally, a grave new problem has arisen in currency rate movements. As electronic transfer techniques developed in the eighties, increasingly large sums of money could be moved instantly from country to country by financiers in search of gain from currency rate movements. Consequently the rates began to fluctuate violently, jeopardizing the stability of international prices and trade. The problems of exercising control are formidable. The financiers have an obvious interest in currency movements as their profits are derived largely from commission on transactions, while the scope for control by individual governments is restricted by the fear that the profitable operations could be fairly easily shifted to less restrictive states. The stakes are very high— in Britain the City produces more export income than the oil industry. Moreover, the magnitude of the sums involved is increasing. It is possible only to guess the actual size of the currency flows, which are clearly many times larger than those of international trade—by the late eighties they were some twenty to fifty times larger.

Some progress has been made within the European Community, which successfully stabilized and institutionalized exchange rates among its members, although Britain did not join in. A similar arrangement between the world's main currencies, especially the dollar and the yen, has, however, proved intractable. From the mid-eighties the Group of Five has sporadically managed to exercise a limited influence over the financial markets through persuasion, but institutionalization does not seem likely despite the clear need for an international regime. The establishment of such a regime has been obstructed both by national governments insisting on the preservation of their economic sovereignty and by the powerful financial interests concerned with their profits.

9

Instruments and agencies of international society

International society and its members

It has been repeatedly stressed that international systems are more than the mechanical sums of interaction among their members, that they exhibit a certain structure and develop sets of norms for state behaviour. We shall now discuss how the historically evolved institutions of the contemporary international system cope with the issues confronting us.

International society does not include many units—only in the second half of the twentieth century did the states surpass 160 and other organizations become distinct international actors. Like many organizations with few members, international society has not developed many specialized organs and instruments; in fact, until recently nearly all the activities carried out on its behalf were undertaken by the great powers. However, harmony of interests between international society and the members acting on its behalf cannot be assumed to exist in all situations. As has been argued, states act primarily in order to secure their individual national advantage and it is hard to imagine that they would ever refrain from pursuing it. Indeed, if we look into the operation of the Concert of Europe, we readily perceive how complex is the connection between individual and social roles; sometimes the suspicion arises that the ostensibly social role serves as a mere disguise for the pursuit of purely selfish national interests.

While we recognize the confusion and hypocrisy implicit in the situation, we must bear in mind that international order fully depends upon the co-operation of the great powers and cannot possibly work if the vital interests of any of these powers are adversely affected. Practical difficulties do arise and have to be solved in each single case. In theory the conundrum can be explained fairly easily. On the one hand, actions against the vital interests of one's state cannot be in the interest of the system to which the state belongs, since the system would automatically become not worthwhile; on the other, once the preservation of international order in general is accepted as a vital national interest, the state may have to go quite far in overriding its more selfish interests and values.

While the two superpowers remain the dominant agents of the international system, over the last hundred years, but mainly since the Second World War, there have arisen numerous agencies and institutions working for international society as a whole. They act simultaneously on behalf of their individual state-members, and occasionally in the interests of a group of them or even of a single power alone, but their major function is to act on behalf of international society. The new institutions express the evolution and sophistication of international politics just as division of labour and specialization express them in economics.

The operation of the post-war international system is not only complicated by the rise of non-state actors; the system shares the difficulties of all organizations consisting of a small number of members because its most important units—the states—are few. Theoretically, all states interact on the footing of sovereign equality, as if they were similar in most significant respects. In fact, they differ not only in power but also in their political systems and institutions, in the ideologies they profess, in the attitudes they adopt to the international order. They are pronouncedly individualistic and must be realistically accepted as being so. Failing large numbers, it is impossible to impose any far-reaching codes of behaviour which would rigidly apply to all, or to arrive at any significant statistical rules according to which such behaviour could be predicted. In a domestic society which numbers millions of individuals, norms of behaviour do not lose their general validity if they are occasionally infringed by a few; it is even possible to predict the frequency of such infringements. In international relations any statistical prediction of the probability of behaviour of units which are so different in some vital respects would be very unreliable; moreover, violation of the norm by one single state may deprive it of its significance. What, for instance, would be the value of outlawing war or nuclear or any other weapons of mass destruction if one great power refused to submit? The superpowers and often also other powers can be compared with the mighty feudal barons who could not be expected to accept all general norms of behaviour; not statistical forecasts but an analysis of their individual policies and attitudes is required for most purposes.

Hence, while it is possible to analyse an issue in a domestic society in the abstract, without going into the identity of the parties, such analysis does not take us far in international relations. The identity of the state involved is as important as what is at stake. It is, for instance, clear that the Irish claim to Ulster creates an issue of quite a different nature than would a Soviet claim to a part of Finnish territory. An objection to a trivial infringement of diplomatic etiquette by one of the superpowers can create an issue very much graver than the Albanian claim to the southern part of Yugoslavia. Weaker states have always found it difficult to deal with those more powerful. They have often been forced to seek the protection of greater powers, arriving at a position of dependence similar to that of vassals in the feudal system; sometimes they were eventually absorbed by these powers. Otherwise they formed combinations, like the Swiss or the American Federations, which reduced their inequality in relation to the more powerful states. Discrepancies have greatly increased today because the accumulation of power by the two superpowers can scarcely be matched while, under the aegis of the United Nations, very weak new states have been coming into existence; they could never have reached independence in the harsher climate of the pre-UN world.

Through their oscillations between periods of stability and change, the relations between international society and its members have greatly increased both in scope and intensity over the last few centuries. In every period of change they have to be rearranged, and, the more ramified and intensive they are, the more difficult does the task become. The problems of our own generation are considerably more involved than those following the French Revolution not only because they are graver in themselves but also because we have to deal with them in a much more complex framework.

Until now international societies have been subservient to their members, although, depending on the type of structure, not always to the same degree. On the whole, since the Second World War the two superpowers have been more able to influence international order and less subordinate to it than the several great powers participating in the balance of power in the nineteenth century. If, however, as seems likely, international society continues its evolution towards polycentrism, its structure and the operation of its agencies will logically become more autonomous; indeed this seems to be happening already.

Norms regulating the behaviour of states

A society cannot operate without some normative social control of the behaviour of its members. When every member is a law unto himself, anarchy prevails, behaviour is unpredictable, and no social order can be maintained. International society differs from national societies in that it consists of states instead of individuals and is only loosely organized. Nevertheless, analogies from a society of individuals are not unwarranted, provided they are not pushed too far and the differences are kept in mind.

A legal system is the most highly evolved form of expressing social order; but human behaviour is governed also by many other, non-legal norms, by those of morality and by what are often called *mores*, such as custom, etiquette, or fashion. Some thinkers prefer to derive the highest of these norms, those of law and morality, from higher superhuman principles, but it is possible to explain them, together with the other norms, as a mere rational expression of social needs. Societies differ in the degree to which they permit variety in human behaviour and in the emphasis they put upon conformity. On the whole, the nature of the rules is governed by their social importance and is expressed in the type of sanction provided in cases of breach. If the social importance of the rules is slight, mild social disapproval suffices. For instance, a woman waiving the dictates of fashion may be slightly ridiculed or hampered in her social intercourse with more fashion-conscious individuals. If the dignity of an institution or occasion calls for the wearing of customary attire, anyone not so dressed may be refused admission—thus a woman in a sleeveless dress may not be allowed into an Italian church.

Social sanctions increase with the degree to which human behaviour seriously affects others. Some norms are incorporated in the law of the land and are enforced by central authority which tries to prevent their infringement and punishes their violation; law cannot, however, meet the whole range of socially undesirable possibilities, and is therefore supplemented by the rules of morality which are not enforced in the same way but are generally considered to be important. The sanctions for the violation of moral rules lie not only in individual conscience (which is assiduously trained in the desirable direction at home, at school, and in all social intercourse) but also in strong social pressures. If cruelty to children is to be avoided, law can define only a limited number of punishable offences, but a person treating children cruelly, although not committing any of these offences, is likely, if discovered, to be condemned by his friends and neighbours. This too is a strong form of sanction.

These well-known and rather simple distinctions are mentioned here because they illuminate the more abstruse nature of the norms regulating the behaviour of states. As in domestic societies, the scope and nature of international norms are determined by those of social needs, but there is an important difference in the degree of social agreement which can be reached about them. By definition, domestic societies embody a considerable measure of fundamental social consensus, without which they would not have come into being or would disintegrate. If such social consensus existed internationally, it would lead directly to world government. International order is based not so much on the consensus of its participants as on the physical fact that states coexist and cannot escape from interaction. It is a world characterized mainly by the stark necessities of a Hobbesian society which has not yet evolved a fully articulated social contract.

Interaction among states is much less varied than interaction among individuals; the customs and conventions, the *mores*, of international society are therefore not quite as complex and voluminous as those among individuals. As in a domestic society, the sanction for their infringement is social disapproval of suitable severity. In stable periods, such as much of the fairly homogeneous balance of power system, the customs are generally accepted and observed; in revolutionary periods, however, they are deliberately and flagrantly violated. A good illustration may be found in the determination shown by the Bolshevik rulers of Russia, after they had come to power, to substitute direct relations with the people of other countries and later with their Communist parties, for traditional diplomatic relations. In a few years, when the dust had somewhat settled, the Russians reverted to the traditional forms of diplomacy, including ceremonial dress and titles, although they did not abandon their attempts at subversion.

One source of the norms of international behaviour is found in history, in the way in which states, especially the great powers, have actually been behaving. Hence the great importance of precedent. International relations abound in situations in which states seem to be governed less by the merits of the specific case than by the fear that they would establish an unwelcome precedent. For instance, it seems very likely that the adamant Soviet refusal to consider the Japanese claim for the return of the 'Northern Territories', the four small islands of the South Kurils, is not due mainly to the strategic and fisheries interests involved; rather the Russians are determined to avoid a precedent for allowing the Chinese to press for the revision of the 'unequal' Amur Treaty which established the Sino-Soviet boundaries in Siberia in the nineteenth century.

Further-reaching is the concept of 'legitimacy', which denotes some form of international recognition of certain norms of behaviour. This can be based on a bilateral relationship alone— the leaders of both superpowers occasionally refer to the 'rules of the *détente*', meaning the norms of mutual behaviour arising from their past behaviour and understandings, though the substance of these is admittedly often disputed. Legitimacy can be conveyed by decisions of international organizations, not only the United Nations, but also regional ones. Thus the United States was helped by the OAS in confirming the legitimacy of its 'quarantine' declared in the crisis arising over the Soviet missiles on Cuba in 1962, while the OAU was the decisive legitimizing agency for the Soviet-supported Cuban military interventions in Africa in the late seventies.

Legitimacy is increasingly achieved by what is sometimes termed 'organized persuasion', international debates about what the norms should be, in which individual states become so strongly aware of the views of others and of the repercussions of their behaviour that they can be persuaded, sometimes more or less coerced, to accept rules which they do not find readily acceptable. When the cost of opposing the opinion of other states becomes prohibitive, it becomes rational to adopt the prudential policy of adaptation, of abandoning or attenuating the pursuit of national interests, however much cherished. An outstanding example is the way in which Western powers gradually accepted the powers of the General Assembly to deal with colonialism and with apartheid in South Africa, both of which they justifiably considered as being of essentially domestic jurisdiction and hence not within the competence of the United Nations. Another example referred to in the next chapter is the British acceptance of an extended Exclusive Economic Zone contravening the principle of the open seas cherished by the British. The General Assembly, being the 'town meeting' of the world, acts as a central source of organized persuasion on a world-wide scale. It is of particular importance in a world rent by ideological, racial, cultural, and economic conflicts which render accommodation difficult. In a lesser geographical or functional scope, the same process goes on in all international organizations, notably in the European Community. The total result is of fundamental importance to the functioning of the international system: from being essentially self-centred in the past, states have now inescapably become what some sociologists call 'other-oriented'. Needless to say, this does not mean that they necessarily yield to the desires and susceptibilities of others but they are forced to take them into account and to assess the cost of overriding them.

Justice and international morality

When public debates over the justification of national policies arise internationally, invariably some resort is made to the principles and ideals of justice and of international morality. Each is referred to under a variety of terms and meanings, all of which boil down to one basic consideration—a justification which is internationally acceptable.

It is extremely difficult for us to conceive of principles which are universally acceptable: first, because decision-makers remain bound by the priorities they have in accordance with their respective national interests and, second, because it is operationally difficult to conceive of a world community within which we could apply such principles on an equal footing, without giving priority to one's own nation and special obligations. The problem can be readily demonstrated by looking at the obstacles besetting the practical application of the now generally accepted principle that rich states have some obligation to help those which are very poor. The degree of sacrifice and the nature of the incentives vary greatly. In the late forties, the Americans found it easy to spend about 2 per cent of their GNP on the Marshall Plan, not only because their economy was buoyant but also because they found the expenditure well worthwhile owing both to what they perceived as urgent security reasons and to the high chances of success. At the end of the seventies, when faced with the issue of accepting as members three relatively poor Mediterranean countries, the existing members of the European Community were hesitant about a similarly generous policy—the decision-making machinery, involving the consent of all the nine members, the relatively lower security benefits likely to accrue, and possibly also greater doubts about the likely efficacy of large-scale aid, all played a part. On a world-wide scale the United Nations has not come anywhere near the achievement of its proclaimed principle that the rich countries should devote at least 1 per cent of their GNP to aid. Underlying the hesitations in all these cases, apart from the Marshall Plan, are the justified doubts about the efficacy of aid: striving towards economic equalization at the international level cannot be reasonably conceived as purely a matter of redistribution—aid flowing from the rich to the poor—but must perforce involve the improvement of the domestic performance of the recipients, over which the donors have insufficient influence.

What makes the notion of international morality so ambiguous is that its meaning has never been clearly defined nor has there been agreement concerning the relations between the norms of individual and international morality. One school of thinkers, following Machiavelli, denies the existence of international morality altogether, others, like Kant, equate international morality with private morality; most thinkers accept the existence of international morality but differentiate between it and individual morality.

A realistic analysis of international relations cannot accept at their face value the repeated protestations of statesmen of all countries that they are governed by moral rules. Clearly morality is often invoked under various names merely to provide a respectable garb for the pursuit of selfish state interests; it is a convenient common justification for claims which run counter to somebody else's legal rights. Since law is conservative and allows no claims in equity or ways for revision, those demanding revision invariably invoke morality. The Versailles Peace Treaty was a binding legal agreement, but the Germans represented it as an immoral dictate of the victorious powers determined to oppress them; it is similarly possible to question many legally established boundaries on the basis of national self-determination.

Nevertheless, it does not follow that Machiavelli was correct in rejecting the existence of international morality. Despite the lack of agreement as to its extent, international morality cannot be adapted to selfish ends in all circumstances. In our generation a claim for the revision of frontiers for the purpose of uniting a nation can be advanced and accepted as being morally justified, but, if made on grounds of strategic or economic necessity, such a claim would receive little sympathy from other states and from international public opinion so that no statesman would think of advancing it. This is the first important reason why moral norms must be accepted as an influence upon the behaviour of states: this behaviour is perceived and evaluated in moral terms. Even if, in order to pursue a vital national interest, states sometimes ignore or flout international public opinion, they are generally interested in finding favour with it.

Second, the demarcation lines between domestic and international affairs and between states and individuals are not quite as sharp as they used to be. In the nineteenth century states alone had a standing in international law, and their treatment of individuals, provided these were their own subjects, was their own domestic affair. The excesses of Nazism led to the extension of some rules of individual morality to the treatment of individuals by states. Human rights are now covered by a number of norms of behaviour some of which have hardened into law although most of them are limited to declarations and belong to the realm of morality. The Final Acts of the Helsinki Conference of 1975 have, however, renewed the early post-war interest in human rights and have provided the basis for important subsequent international disputes about their application to the Soviet Union.

The moral sentiments of statesmen as individuals must also be remembered. It is safe to assume that, at least when their national interests are not seriously affected, they usually prefer to act in a way they consider moral rather than otherwise. This is particularly true about the practice of the United Kingdom and the United States. With the exceptional security these countries enjoyed in the nineteenth century, they had the opportunity to think in moral terms rather than in terms of necessity, of the *raison d'état*, as continental statesmen usually did. There is, however, some substance to Reinhold Niebuhr's contention that, far from extending their moral rules to international politics, men tend to use these politics as an outlet for their immoral propensities—that they are moral men living in an immoral society.

The extreme Kantian proposition that international moral norms are identical with those governing individuals belongs to the realm of the 'ought'. Everything ultimately should be reduced to the measure of man, but this does not alter the fact that states are not individuals and that the individuals acting on their behalf consider first their national advantage. Morality constitutes only a vague corrective to their behaviour, perhaps most concretely by providing advanced standards for the interpretation and evolution of international law. Beyond that, a vague obligation to respect some basic human rights and to meet the urgent needs of individuals, even if they belong to another state, may be on the way to becoming a generally accepted norm of international morality; in the case of large-scale natural calamities, when the national government has insufficient means for coping with the distress, other states which can afford it are expected to help, and a similar sense of responsibility for assisting the poorest countries is gradually growing.

International law

Just as the most important norms governing the behaviour of individuals are embodied in domestic or, as the lawyers call it, 'municipal' law, so some norms governing the behaviour of states are embodied in international law. Even so, the identity of name does not indicate an identity of nature. International law operates in quite a different social context, without the foundations of an overwhelming social consensus and of a central authority which endows its rules with sanction. States differ from individuals in that they are not subject to law; international law is not a law above states but one between them. This is a situation so anomalous for a legal system that some professional lawyers used to deny the legal character of international law altogether, claiming that it lacked the distinctive characteristic of effective sanctions. Sovereign states and an international legal system of the same type as domestic legal systems are logically incompatible: either the states are truly sovereign and recognize no superior, in which case there can be no legal rules binding them; or, if such rules exist, then states are not truly sovereign. The contradiction is resolved by the theory of consent which claims that the binding character of international legal norms is founded upon their acceptance by states, explicit or implied. Thus being bound by international law becomes a form of exercising sovereignty. In the classical definition of sovereignty in the Wimbledon case, the World Court emphatically declined 'to see in the conclusion of any Treaty by which a State undertakes to perform or refrain from performing a particular act an abandonment of sovereignty'.

Since international law is based upon such an uneasy compromise, it is not surprising that the evaluation of its significance ranges so widely. Some regard it as a sham, while others claim that, if only given a chance by politicians, lawyers could draft a comprehensive code which would ensure peace upon earth. Neither view does full justice to the true nature of international law which tries to reconcile the contradictions inherent in the coexistence of sovereign states and international order and is the expression both of state sovereignty and of its limitations.

International law is universal: its norms apply to all states, independently of their power, status, geographical position, ideology, and so on. Variations do, however, appear in the relations within certain groups of states. Some are regional, for example, those in the last century in Latin America and, since the Second World War, in Africa, the Middle East and, in a particularly pronounced form, in Western Europe. Others are according to membership of military–ideological blocs, the membership of NATO or the Warsaw Pact. Finally, a dual system of norms has been developing along the North–South axis in favour of the new, developing states. The customary standards governing both international and domestic behaviour have never been applied to them with full rigour; furthermore, by the seventies, as part of their demands for a New International Economic Order, a dual system of rules was emerging, imposing on the developing states some rights without corresponding obligations.

The norms of international law can be divided into three categories. First, there is the 'law of power', which consists of the rules that help to maintain the political framework, the existing hierarchies based upon power. Here belong norms ensuring the independence of states and non-interference in their domestic affairs, peace treaties, boundary agreements, alliances, etc. Then there is the 'law of reciprocity', which regulates areas less vital for power purposes where the states are willing to accommodate the interests of other states in order to obtain reciprocal benefits. This is the most numerous group of international norms, and covers many fields—for instance, diplomatic immunities and extradition, trade and communications, and limitations of warfare. Finally, there is an international 'community law', still at a rudimentary stage; examples can be found in the regulation of the slave trade, or of international rivers, or in the standards of economic good neighbourliness embodied in the GATT.[1]

Like all normative systems, international law incorporates certain principles of natural law, but a historical survey of its development shows that it has developed more through state practice than through logical deduction from such principles. It is intimately linked with the balance of power system within which law performed the important task of laying down the rights and duties of states in relation to one another; most of its basic rules were developed in the fifteenth and sixteenth centuries when the system was coming into being.

International society is fully decentralized and possesses no legislature; it nevertheless incorporates such a fundamental rule as *pacta sunt servanda* which enables states to develop the law through numerous reciprocal treaties. Some arrangements and clauses recur in the treaties regulating a given subject-matter and often serve as a basis for international customary law; this simply means that after a time they are taken for granted and need not be explicitly written into new treaties.

Another important consequence of the decentralization of international society is the absence of a central executive authority which could enforce the law. This does not matter overmuch, however, because international law does not attempt the unenforceable—it does not impose upon states rules liable to infringe their vital interestes. States thus retain the ultimate right to use force and resort to war and preserve an exclusive jurisdiction over domestic matters; despite some attempts to do so, intervention has never been established as a legal institution. Breaches of legal rules do not entail penal consequences, but they are nevertheless rare. Social pressures within international society usually provide a sufficient sanction since all states wish to have the reputation of being law-abiding; this makes treaties with them more respected and desirable and, to some extent at least, shelters them from the blackmail and hard bargaining to which less principled states can be subjected.

Within the balance of power system, international law was fairly adequate; despite the partial break during the French

Revolution and the Napoleonic Wars, it gradually developed into a fairly comprehensive system of rules. The general moderation and acceptance of the system made workable the law of power, despite its rudimentary nature; against the background of security, reciprocal interests gave rise to a rapid proliferation of treaties, especially regarding commerce, while numerous conferences and a few permanent institutions began to develop the law of community.

When the balance of power system began to decline in the twentieth century, the many efforts to spread the 'rule of law'—to develop international courts, to extend international law to the prohibition of the use of force—were bound to fail. Law is an expression of social order and constitutes only a marginally formative element within it. The main reason why these attempts failed was that the reformers confused the law of power with other groups of norms. The laws of reciprocity and community could develop and prosper only against the background of the security ensured by the operation of the balance of power. When this security disappeared and the law of power had to be fitted to a new international system, any attempts to extend community norms to the field of power were extremely naïve. Moreover, the legal system had a European and Christian basis and so required adjustments to accommodate non-European and non-Christian states.

Since 1945 international law has lost much of its traditional meaning. The basic distinctions between domestic and international matters have disappeared and those between private and public acts have become blurred; many rules concerning territorial jurisdiction or the law of war and neutrality have been violated to the point of nullifying them; the new problems of nuclear weapons, outer space, the exploitation of the sea-bed, or propaganda, cannot be readily solved. The conflicts in the bipolar world were so sharp that no security could be found within it; the relations between the two hostile blocs were so unsettled that the law of power could not provide a reasonable background for reciprocity and co-operation, and in fact neither reached its previous level. Simultaneously, the interaction within the blocs became so intimate that in some respects it superseded traditional international patterns and began to resemble interaction within integrated political societies.

The sharp dichotomy of the bipolar world may now be resolving into a new polycentric order and, instead of becoming sharply differentiated into intra- and inter-bloc relations, international law is reverting to its more general function. It would, however, be unrealistic to expect a return to the norms of the golden age of international law based upon the balance of power. There has been no break in the continuity of international law, as it is easier to adapt old concepts and institutions than to build up from scratch, but obviously the law of the new order will have to be a new kind of law. Much of it will be conceived to satisfy the functional needs of international society as a whole rather than to deal with security and power; it will therefore fall within the hitherto rudimentary category of rules of 'community law', sometimes called also 'new international law'. So much has been done in this domain since the Second World War that, following Myres McDougal, some international lawyers suggest that we should regard the making of international law as a form of international decision-making, differing from the political one only in that it employs legal or quasi-legal forms.

A good example of this process is found in the evolution of the law of the sea, arising primarily from the development of technologies which made possible the exploitation of the sea-bed for minerals and led to serious over-fishing and depletion of the most popular and accessible species of fish. New norms were arrived at in many ways. The earliest post-war measures were established through unilateral national declarations which were then repeated by other nations, sometimes fairly readily, like the extension of exclusive national rights to the continental shelf by the United States, sometimes with a long delay, like some Latin American claims to exclusive fisheries rights over a 320-kilometre zone. International conferences of the major states involved were periodically convened to ensure the conservation of whales and of fish stocks in the North Sea.

The most important element in the development of the law of the sea, and the one which offers most promise for other important issue-areas likely to arise in the future, proved to be a series of general UN conferences on the law of the sea. Two of these were held in the late fifties and codified the law, especially that dealing with the delimitation of the continental shelf. They also came close to an agreement on the width of territorial waters over which states hold exclusive jurisdiction, the width of which has been historically developed, varying as much as between five and nineteen kilometres. A series of sessions of a new conference were convened in the seventies, demonstrating the expedient of collective persuasion as a method of international law-making. Debates were prolonged, the deadlines were never met, and the ultimate solutions arrived at can be regarded as only a minimal programme, nowhere near solutions optimal for the international community: they merely extended the jurisdiction of the individual states over what used to be the open seas, the common heritage of mankind. At the same time, however, they made progress towards halting the continuing depletion of fisheries and made sufficient headway towards a legal framework for the exploitation of sea-bed resources to prevent the recurrence of acute international conflicts. Although the conference was unable to reach agreement about a proposed new International Sea-bed Authority to control the exploitation of the sea-bed outside the domain of individual states, it did reach one on the principles of 19-kilometre territorial waters and of a 320-kilometre Exclusive Economic Zone. There is little doubt that a similar procedure will be adopted if and when technological advance makes likely the exploitation of Antarctica, the only unappropriated part of the land masses of the globe.

A large proportion of the new international law is, however, likely to take the form of the law of international institutions.

10

International institutions

Global international institutions

International institutions will be considered here only in their role as agencies of international order. They constitute too specialized and complex a field to allow more than the broadest outline of their historical development, structure, and activities.

Individuals can save themselves much effort in personal life by developing routines to deal with recurring needs and situations; in social behaviour such routines take the form of institutions. In a broad sense the word 'institution' includes such *ad hoc* arrangements as international conferences to settle a specific matter, but generally the name is reserved for establishments which operate continuously. The majority of the existing several thousands of international institutions (or organizations) are non-governmental; they combine national associations and individuals, and many of them represent relatively esoteric interests which have no direct bearing on politics. But even if singly these institutions exercise only a negligible impact on international relations, the thin strands, when woven together, constitute quite a strong rope. They represent so many individuals and organizations with transnational affiliations that they amount to substantial links between the national states.

Over 200 international institutions are intergovernmental, more than half of them regional. These include some which are politically important; only these will be discussed here.

The first international institution, the Geodetic Union, was established only in 1864, so the subsequent proliferation of others clearly reflects an increased intensity in international relations. This was made possible by the exceptional stability of the balance of power order in the latter part of the nineteenth century, but subsequent disturbances of this order did not spell the end of the existing institutions; on the contrary, they led to the establishment of additional ones, including those of greatest political significance, the League of Nations and the United Nations. History is important in explaining the nature of these institutions. They are not as closely connected with the balance of power system as is international law. In fact, they largely represent twentieth-century forces and ideas which came into being after the balance of power system had stopped functioning effectively. There is nevertheless a close link between law and institutions. Some of the most important institutions have pronouncedly political objectives and are run by politicians and statesmen, but the drafting of their charters and their interpretation remain in the hands of lawyers. Legality, conformity with the constitution, is a necessary feature of any state policy which intends to win the support of the other members. Legal arguments can stretch interpretation of the constitution to great lengths, but there is a limit to its flexibility and the other members sit in judgement.

Here we come up against the fundamental difficulty of all international institutions inherent in their dual role which theoretically need not, but actually sometimes does, lead to incompatibilities. On the one hand, institutions pursue certain international objectives and work on behalf of international order. On the other, the member-states enter these institutions with the same interests as they had before, and expect them to be satisfied, or at least not infringed. Ideally there is a harmony of interests—co-operation within the institution improves the chances of satisfying the interests of states, thus compensating for incidental inconveniences—but this is not always the case. Britain, for instance, a faithful though not very enthusiastic member of the United Nations, has found it difficult to accept UN actions directly affecting British policies, such as the condemnation of the Suez expedition in 1956, or the violent and often uninformed and unrealistic attacks on British colonial policy.

In order to estimate the dual role of international institutions as instruments both of international order and of the national policies of the members, we should consider their place in the three realms of international politics dealt with by the laws of power, of reciprocity, and of community. As is the case with international law, institutions succeed in direct proportion to their distance from power politics: the less they affect the power-position of states, the more are these states likely to co-operate. Immunities for diplomats were thus more acceptable than the outlawing of war; since mail is strategically much less important than telegraph and radio, the Universal Postal Union has been more successful than the International Telecommunications Union.

The lines between reciprocity and community cannot be sharply drawn because, once reciprocity among states reaches a certain level, it leads to the development of the rudiments of a community; reciprocal trade agreements, for instance, have now established the good neighbour principle which has become incorporated in the relevant international institution, the GATT. International organization has been both the result of certain common objectives and the agent for the development of community ties. Where reciprocity has remained the rule, it serves as a convenient specialized channel for reciprocal arrangements.

Co-ordination and reciprocity were successfully carried over from the nineteenth century and further developed in the twentieth, when many new institutions were added to those few previously existing. The development of institutions concerned with power politics began only at the turn of the century. The two Hague Conferences in 1899 and 1907 unsuccessfully attempted to provide a legal framework intended to limit the use of force and to facilitate the solution of disputes through non-violent means. The conventions concluded did not go very far and the only institution established, the Permanent Court of Arbitration, was not in fact either permanent or a court, but merely a panel of names from which the parties could choose arbitrators for the settlement of any issue they might wish to submit. International institutions concerned with power politics arose only in the wake of the First World War, as a result of the bankruptcy of the old order based on the balance of power. Although the political relevance of the League of Nations in inter-war politics was not perhaps great, it is well worth returning to the assumptions underlying its establishment, assumptions which illuminate the nature of international organization although they are not widely accepted today.

The League of Nations and the United Nations in historical perspective

The League of Nations was conceived as a comprehensive institution. In President Wilson's words, it was not to be 'merely a league to secure the peace of the world' but also 'a league that can be used for co-operation on any international matter'. The League was born out of the shock caused by the First World War, and its main activity was to maintain peace. Hence its work in pursuing international co-operation on the lines developed in the nineteenth century did not become fully appreciated until its political activities had failed in the mid-thirties. Discussion of the non-political activities can be left to the following section; historical perspective depends mainly on the setting within the international system and the relations among the great powers of the period.

The framers of the Covenant of the League of Nations did not agree in their attitudes to the problems of peace. At the one extreme there was President Wilson, whose approach to international relations was evangelical, who wished to achieve through the League what another prominent statesman, General Smuts, called 'an inner transformation of international relations and institutions'. A concert of power was to end entangling alliances, which he blamed for the war; a collective security system was to replace power politics. This was not, however, the attitude of the British, who played the next most important part in the establishment of the League; they regarded the League largely as an improved contemporary version of the Concert of Europe which had so well served their national purposes in the nineteenth century. The French were concerned with guarantees against renewed German aggression; hence they were particularly interested in the machinery of sanctions against a convenant-breaker, and their first draft included far-reaching provisions in this direction, including the establishment of a commander-in-chief with a permanent staff. Thus, while Wilson conceived the League as an instrument of international order, the British and the French saw in it mainly a new instrument to serve their respective and differing national interests and tried to mould it accordingly.

During the twenty years of its active existence, the League changed its character several times. When the Americans did not join it, rather unexpectedly the small neutral states became the spokesmen for collective security and the principles of international order. Their views did not, however, prevail since they were merely 'consumers of security'. The character of the League depended on the views of its great power members, the only ones capable of effective collective action.

France and Britain deliberately pursued their respective national interests and did not therefore see eye to eye about the treatment of Germany and the role of the League. At first Germany and the other defeated countries were kept out and the League amounted to a loose association of victors and neutrals to preserve the peace settlements. In the mid-twenties, in conformity with British views, Germany and the other defeated states were admitted in the vain expectation that they would co-operate from the inside in the maintenance of international order. After the danger of Nazism had become clear and Hitler had left the League, the Soviet Union joined it and vainly tried to shape it into a fully-fledged anti-Nazi alliance. For most of its existence the League stubbornly but futilely pursued general discussions about international order which will be analysed later.

In 1945 the victors at least did not fundamentally disagree about the treatment of the defeated enemies. They formed the new international organization, the United Nations, as an association of 'peace-loving' nations directed against the potential aggressors, which in 1945 meant the defeated states. The United Nations was to be tougher and more realistic than its predecessor; the Americans made sure that this time neither the United States nor the Soviet Union would stay out.

The Charter was signed in June 1945 but, before the United Nations even started its operations, it had become obsolete. The new nuclear weapons were first exploded in July and used with telling effect against Japan in August. The preponderance of the two superpowers and the differences arising between them made unimportant the original agreements on the treatment of the defeated states—and, in any case, both sides soon deviated from their drastic provisions. Until 1947 the United Nations uneasily tried to bring the Charter into operation, working, as envisaged, mainly through the Security Council, in which the superpowers tried to reach agreement, usually in vain.

In its early period the United Nations served, to a large extent, the ends of American national policy. The Russians could paralyse the Security Council by their power of veto, but the Americans made extensive use of the large majorities they could command in the General Assembly, which they succeeded in making the centre of political activities. The process culminated in 1950 when the Russians temporarily withdrew from all the organs of the United Nations; it is possible that they were preparing for a final withdrawal and were grooming a rival Communist organization, the Partisans of Peace. However, when the Americans made use of their absence and secured UN support for their action against the Communist North Koreans who had attacked American-protected South Korea in June 1950, the Russians immediately returned in order to impede further action in the matter and to safeguard themselves against the repetition of such happenings.

Between 1955 and 1957 the composition of the United Nations changed dramatically with the mass admission of Asian and African states. The United States, its European allies, and Latin American supporters were no longer in the majority in the General Assembly. The new members were interested not in the cold war but in anti-colonialism; the Soviet Union supported them in accordance with her traditions and secured their reciprocal support or at least neutrality. Since 1958 the United Nations has become increasingly identified with the Afro-Asian bloc and its aspirations.

Anti-colonialism was, however, bound to abate with the rapid emancipation of colonies, and the Afro-Asian members then began to take an increasing interest in other aspects of the international order. On the whole they are treating both superpowers with suspicion and are refusing to side with either. They have repeatedly urged them to refrain from behaviour endangering the peace of the world and to get on with disarmament.

But the Afro-Asian states are not exclusively 'consumers of security'. They have, for instance, established the principle that UN intervention forces should consist only of contingents drawn from themselves and not from the great powers; the UN force on Cyprus was exceptional in including British troops, and this was only because they were available on the island and were indispensable for the constitution of the force. So far international organization has been unable to make much progress towards a new type of international order, mainly because its great power members could never agree. Although there is no guarantee that the smaller powers will be capable of agreeing on much beyond their anti-colonial objectives, it is at least not impossible.

We will turn now to the organization and the activities of the League of Nations and the United Nations, which are of more than purely historical interest. The existing traditions may not be perpetuated by a United Nations in which the smaller powers are preponderant, but they will serve at least as a starting point.

The structure of global institutions

World-wide international institutions centre round the United Nations with a membership of over 160 states and with a wide competence in security, political, and non-political matters. Loosely co-ordinated and connected are thirteen specialized agencies which deal with more limited technical aspects of world co-operation and generally have a somewhat more limited membership. Some of them, such as the ILO, the Universal Postal Union, and the International Telecommunications Union, date back to pre-UN days, but most of them, for example the World Bank, the IMF, the Food and Agriculture Organization (FAO), UNESCO, and the World Health Organization (WHO), were established towards the end of the Second World War or soon after it.

The structure of all these institutions is basically similar, although it shows some variations according to how relevant their activities are for power politics and to the role played by the great powers. All the members are represented in some form of assembly, in the United Nations itself called the General

Assembly. The principles of sovereign equality and of unanimity are sometimes slightly modified; in the World Bank and IMF, voting is weighted by the amount of contributions made by the members; and in the General Assembly of the United Nations, recommendations—which have no legally binding force—require only a two-thirds majority even on important matters.

The position of the great powers and main contributors is reflected by another body, generally called a council, in which they are either assured seats by the constitution or given them in practice, together with a small number of other members. The relations between the council and the assembly vary from institution to institution, and within them, in different periods, but in no case is the council an executive body acting on behalf of the assembly. The United Nations has in addition three specialized councils—a Security Council of fifteen, with five great powers permanently represented (Britain, China, France, the Soviet Union, and the United States); an Economic and Social Council of twenty-seven, without permanent membership, and a Trusteeship Council in which countries administering and not administering trust territories are equally represented.

From the point of view of international order, extremely important organs of the institutions are their secretariats. Whereas the assemblies are based on the principles of sovereign equality of all members, and the councils, however imperfectly, endeavour to give some expression to power gradations, the secretariats act on behalf of the institution as a whole, as distinct from its individual members. Although he commands no state machinery, the Secretary-General of the United Nations is an internationally important personality. He cannot exercise much initiative on behalf of international order because he cannot afford to antagonize any one of the powerful members, but he is responsible for implementing a policy, once it has been agreed by the organization, and he can interpret his instructions with some degree of latitude.

The position of the Secretary-General acting on behalf of the United Nations as a whole, maintaining international order even against the national interests of powerful members or their blocs, is extremely precarious. He represents an organization which has no power or means except those provided by its members. The only tangible element of power which he can wield is international public opinion as expressed by these members. He must be always watchful in estimating what this opinion is and, even with the greatest care, he cannot avoid clashes. This was the fate of Trygve Lie, the first Secretary-General, who accepted the American view that the Communists had committed aggression in Korea and allowed full UN support for American action. It happened also to his more cautious successor, Dag Hammarskjöld, who pursued an active UN policy in the Congo, thus thwarting Soviet designs. Khrushchev's contention that no individual can be neutral is justified in the conditions of our generation, but his demand that the position of the Secretary-General should be split into a 'troika', a committee of three representatives of the three blocs (Communist, Western, and non-aligned), would have led to a complete paralysis of the organization. While the blocs would be able to exercise their veto, the organization could not conceivably do much for international order. Following the successful part played by the Secretary-General in the Cuban missile crisis in 1962, the Russians abandoned their proposal.

Both in the League and in the United Nations, members retained their sovereign positions and the immunity of their domestic affairs from interference. In the United Nations, however, this immunity has become somewhat conditional, limited to matters 'essentially within the domestic jurisdiction' of the members, and the General Assembly has further eroded it. Arguing that any domestic affair which affects international peace and security stops being essentially within domestic jurisdiction, it has been freely discussing and making recommendations upon colonial matters, human rights, and some aspects of the governmental system of the members, all of which would have been considered entirely out of court by the Assembly of the League of Nations. Moreover, according to Article 25 of the Charter, the members agree 'to carry out the decisions of the Security Council in accordance with the present Charter'. This means that, provided the five permanent members concur, they, together with an additional four members of the Security Council, can impose far-reaching obligations on other states. The permanent members are immune because they can prevent an unacceptable decision by exercising their power of veto.

Maintenance of international peace and security and other activities of comprehensive international institutions

The attempts to ensure the maintenance of international peace and security through suitable institutional means is best explained by a comparison with the maintenance of peace in a domestic society. In 1918, when the Covenant of the League was written, international society was still in an anarchic condition. Traditionally, when negotiations and other methods for settling differences failed, states resorted to force and, in turn, could be restrained only by force or its threat. While in domestic societies the widespread use of violence was prevented by a degree of social consensus on the vesting of the monopoly of force in a central authority and by the establishment of such an authority, only very radical thinkers could believe that these were feasible, at least within the foreseeable future, in international society. The institutional devices did not go quite so far but constituted an attempt to adapt some domestic institutions serving the maintenance of peace to the looser structure of international society.

One group of these institutional devices dealt with force. Its use by individual states was strongly circumscribed, or even prohibited; plans for collective security envisaged internationally administered sanctions against a peace-breaker; proposals for disarmament aimed at eliminating the danger of armaments races and the temptation to resort to war because armaments were abundant. Another group of devices imitated the domestic machinery for negotiations and adjudication of disputes, including the courts of law, and tried also to find some method for making peaceful changes in legal relations to correspond with social changes. Finally, since satisfied states are more likely to remain peaceful than dissatisfied ones, various welfare measures, generally desirable for their own sake too, had the primary aim of preserving peace.

The League of Nations Covenant circumscribed the legality of war. Members were allowed to resort to it only after certain prescribed procedures and 'cooling off' periods had been adhered to. Moreover, the members expressly undertook to preserve each other's territorial integrity and political independence against external aggression (Art. 10). In the twenties, many international efforts went into 'closing the gaps' in the Covenant and outlawing war altogether. This was ostensibly achieved by the Briand-Kellogg Pact in 1928, which was signed by all states, with only insignificant exceptions. The signatories renounced war as an instrument of national policy and undertook not to seek the solution or settlement of disputes of whatever nature or origin by other than peaceful means. Although at the time this was not generally realized, war nevertheless remained lawful in at least five instances, notably in self-defence. The Charter of the United Nations, the signatories to which undertook to refrain from the use and threat of force in their international relations, explicitly authorized self-defence (Art. 2, para. 4, and Art. 51).

States could scarcely be expected to rely upon agreements alone, and the Covenant of the League therefore provided for collective sanctions against a convenant-breaker (Art. 16). There were to be diplomatic and economic sanctions which would be applied by the individual members automatically, simultaneously, and comprehensively, and optional military sanctions to be applied at the recommendation of the Council. The United Nations Charter introduced centralized sanctions and did not differentiate between the non-military and the military ones. All sanctions were to be applied on the binding orders of the Security Council, which was to have at its disposal a collective security force. Finally, both World Wars ended in the disarmament of the defeated aggressors; while the Covenant provided also for a general disarmament or limitation of armaments, the Charter, having proposed a collective security force, limited itself to a provision for their regulation.

In the light of the historical record, all these attempts to circumscribe the use of force in international relations have been unsuccessful. Plans have not materialized, agreements are hedged with escape clauses or interpreted so narrowly that they become meaningless, force has been used in many minor conflicts and also on the largest scale in history in the Second World War.

The activities of international institutions in this field have largely amounted to statements of goals and aspirations. They are not, however, totally devoid of practical effect. Even the most limited form of UN intervention, such as inscribing an issue on an agenda and passing resolutions, is an influence, though admittedly not an imperative one, which is taken into account by states contemplating the use of force. The United Nations has been unable to stop some outbreaks of violence but it can sometimes effectively confine them and facilitate their termination.

A UN 'presence' is now an important international factor in many minor conflicts which do not directly affect one of the superpowers. Sometimes a group of impartial observers is employed, such as the UN Commission on India and Pakistan; sometimes a body of trained military personnel is used for supervision, signally in Palestine (UN Truce Supervision Organization); finally, there can be a military peace-keeping force. The first force of that type (UN Emergency Force) was used in the Suez zone to supervise the cease-fire and the withdrawal of the attacking forces. It was a brilliant improvisation due largely to the drive of Dag Hammarskjöld who recruited it among the few neutral states who made contingents available. Another, even larger force was used for various tasks in the Congo, including the politically explosive one of preserving the unity of the state. This force was involved in actual fighting and acquitted itself well. UN intervention forces are difficult to organize. They have to be recruited from states acceptable to the host country and they are not assured of finance. For a while the very survival of the United Nations was threatened because of the debts accumulated for the maintenance of the forces in the Middle East and in the Congo, to which the Soviet Union, France, and some other states refused to contribute. Even so, a small UN force facilitated the transition from Dutch to Indonesian rule in West Irian (New Guinea) in 1963, another small force was sent to Yemen in 1964, a larger one to Cyprus, and in 1978 one to the Lebanon.

In the field of pacific settlement of disputes, international institutions have not only added conciliation by their organs and judicial settlement by the World Court to the previously existing procedures, they have also prodded and encouraged states to resort to pacific settlement instead of fighting. The achievement is, however, largely procedural. Many procedures exist, but resort to them does not ensure that settlement will be achieved. The standards by which international disputes are solved remain vague. The maintenance of peace without qualifications can easily lead to appeasement, to the satisfaction of aggressively-minded states at the cost of the weaker ones. 'Justice' is mentioned several times in the Charter but is insufficiently articulated to provide a practical criterion.

The trouble is that most disputes are not legal, not about the respective rights and duties of the parties, but political, aiming at the alteration of such rights and duties. Both the League and the United Nations were established in the aftermath of World Wars primarily to maintain the status quo, the settlements arising from these wars. Both had only extremely vague provisions for procedures to be employed in revision of treaties and in peaceful change. The main 'peaceful change' (meaning one not involving a major war) in the inter-war period was the revision of the Peace Treaty of Versailles, which took place outside the League. By contrast, the United Nations has partaken in much of the change since 1945, notably in accelerating progress towards colonial emancipation. Pressure from the United Nations has occasionally been instrumental in forcing colonial states to abandon their legal rights and to agree to change; needless to say, however, the influence of international organizations both in the processes of conciliation and of peaceful change depends, to a very large extent, on the power of the parties—by and large the superpowers are very much harder to persuade than smaller powers. No states readily yield on really vital interests, for instance South Africa on apartheid.

The preamble of the Charter states the determination of its members to 'promote social progress and better standards of life in larger freedom' and for this end to 'employ international machinery for the promotion of economic and social advancement of all people'. This so-called 'functional co-operation' includes three distinct objectives. First of all, international co-operation in technical matters—which was already being dealt with by international bureaux in the previous century—has been maintained and extended to other fields, for instance, civil aviation and peaceful uses of atomic energy. Second, as a reaction against the excesses of totalitarianism and the sufferings caused by the Second World War, humanitarian influences have found expression in attempts to secure internationally the observance of human rights and the achievement of higher standards of social welfare. Third, since legitimate grievances could cause wars, economic and social progress could provide an additional way of preventing them.

From each of these three angles the record of international functional co-operation looks different. Technical co-operation has advanced further, for example in economic or cultural matters, or regarding outer space, but scarcely in accordance with the growing needs of international interaction; where power considerations and selfish national interests are affected, progress has been painfully slow. The humanitarian influence has undoubtedly been established as part of international life. The very acceptance of the fact that the human rights of anybody, anywhere, are an international concern, and that the whole of international society is, at least to some vague extent, responsible for the economic and social welfare and progress of all its members, constitutes an important departure from the pre-war state of affairs.

Somewhat dubious is the assumption that the elimination of economic and social grievances is likely to help in the prevention of war. It would be more convincing if conceivably such grievances could be fully eliminated. In fact, they can only be alleviated. There is no need for cynicism, for the humanitarian justification of international activities in this field is in itself sufficient, but it is rather illogical to assume that the hungry who are given half a loaf will become more peaceful. On the contrary, not being fully preoccupied with their struggle for existence and having more energy, they may become even more turbulent.

With its nearly universal membership, the United Nations is a meeting place of the states of the world and a symbol of world unity. The representatives of all states are forcibly reminded of the fact that their foreign policies and, increasingly, also their domestic affairs cannot be conducted exclusively in pursuit of selfish national aims. If the interests and feelings of other nations are affected, the issue comes under the discussion and scrutiny of the General Assembly. Every one of its members still pursues primarily an individual national interest, but the Assembly forces them to take other members into account as well. Many disputes and situations lose much of their potential danger when they receive publicity at an early stage, even though others thus become exacerbated.

When the General Assembly listens uneasily to acrimonious speeches and grapples with its overloaded agenda, maybe it is reflecting a laborious but steady progress towards an international order which is gradually emerging from the countless permutations of the national interests voiced.

Non-global intergovernmental organizations

Much of the greatly increased post-war interaction has not been taking place at the global level but within a narrower scope, be it geographical regions or functional co-operation embracing only the states directly involved. To some extent these two bases have now fused and there is no marked difference between regional and functional organizations; indeed, the majority of regional organizations concentrate upon a specific function. If institutionalization can be regarded as a rough index of the intensity of interaction, a steadily increasing amount of international interaction is taking place not at the global level; the non-global institutions established after 1945 outnumber global ones. The distinguishing characteristic of these non-global, especially regional, organizations is that they tend to conduct their policies separately from the mainstream of global politics, although the latter occasionally intrude. The United Nations does not obstruct these trends towards regionalization; on the contrary, General Assembly sessions provide an additional opportunity for interaction and for countries to vote together, whether to take a common stand on issues of common concern or to choose regional representatives.

A few relevant criteria for the evaluation of the role of a non-global intergovernmental organization in world politics can be found in the importance of its scope and domain and in the adequacy of its decision-making. The impact of the geographical scope is simple—an organization embracing nearly a whole continent is *prima facie* more important than one limited to a subregion: this is the relationship between the European Community and Benelux, or the OAS and organizations in Central America, or the OAU and institutions in East or West Africa. The importance of the functional domain and of the weight of the organization within it is also clear. The European Community is primarily engaged in world trade and is the largest world trader. OPEC is concerned with oil production and distribution and includes the majority of oil exporters. NATO and the Warsaw Pact are concerned with the major area of confrontation between East and West.

One has to consider also the capacity to act, which is largely the function of the decision-making processes. In the past, much used to be made of the constitution of each organization, whether it assumed a 'supranational' character—that is, was capable of making decisions binding on the members—or remained dependent upon the consent of all members. The evolution of the European Community since the so-called 'Luxembourg Compromise' has demonstrated the limitations of this distinction. Although constitutionally a majority vote is possible on some issues, a member can block the process whenever it deems that a vital national interest is at stake. The constitution apart, two other variables are also important: the size and efficiency of the secretariat, and the cohesion of the members and the degree to which they share basic attitudes on the issues within the ambit of the organization. For instance, OPEC's significance, great as it is owing to its domain, is diminished by the deep divisions between the moderate and the radical and between the Arab and non-Arab members; whereas the Warsaw Pact is dominated by the Soviet Union, NATO allows a great degree of freedom of national behaviour which results in the absence of any significant standardization of arms and allows violent disputes between members to erupt.

Finally, one has to consider the dynamics of the organizations. once functioning, they not only stabilize and often increase interaction within their scope but they also offer an established channel for additional interaction for which need may arise. This may take the form of the broadening of the geographical scope of the organization—for instance the CMEA has included non-European members, and Japan is a member of the OECD, which was originally limited to the Atlantic area. The extension can also be functional. NATO, for instance, being concerned with the Soviet military threat, has also logically become the channel for the co-ordination of the members' general policies towards the Soviet Union. Perhaps most spectacular has been the functional extension of the European Community to co-ordinate the foreign policies of the members, although these do not fall within its competence. This was at first limited to informal periodical meetings of all the EEC ambassadors in each capital and then extended to periodical meetings of the heads of the official machines of their foreign ministries. Although no decision-making is involved, exchange of information and views at the formative stage of policies constitutes an important step towards co-ordination, and may well eventually lead to a degree of political unity.

11

The problems of today and tomorrow

The new stakes of conflict

In order to facilitate comparisons, the post-war international system has already been surveyed in terms of the 'stakes of conflict', the expression being used in a manner identical to that in the discussion of the preceding systems. This brief outline will now be supplemented by a discussion of the features distinguishing the contemporary system from its predecessors. What follows is a rather subjective assessment of the problems which appear to be of the greatest moment today and are likely to affect the future. Most of them have already been touched upon from different angles; their full evaluation will, of necessity, have to await a historical perspective.

First of all, the post-war international system is characterized by a greatly increased *complexity* which is manifested in many ways. The actors have multiplied and become heterogeneous in many essential respects: it is hard enough to conceptualize and understand the interaction among the more than 160 states now in existence, let alone all the new non-state actors, the exact roles of which are by no means clear. There is, moreover, a similar increase in the lines of conflict—the power-political/ideological East–West conflict has developed partly separately from and partly in interaction with the North–South conflict, while the issues of conflicts over economic issues and resources sometimes constitute a separate domain and sometimes interact with either line or with both.

Second, it is important to note the greatly increased *intensity* of interaction. Against the background of a rapidly developing technology, especially of transport, communications, and warfare, interaction across national boundaries has been growing with tremendous speed although this has been matched, and, in the case of the largest states, possibly even surpassed by a similar increase in domestic interaction. In absolute terms, however, international transactions have increased by a very large factor, according to any significant yardstick available: international trade, travel, diplomatic relations, etc.

Third, ours has been a period of very extensive and also very rapid change. There has been change in the nature of the major issues: the cold war turned into a *détente* which later petered out; the North–South conflict, which started over the issue of anti-colonialism, and still continues over South Africa, has largely shifted to problems of economic growth; there has been change in the salience of issue-areas—the gravest international conflicts have extended from security to economics, resources, and ecopolitics; the major danger spots have gradually shifted from Europe to the Middle East and Africa; there has been a change in the power and status of states—after a long period of prostration China has become a great power, following the Communist victory in 1949, and Japan and the Federal Republic of Germany have made a spectacular economic advance. Following the rise in the price of oil in 1973, Saudi Arabia acquired for a while much larger liquid financial resources than those of any other state, only to be suddenly depleted by the eighties; by 1986 the United States, the country predominant in 1945, had become the world's largest debtor with an apparently incurable trade deficit while, despite her large oil income, Britain's economy had slipped well behind that of her rivals.

Closely connected is the fourth characteristic, the tendency for all the issues to grow in magnitude, or, as it is sometimes rather loosely put, 'exponentially'. The rise of the population of the earth from around 2,500 million in 1950 to 5,000 million in the mid-eighties; the growing consumption of oil; the increase in world expenditure on armaments to almost $1 trillion; and the calculation of the casualties likely in a nuclear war in terms of many millions of deaths—all testify to this tendency.

Fifth, the linkage between domestic and international affairs has greatly grown in both directions. On the one hand, rapidly growing domestic needs and demands have become increasingly dependent upon international politics; on the other, international politics has become increasingly affected by domestic conflicts. The process can be conceptualized as diffusion, spill-over, or esclation; it is particularly well illustrated by the great growth of terrorism from the sixties onwards.

Finally, the instruments and agencies of international order have not been able to keep pace with the changes. As this point is by no means self-explanatory, it requires some elaboration.

The two superpowers have been performing the traditional great power role of keeping a degree of strategic equilibrium within the international system, but increasingly less effectively. This can be partly attributed to the growing difficulty of the task and partly to the increasing inadequacy of their resources and the ineffectiveness of their foreign policies. When they had gained a degree of experience in dealing with each other, both super-powers underwent severe setbacks in their domestic affairs and in the leadership of their respective blocs.

The phenomenon had several roots, similar in both countries. To start with, there was the economic strain. With great effort the Russians successfully rehabilitated their war-shattered economy and developed nuclear weapons and space technology. By the mid-eighties, however, their economic growth was grinding to a halt; they were unable to keep up with the American information technology or the SDI; their collectivized agriculture remained hopelessly inefficient and the prospects of the Gorbachev attempts at a drastic reform of the economic system were uncertain. The Americans were facing an apparently incurable problem of colossal budgetary and balance of payments deficits. Both countries suffered technological disasters in 1986: the Russians with the nuclear power station at Chernobyl which jeopardized their whole energy policy, the Americans with their space shuttle *Challenger* which set back their space programme. Both underwent a crisis of faith, not only in their technological prowess but an ideological one too. The Americans were slowly recovering from their setback in Vietnam, the subsequent Watergate scandal, and the Iranian hostages crisis when, at the end of 1986, they were faced with a new scandal over President Reagan's clandestine sale of arms to Iran. In 1979 the Russians became involved in the debilitating intervention in Afghanistan from which they started to extricate themselves only in the late eighties, when they became involved in an urgently needed fundamental reform of the economic and social system, strenuously resisted by some conservatives.

The capacity of the superpowers has been affected not only by the weakening of their domestic bases but also by external changes. Soviet leadership of the world Communist movement was successfully challenged in turn by the Yugoslavs, the Chinese, and the Western European Communist parties; dissent had to be forcibly suppressed even within the Communist bloc in Hungary, Czechoslovakia, and Poland. In the Third World, the socialist model for development has become increasingly less attractive and the Afghanistan intervention unpopular.

Likewise the American leadership of the 'free world' has been weakened. Parallel with the loss of economic preponderance due to the rapid economic growth of Western European and Japanese economies, the United States also lost much of its political influence as not only neutrals but also allies began to assert their differences. Notably criticism abounded of the American involvement with the 'Contras', the ineffective opposition in socialist Nicaragua, and of American attitudes to arms control.

Simultaneously international arrangements have been negotiated and international institutions established to cope with a variety of the new tasks, often with great ingenuity but, on the whole, with success limited to technical matters. Certainly the United Nations has not fulfilled the early expectations of its enthusiasts and has proved incapable either of resolving acute international conflicts or of co-ordinating a fully-fledged international co-operation.

There is no simple way of bringing all these characteristics of the contemporary international system into a comprehensive framework of analysis. This is best demonstrated by the fact that a different periodization is required by each angle from which one undertakes the analysis. From the systemic point of view, the differing stability of the security and the economic systems seems to indicate opposed trends: after a period of acute cold war, relative stability in the former; after a period of sustained economic growth, a definite slowing down in the latter, with the dangers of stagnation and even collapse from the late seventies. The picture looks quite different from other points of view. Thus in the Atlantic bloc, both in the area of security and in that of economics, periodization would be most convincingly based upon the vigorous exercise of American leadership in the early post-war period and its weakening in the sixties and seventies. From national points of view, however, the crucial events for each nation are different: Vietnam for the Americans; Suez for the British; the Cuban missile crisis, Afghanistan, and Chernobyl for the Russians; also the change of leadership in countries which have no adequate constitutional provisions for the purpose—the death of Stalin, Mao, and Tito in Communist states; the death or removal of the first leader or generation of leaders in new states.

Capacity for problem-solving

Another even more fundamental effect of the confusion in the contemporary international system is the mixture of elements conducive both to its stability and its disruption. This is best demonstrated by a few concrete examples. The so-called cold war has undoubtedly been the central issue of post-war international politics, leading both to pessimistic forecasts of an inevitable armed clash between the two titans which would engulf mankind in a real catastrophe, and to optimistic ideas about the possibility of accommodation. As decades pass, neither estimate has proved right. On the one hand, despite several 'eyeball-to-eyeball' confrontations, notably during the Cuban missile crisis in 1962, the two superpowers have gradually engaged in a slow but distinct *détente*. On the other, the basic hostility and difficulty of accommodation have remained strongly in evidence.

If one recognizes both the power-political and the ideological roots of this central conflict, it seems inevitable that the two dominant powers should engage in military and political competition, but the tendency towards rigid bipolarity in the immediate post-war decade has been replaced by a tendency towards polycentrism. Likewise the clash between the commanding collectivist ideology of the Soviet Union and the individualist one of the United States exacerbates the antagonism, but the edges of both ideologies have now become somewhat blurred. The fundamental differences between them are apparently narrowing; perhaps it is significant that both are the offspring of the ideas of the Enlightenment about social progress based upon rationalism. The Americans, despite their fears of 'creeping socialism', have introduced a range of collectivist arrangements for social welfare while, from the seventies, the Soviet rulers have come under increasing domestic pressures for improved economic performance as well as for greater individual freedom and protection of human rights. Finally, centrally important common interests have emerged: both the Russians and the Americans have firmly recognized that they should avoid a nuclear war, and the Chernobyl disaster has made nuclear co-operation desirable; although reluctantly, as developed industrialized countries they have occasionally come close to a common stand on North–South issues; they have also engaged in slightly increased trade exchanges—to allow the Russians a much-needed access to Western technology and to give the West equally much-needed additional markets.

The nature of Soviet–American relations is most clearly revealed in the field of armaments. Once the Russians had achieved a 'second-strike capability', meaning a nuclear force capable of surviving an American nuclear attack and striking back, a basic stability was reached, despite the uncertainties engendered by waves of technological innovation. The relationship is, however, infinitely more complex than the balance of power in the nineteenth century. This is manifested by the great variety of levels at which the issue of arms control and disarmament is dealt with: though the bilateral SALT and Strategic Arms Reduction Talks (START) were the most important, NATO–Warsaw Pact Mutual Balanced Force Reduction talks and global UN disarmament talks have taken place simultaneously, and occasional international conferences. There has been some ostensible technical progress towards a degree of containment of armaments—the prickly question of inspection, for example, which involves accepting a crucial breach in the prerogatives of sovereignty, has been partly resolved by the increasingly effective surveillance from satellites; the testing of nuclear weapons has also been greatly circumscribed through a series of treaties. The negotiations at the various levels have not, however, been co-ordinated and there is a strong element of unreality in all of them: often quite unrealistic aspirations continue to be professed; sales and grants of ever more sophisticated weapons to a growing number of states are becoming an increasingly disruptive element in regional arms balances; China and quite a few other potential and possibly actual possessors of nuclear weapons are refusing to become bound by the nuclear agreements; potentially equally lethal biological and chemical weapons, though proscribed, are being developed; perhaps most importantly, during the seventies and eighties the pace and scope of technological change made questionable the use of any agreements whatsoever. In 1987, after a year in power, the new Soviet leader, Gorbachev, engaged on what appeared to be a serious attempt at a fundamental reform of the domestic system, which would make it more acceptable to the West, as well as of foreign policy. Under the weakening leadership of its ageing president, Reagan, the United States was incapable of responding.

Outside the central superpower relationship, intractable conflicts of the traditional type, over territory and political independence, continue to abound. The most prominent among these has been the Arab–Israeli conflict, which led to four major Middle Eastern wars in 1947, 1956, 1967, and 1973. The fundamental nature of this conflict has remained identical but the identity of the actors has been constantly changing, fluctuating between a largely regional context and a global one. The protagonists were at first Israel and the Arab 'confrontation states'; the PLO then became an important actor, but it was considerably weakened in the late seventies owing to inner splits and was temporarily deprived of its base in the Lebanon by the Israeli invasion in 1982; first the British and the French, then the Russians and finally the Americans became involved; the United Nations have played an intermittent part.

An incredible variety of diplomatic procedures have been employed, many of them under the auspices of the United Nations: armistice commissions, 'proximity talks' between the Arabs and the Israelis—as the former generally refuse to deal with the latter directly—UN resolutions, missions by UN special representatives, the round-table Geneva Conference. There have also been high-level bilateral meetings, first in secret, and then, since President Sadat's visit to Israel in 1977, official and public; there have been, finally, repeated American initiatives, notably a long period of 'shuttle diplomacy' under Dr Kissinger, and, in 1978, a trilateral summit meeting between the leaders of Israel and Egypt and the US President, at the latter's invitation. The basic conflict between Israel and the Arabs boils down to the traditional issues of security and territory; despite all the regional and international efforts it seems impossible to find terms for a concrete arrangement to produce a mutually acceptable compromise between Israel's demands for security and Arab demands for the return of territories occupied by Israel in 1967. The richness of diplomatic inventiveness has not prevented recurrent outbreaks of violence nor the possibility of its escalation to a global level, though it did lead to the Egypt–Israel peace treaty of March 1979.

Equally futile have been the international attempts to deal with the problems of terrorism: bomb outrages, the hijacking of planes, the taking of hostages. The terrorists have been successful partly owing to the ready assistance from sympathetic states, especially Libya, Syria, and Iran, and partly owing to the legitimacy enjoyed by some of the 'liberation movements'. Despite many declarations and several agreements, concerted international action has proved difficult; in violation of their professed policies, governments have occasionally agreed to negotiate and offer concessions to terrorists holding their nationals as hostages.

Drug traffic has also created a need for concerted international action. Drug-taking, which has become a scourge of all industrialized societies, furnishes colossal illegal, and hence untaxed, incomes for those involved in the trade. Much international as well as national activity takes place to prevent the production, manufacture, transport, and distribution of drugs and the 'laundering' of the proceeds. The interests involved are, however, powerful and well organized to the point of being able to corrupt governmental agencies, especially in the poor countries where cultivation takes place.

As in the field of security, the variety of agencies and instruments devised to cope with economic issues is enormous. The most important of these are the Organization of Economic Cooperation and Development, a loose umbrella organization of the whole Western world, and the European Community, the more tightly binding regional organization of Western Europe. National sovereignty does not obstruct a degree of international management in the field of economics as starkly as in the field of security; indeed, the international economic system has weathered several severe crises. Notably, through establishing special oil credit facilities, the IMF maintained a degree of stability in the international monetary system after the global balances of payments had been drastically and fundamentally disturbed by the quadrupling of the price of oil in 1973. In the late seventies, it became an important international agent in curbing inflation by making the large credit facilities required from it by many members conditional upon anti-inflationary governmental policies. Perhaps even more significant was the relatively limited turn away from the principle of a free international trade by states threatened by large trade deficits—the recession in international trade did not, therefore, result in a return to the disastrous protectionism and trade wars of the thirties. Characteristically, in the late seventies, the loose management of international economics became somewhat institutionalized by the periodic summit meetings of the leaders of the major industrialized powers, the Group of Five, an institution basically similar to the Concert of Europe in the nineteenth century.

The North–South conflict has both a political and an economic dimension. Decolonization, which constituted the main political demand, has been highly successful: by the late eighties nearly all entities demanding independence had achieved sovereign statehood. The non-alignment movement has, however, been much less successful: the emancipated states could not prevail with their desire to be treated primarily in their own right and not as a playground for Soviet–American rivalries—partly because their aspirations at national integration and economic development have proved to be generally unattainable.

The economic demands of the Third World countries

crystallized in the shape of pressures for a New International Economic Order in which they would secure better conditions for development, especially through improved terms of trade and substantial aid. The industrialized countries reluctantly accepted the principle. They gave aid, though much less than demanded, and made limited trade arrangements, to the extent of allowing developing states a somewhat privileged position under the terms of the GATT and also under successive agreements concluded by the European Community with selected developing countries. In the seventies the situation became further complicated by the world recession, which resulted in drastic falls in commodity prices, and by the predicament of the poorest nations faced with swollen oil bills; the latter problem was largely met by grants from the members of OPEC. The Group of 77 organizing the less developed states, which has now risen to over a hundred, has not, however, reached the previous cohesion of the Third World over anti-colonialism. This is understandable in the light of the increasing economic disparities between the incomes of the oil exporters, who have remained members, although they have become the richest nations on earth as the result of their oil earnings, and the consistent poverty of others. Moreover, it is becoming increasingly clear that effective relief of poverty cannot be achieved by international action alone because it requires a rational restructuring of the economies and hence also the societies of the Third World. Effective action in this direction is not within the power of the industrialized countries and they are politically inhibited even in making demands for it as a condition for further concessions. Finally, by the seventies, both the Western and the Communist models of economic development had become tarnished by the adverse experiences of both systems and the international trade and finance systems had slid into a chronic crisis.

The rapid growth of population and of world economies since the Second World War raises the spectre of several possible dangers to the future of mankind, which were widely publicized by the influential volume *Limits to Economic Growth*, produced by the Club of Rome, and by numerous subsequent analyses. Although the recession of the seventies has slowed down the hitherto incessantly growing demands for food and raw materials, especially oil, the question remains insoluble as to how the demands of the Third World states, following the same path of industrialization as the Europeans, can possibly be met, especially when, after Mao's death, the rulers of China decided to turn to the West for help with modernization and industrialization. Pollution dangers remain potent, as shown in 1986 by the disastrous breakdowns of the Soviet nuclear power station at Chernobyl, with a fall-out throughout much of Europe, and of the Swiss chemical plant which polluted the Rhine. Preservation of health is likewise facing severe problems, notably the inexorable spread of the virus-induced epidemic of AIDS and the conceivably losing fights against the world-wide staphylococcus infection of hospitals and the rat infestation of large cities.

It is important, however, to stress also the other side of the picture. Internationally concerted action has only occasionally been attempted, generally by the United Nations, and often has not gone beyond exchanges of views and sometimes statements of principles. Nevertheless, the ecological disasters prophesied have not taken place, mainly as a result of the operation of market forces, some relatively uncoordinated national activities, and the diffusion of ideas and technology. Thus, despite low standards of nutrition and occasional famines, a near-balance between population and food has been achieved, partly as a result of a slowing down of population increases due to urban pressures, partly as a result of deliberate governmental policies, the development of high-yield hybrid grains, and a greater use of artifical fertilizers and irrigation. The rapidly growing energy demands have been satisfied by oil, which has largely replaced coal; when oil shortage was looming in the seventies, many additional sources of oil supply were found and exploited, most spectacularly from the sea-bed; even when Middle Eastern oil supplies were temporarily disrupted during the Yom Kippur War in 1973, distribution was efficiently continued by the major oil companies. Awareness of the dangers of pollution has spread so widely, particularly during the seventies, that pressure of public opinion has halted and partly reversed its increase in the industrialized countries. Thus, despite our inability to secure concerted international action and our lateness in responding to problems, mankind has so far weathered the ecological and resources crises and near-crises much better than could reasonably have been expected.

Prospects

The few examples of current international problems hitherto discussed are scarcely adequate to give a full idea of the complexity of the contemporary international system. They do, nevertheless, allow us to make an informed guess about the possible direction in which this system might evolve towards the end of the twentieth century.

This book started with a working hypothesis that mankind is loosely organized into an international society of sovereign states which rely mainly, although not exclusively, on power in their mutual relations. These states are represented by individuals holding certain official positions who determine state policies under the complex, often conflicting influences and pressures from their domestic and international environments. Inevitably, international society is subject to repeated crises and to the recurrent danger of war; it cannot effectively cope with a growing number of political, economic, and ecological problems, although lately co-operation among states in all these fields has been growing.

We are undoubtedly faced with a major crisis of the territorial sovereign state in its traditional form. No state is any longer self-sufficient or safe within its boundaries, not even the superpowers, let alone the new mini-states; all are facing a diminution of their sovereignty. Nevertheless, it is hard to see how the present division of mankind into states could lose its importance in the foreseeable future. This supposition readily leads to one possible future—an international system continuing much as it is now, but with states probably somewhat readier to co-ordinate their activities at the cost of further inroads into their sovereignty, and new non-state actors and transnational activities further supplementing their activities. Envisaging such a future is, however, no more than a simplistic, and naïve, projection into the future of the trends of the present and the immediate past.

Legitimate doubts about the validity of this forecast can be raised on the basis both of the seriousness of the individual problems with which the system will have to cope and the cumulative effect of the number and intensity of these problems.

The only rational model for the future would be one of some form of world government. Without it no satisfactory solution to the core-problems of our times can be envisaged—whether ensuring the prevention of a major war or some form of world-wide economic growth with a degree of redistribution and without disastrous ecological side-effects—because all of these require political decisions not limited to individual nations but within the global or, at the very least, some broad regional context. Although this is acknowledged not only by theoreticians but also quite frequently and openly by statesmen, advance from our plural system to a unitary one seems not only to be politically impossible but, on reflection, also undesirable. Even within individual states unification for basic political purposes has been achieved at the cost of overriding the interests and aspirations of some of the various subgroups and minorities. Pressures for supranational solution of broader than national problems are nowadays matched by pressure for subnational solution of problems peculiar to national subgroups. A wholesale or even a substantial partial transfer of powers to a supranational authority could further aggravate the existing subnational conflicts and would add to them a new and even more important layer of national ones.

There is, however, a third future international order possible which would combine some features of the two already discussed and could therefore be both more feasible and more effective than either. For lack of a better term we could call it one of 'mixed management'. On the one hand, it would be firmly based upon the present pluralist system of mixed actors, with states being most prominent among them; on the other, it would introduce an element of rational planning for international order, both at the global and at regional levels. It is possible to interpret the present situation as being the initial stage of such a system. States still occupy a central position as the sovereign entities with the ultimate power of political decision, but are rapidly adjusting their authority in two directions: delegating it both to some broader bodies—global and regional—to deal with problems with which the state on its own is helpless, and downwards, where minorities feel dissatisfied and press for devolution. In order to avoid arid debates over sovereignty and its clashes, it may be useful to think about such a system in terms of functional needs and of what may be termed delegation sideways, not through accepting supra- or transnational authority but through depoliticizing some politically less sensitive activities and having them run by international or transnational organizations; the Universal Postal Union provides a good example. Similarly intractable *national conflicts* like the one between the Arabs and the Israelis or even the Americans and the Russians may become at least partially transformed into *international problems* which, although remaining difficult, offer somewhat more scope for rational solution.

There is general agreement about a desirable broad direction—that international order should ensure freedom from a major war, economic growth without disastrous ecological effects, and some minimum human rights. There is, however, basic disagreement about the appropriate means for securing these major objectives, as expressed in the varying lines of contemporary conflicts. It would be unrealistic, therefore, to expect that any rationally designed major international policies would command general acceptance. In the light of the post-war experience it seems, nevertheless, quite realistic to expect that actual or anticipated severe crises in specific fields and on specific issues may lead to global or regional action and ultimately institutionalization. If the experience of the European Community can serve as a guide, in the longer run it seems likely that the states will delegate some of their authority upwards, although this is likely to take place in an erratic fashion and not according to a blueprint, and also to be obstructed by reassertions of national sovereignty.

It is relatively easy to classify factors which will determine the future shape of the international system—they fall into the categories of functional needs, political will, and a residual group of random though often important elements—but it seems impossible to evaluate with any degree of certainty how these elements will shape and interact. One possible line of development is a substantial increase in the hitherto limited impact of movements directed towards a world order: the pacifists; the 'Greens' concerned with ecology, especially nuclear pollution; organizations concerned with human rights; last but not least, the various theoreticians who advocate a complete change of perspective in our thinking about international relations, taking us right away from the focus of state-centred power politics towards some form of world order. The theoreticians include not only Utopian idealists but also thinkers with extensive high-level military or political experience who have in the course of their work become pessimistic about the present and the future unless some fundamental change takes place. Although it is hard to deny that some of these alternative approaches exhibit elements of common sense and even wisdom, they tend, at least by implication, to be normative. Inevitably, 'world order' is an ideologically laden notion and agreement on its pursuit inevitably brings us back to the clash of ideologies attempting to define its moral basis and thus, ultimately, to the conflict between the superpowers. What is often passed off as an ecumenical movement above all ideologies merely skips over the underlying basic disagreements.

At the same time, one should remember that persevering with the conventional power-political approach is likewise, by implication, normative: it assumes the basic continuation of the status quo. To avoid the obvious dangers of closing one's mind to the necessity of adaptation and change, it is essential to maintain as open-ended an approach as possible; to prevent a tyranny of the present, one needs both to study its historical origins and to probe into the possibilities for the future, often supplementing the analysis with some alternative approach.

In sum, it is hard to accept the idea that the conventional power-political model merely represents the past, the remnants of which linger in the present, whereas the alternative approaches represent the future. We cannot foresee how much of these new perspectives will materialize, although it would be foolish to deny that some of them are already making an impact on the operation of the international system; it is possible that this impact may greatly increase, although, as has been argued, scarcely leading to an international government. Consequently only a vague and impressionistic prediction is possible about the shape of things to come at the end of the century: it seems likely that the international system will remain pluralistic and untidy, with states continuing to play a leading though probably increasingly more circumscribed role.

Notes

Chapter 1: Thinking about international relations

1. Cf. J.Frankel, *International Politics: Conflict and Harmony*, Penguin, 1969.

Chapter 2: States 1

1. Sir Halford Mackinder, *Democratic Ideals and Reality*, London, 1909.
2. K.Wittfogel, *Oriental Despotism: a Comparative Study of Totalitarian Power*, Yale University Press, 1957.
3. Hedley Bull and Alan Watson (eds.), *The Expansion of International Society*, Oxford, Clarendon Press, 1984.
4. L.Oppenheim, *International Law*, Vol. 1, 8th edition, 1957.

Chapter 4: Non-state actors

1. John Herz, *International Politics in the Nuclear Age*, Columbia University Press, 1959.

Chapter 5: The making of foreign policy

1. This chapter condenses part of the contents of *The Making of Foreign Policy* (Oxford Unversity Press, 1963, 1967) and *National Interest* (Macmillan, 1970) by the author.

Chapter 6: Interaction among states and state power

1. Cf. J. Frankel, *International Politics: Conflict and Harmony*, Penguin, 1969.
2. Thomas C. Schelling, *The Strategy of Conflict*, Oxford University Press, 1963.
3. H. and M. Sprout, *The Foundations of International Politics*, 1962.

Chapter 8: The international system

1. Cf. E.H. Carr, *The Twenty Years' Crisis, 1919–1939*, 2nd ed., Macmillan, 1946.

Chapter 9: Instruments and agencies of international society

1. Georg Schwarzenberger, *Power Politics*, 3rd edition, Stevens & Sons, London, 1964.

Further reading

Aron, R., *Peace and War*, Weidenfeld and Nicolson, 1966.

Bull, H., *The Anarchical Society*, Macmillan, 1977.

Carr, E.H., *The Twenty Years' Crisis, 1919–1939*, 2nd edition, Macmillan, 1946.

Claude, I.L. Jr., *Swords into Plowshares*, 3rd edition, University of London Press, 1964.

Clausewitz, K.V., *On War*, Princeton University Press, 1976.

Dougherty, J.E., and Pfalzgraff, R.L. Jr., *Contending Theories of International Relations: a Comprehensive Survey*, Harper and Row, 1981.

Frankel, J., *The Making of Foreign Policy*, Oxford University Press, 1963, 1967.

—— *International Politics: Conflict and Harmony*, Penguin, 1969.

—— *National Interest*, Macmillan, 1970.

—— *Contemporary International Theory and the Behaviour of States*, Oxford University Press, 1973.

Gilpin, R., *War and Change in International Politics*, Cambridge University Press, 1984.

Henkin, L., *How Nations Behave: Law and Foreign Policy*, Pall Mall, 1968.

Herz, J., *International Politics in the Nuclear Age*, Columbia University Press, 1959.

Holsti, K.J., *International Politics*, 4th edition, Prentice-Hall, 1983.

Kaplan, M.A., *System and Process in International Relations*, Wiley, 1957.

Kant, E., 'An Essay on Perpetual Peace', in *Political Writings*.

Keohane, R., and Nye, J., *Power and Interdependence: World Politics in Transition*, Little Brown, 1977.

Keylor, W.R., *The Twentieth Century World: an International History*, Oxford University Press, 1984.

Machiavelli, N., *The Prince*.

Morgenthau, H., *Politics Among Nations; the Struggle for Power and Peace*, 7th edition, A. Knopf, 1985.

Olson, William C. (ed.), *The Theory and Practice of International Relations*, 7th edition, Prentice-Hall, 1987.

Snyder, R.C., *et al.*, *Foreign Policy Decision Making*, New York, 1962.

Spero, J.E., *The Politics of International Economic Relations*, 3rd edition, Allen and Unwin, 1987.

Thucydides, *History of the Peloponnesian War*.

Vasquez, J.A., *The Power of Power Politics*, Frances Pinter, 1983.

Waltz, K.J., *Man, the State, and War*, Columbia University Press, 1959.

—— *Theory of International Politics*, Addison-Wesley, 1979.

Wright, Quincy, *The Study of International Relations*, Appleton-Century Croft, 1955.

Periodicals

British:
The Economist (weekly).
International Affairs (quarterly).
Review of International Studies (quarterly).
World Today (monthly).

American:
American Political Science Review (quarterly).
Foreign Affairs (quarterly).
Foreign Policy (quarterly).
International Organization (four-monthly).
World Politics (quarterly).

Index

Afghanistan: foreign military occupation of, 22; government of, 29–30; Russian experience in, 37, 54, 220–2

Africa: agricultural production in, 183; application of international law in, 196; classification by region, 34; conflict in, 219; Cuban intervention in, 133, 135, 191; demographic expansion in, 118; effect of tradition on stability in, 27; Nigeria's world position, 38; non-alignment in, 179; Russian intervention in, 54, 61; spread of cold war to, 177

agencies, specialized, 46–7, 108, 207–8

aid, 51, 66, 90, 180, 227

alliances, 129, 168, 170–1, 173; *see also* North Atlantic Treaty Organization; Warsaw Pact

America, *see* United States of America

analysis, levels of, 4, 101

anti-colonialism, 128, 206, 213, 219, 227

Arabs: and Arab League, 65; ideal of single nation, 27; influence of OPEC, 216; and Israel, 76–7, 156–7, 224–5; oil exporters, 31, 149

arms control, 62, 131, 221, 223; *see also* disarmament

Asia: American foreign policy and, 43–4, 121; demographic expansion in, 118; effect of cold war on, 177–8; geographical classification of, 34; Russian diplomatic successes in, 54; stability in, 27

balance of power: and bipolar system, 176; collective security and, 174; conduct of diplomacy and, 136, 138; Great Britain and, 132; Greek political theory and, 16; international law, 197–8; stability of in nineteenth century, 201; system, 167–72

bipolarity, 16, 18, 60, 165, 176–81, 222

bureaucracy, 63, 86–9, 123–4, 208–9, 216

capabilities, 113, 115–30

change: international relations and, 187; international systems and, 164–7; in nineteenth-century Europe, 171; since 1945, 18, 181, 219; technological, 224

character, national, 126–7

Chernobyl disaster, 37, 56, 220, 222–3, 228

China: Albania and, 53; America and, 40, 43–5, 144, 179; armistice negotiations on Korea, 156; boycotting British and Japanese goods, 150; Britain recognizes Central People's Government, 29; cold war, 107; government of, 21–2, 31, 123; isolationism of, 11; military policy, 153; negotiating with Lord Napier, 140; in new global order, 37–8; nuclear power, 124, 131; population, 116, 118; role definitions, 104; Russia and, 51, 56, 64, 190, 221; self-sufficiency, 105; status, 219; turning to West, 228; UN sanctions against, 151; weakness post-Second World War, 176

Churches, 67–9, 143

cold war: America and, 43–5, 56, 107; and bipolar system, 165,